THEORIES OF DEVELOPMENT IN THE OXFORD MOVEMENT

THEORIES OF DEVELOPMENT IN THE OXFORD MOVEMENT

JAMES PEREIRO

GRACEWING

This edition first published in England in 2015

by

Gracewing
2 Southern Avenue
Leominster
Herefordshire HR6 0QF
United Kingdom

www.gracewing.co.uk

ISBN 978 085244 825 0

Typeset by Word and Page, Chester, UK

Cover design by Bernardita Peña Hurtado

CONTENTS

ABBREVIATIONS

BOA	Birmingham Oratory Archives.
Halifax Papers	Halifax Papers at the Borthwick Institute of Historical Research, York.
HOU	M. G. Brock and M. C. Curthoys, eds, *The History of the University of Oxford*, VI: *Nineteenth-Century Oxford*, Part I (Oxford: Clarendon Press, 1997).
LBV	Liddon Bound Volumes, Pusey House, Oxford.
LD	*The Letters and Diaries of John Henry Newman*, vols I–X, ed. T. Gornall, I. Ker, G. Tracey and F. M. McGrath (Oxford: Oxford University Press, 1978–2006); vols. XI–XXXI, ed. C. S. Dessain, E. E. Kelly and T. Gornall (London: Nelson, 1961–72; Oxford: Oxford University Press, 1973–7).
Manning MSS Bod.	Manning Papers at the Bodleian Library, Oxford.
PPS	J. H. Newman, *Parochial and Plain Sermons*, 8 vols (London: Longman, Green and Co., 1898–1900, new ed.).
Remains	R. H. Froude, *The Remains of the Late Rev. Richard Hurrell Froude*, ed. J. H. Newman and J. Keble, Part I, 2 vols (London: Rivington, 1838); Part II, 2 vols (Derby: Mozley, 1839).
SAO	J. Keble, *Sermons Academical and Occasional* (Oxford and London: Parker and Rivington, 1847).
US	J. H. Newman, *Sermons Chiefly on the Theory of Religious Belief: Preached before the University of Oxford* (London: Rivington, 1843).

ACKNOWLEDGEMENTS

During the preparation of this volume I have incurred many debts of gratitude to a considerable number of people, and it would be impossible to detail them all. I might single out the librarians and archivists of Pusey House and the Bodleian Library in Oxford for their help and sympathy. Prof. Alan McClelland has been most generous in his advice over the years and some of the materials included in this book were first published under his editorship of *Recusant History*. Francis J. McGrath granted me access to materials from the Newman archives at the Birmingham Oratory, some of which have since been published in the last volumes of Newman's *Letters and Diaries*. I should also acknowledge the help of Dr Andrew Hegarty and Dr Peter Damian-Grint, who read over the original manuscript and offered many suggestions for improving it. Permission to quote from manuscripts in their possession was generously given by the Borthwick Institute (York), The Bodleian Library (Oxford), and the Principal and Chapter of Pusey House (Oxford).

INTRODUCTION

THE PRESENT BOOK is a revised version of chapters which first appeared as part of my *Ethos and the Oxford Movement*. It also includes the two appendices found at the end of that book. The work of revision has involved looking afresh at the subject under study and adding new material to the original text. The conclusions of the previous book, however, remain unaltered, having been reinforced by the work of revision. The study of John Henry Newman's theory of development of doctrine in isolation from the intellectual context in which it grew had led some scholars to misinterpret aspects of it and to draw flawed hypotheses about its origin and growth. The present book does not pretend to be a detailed analysis of Newman's *Development of Christian Doctrine*. It rather aims at clarifying its intellectual roots. In so doing, it also sheds light on the Tractarian theory of religious knowledge which served as the foundation on which Newman's *Development* was to be built. After his conversion, subsequent Catholic criticism made Newman realize that people needed to be introduced to the principles underlying the essay in order to understand it aright; that knowledge could not be taken for granted. As Newman put it, 'they [the principles] had been long familiar to our minds', but that was not the case for many of its readers, both Anglican and Catholic. In that respect, he thought that some of his *University Sermons* – bringing out Tractarian ideas about religious knowledge and the relationship between faith and reason – were the best introduction to the *Essay*.[1] He was interested in having them translated into French to make them more available to a non-English-speaking readership.

The title of the present book – *Theories of Development in the Oxford Movement* – suggests that, besides Newman, other Tractarians also proposed theories of development of doctrine or made important contributions to its formation. The origin of the present study was the discovery of several manuscripts and letters written by Samuel Francis Wood in late 1835 and early 1836. They are to be found among Henry Edward Manning's papers at the Bodleian Library (Oxford) and the Halifax Papers at the Borthwick Institute (York). These papers are of considerable importance. One of the manuscripts in the Bodleian Library, dated 1835, contains an elaborate, though schematic, theory of doctrinal development written by Wood. The emergence of a theory of development in the Oxford Movement, preceding Newman's *University Sermons* of 1843 and his *Essay on the Development of Christian Doctrine* of 1845, had not been previously known to scholars and calls now for a reconsideration of the roots and origins of the concept of doctrinal development, taking into account the intellectual environment in which it was conceived.

Wood's other manuscript published as an appendix also offers some clues for this study. It contains an interesting description of the spirit animating the Oxford Movement and a brief narrative of its history. Wood wrote this paper in 1840, at the request of Pusey and Newman. It was destined for the German theologian Friedrich August Tholuck, a friend of Pusey. Tholuck was at the time editor of the *Literarischer Anzeiger für Christliche Theologie und Wissenschaft*, published in Halle between 1830 and 1859. The journal had already printed some references to the Oxford Movement, and Tholuck wanted to keep his public informed about further theological developments in England. Pusey, committed on many fronts, asked Wood to answer Tholuck's request. In his paper Wood described the genesis of Tractarian ideas and the history of the Movement up to 1840, offering a true insider's account of its origin, spirit and inner counsels. Pusey and Newman considered that Wood's narrative was a fair description of the Oxford Movement, and their endorsement gives the paper a quasi-official character. Their marginalia on the manuscript, though few and brief, are also of great interest, showing that there were subtle but relevant differences among them.

Samuel Francis Wood had been born on 1 August 1809.[2] His elder brother, Charles, after occupying important positions in Government, was to become the first Viscount Halifax. Samuel followed him to Oxford, matriculating from Oriel College on 16

February 1827. There he benefited from Newman's ideas about the pastoral nature of the tutorial system: moral training should accompany intellectual development, and the tutor was to maintain a personal relationship of friendship with those entrusted to his care. That intellectual and moral training left a deep mark on Wood. He joined Newman and Hurrell Froude in some of the spiritual exercises they had introduced at Oriel, and, for the rest of his life, remained a man of deep and sincere piety. At the end of his Oxford studies, having failed to gain an Oriel fellowship, he moved to London to commence studies for the Bar, to which he was called in 1835. His heart, however, remained in Oxford. The practice of law did not fulfil his aspirations. Wood's interests were theological and Church-related, and, for the rest of his life, he combined the study and exercise of the legal profession with a continuous involvement in those questions at a theoretical and practical level. He had always shown great intellectual independence and originality of mind, and while agreeing with his friends on many points, he also differed from them in other respects, defending his opinions articulately. Newman, while appreciating his friend's originality of thought, felt he should caution him about the dangers of theorizing: the fact that Wood was not involved in pastoral care might prevent him from seeing the deep practical consequences which might follow from theories.[3]

In the mid-1830s the concepts of Tradition and the rule of faith were the subject of study and animated controversy. Newman was engaged at the time with the Abbé Jager in a correspondence on the subject. Wood's ideas on the role of Tradition and the possibility of doctrinal development found expression in the short paper which he sent to Henry Edward Manning on 19 November 1835. This is the most complete statement of his hypothesis. The subsequent correspondence and his conversations with Manning and Newman only served to define and develop some aspects of his 'presumptio', as he called it, while keeping intact the substance of its first enunciation.[4] His two friends did not accept Wood's theory that progress and development of doctrine were intended in the divine plan or that it should have continued after the Primitive Church. Wood was unmoved and disappointed by their arguments. He decided to keep the theory to himself, confessing that he would try 'not to be restless or anxious about such difficulties, but wait calmly in the sure trust that if any of us be otherwise minded, God will reveal this also unto us'.[5] If his theory was right – and he had no doubts about it – others would arrive in due time to similar conclusions from the principles they held in common.

As we have seen, Wood's departure for London did not bring about a loosening of his ties with Oxford and the questions being debated there. On the contrary, the fact that some of Newman's former pupils and friends had left the University to start their professional careers in London in the early 1830s opened a new field for Tractarian activity and influence. Wood and those formed like him in the *ethos* inspiring the Movement were kept informed about events at Oxford and about the theological agitation generated by the *Tracts for the Times*. They were anxious to help in whatever capacity they could. Newman, who was in London early in 1836, offered them a new field for their activity. In a letter to Thomas Dyke Acland,[6] he expressed his conviction that there was a harvest to be reaped in London, 'if anyone would set himself to the work'.[7] Newman's comments did not fall on deaf ears: Wood, Frederic Rogers,[8] John William Bowden,[9] and Acland set their hands to the plough without delay. They would later be joined by James Hope, Roundell Palmer and others. Rogers, in July, reported to Newman: 'Wood is most sanguine, and eager to know everyone who holds prospects of being bettered.'[10]

Newman, in his response to Rogers's letter, gave them an initial focus for their activity: 'If you form a knot in London, and set about puzzling the Peculiars [Evangelicals], etc., I shall not regret one bit being left alone [in the ventures he was himself involved in at the time].'[11] Wood and his friends should try to break the 'stranglehold' that the Peculiars had gained in London, and in many Church societies, as a result of the Evangelical revival of the first quarter of the century. William Downes Willis, Rural Dean of Bath, had described the situation vividly in a letter to Newman in May 1836: 'I wish we could see our way clearly in the case of the Society for Promotion of Christian Knowledge [SPCK] and could rescue her as completely from the thraldom of a party as you have saved your Alma Mater . . . It would be a hard thing indeed if the "Record" and Mr. Rochford Clark are to rule us and Calvinize us in London, – while our advowsons are to be Simonized, and our parishes *Pastoral aided*, and the cuckoos our poor mother Church has hatched, are to thrust the nestlings from their home.'[12] The London Tractarians soon got involved in those ventures, with mixed results.

The public debate on education soon offered them a new field for their exertions. The education of the lower classes had come to the attention of Parliament in the 1830s. Since 1834 a number of Education Committees had sat and questioned witnesses from the educational societies (the High Church inspired 'National Society for the Education of the Poor' and the Evangelical and non-conformist 'British and Foreign Schools Society'), and other groups and individuals. Many felt that the neglect of education which recent studies had shown could only be properly remedied by the state taking the reins of education into its hands, as had been done in Prussia, Holland, and more recently in France. Nearer home, Ireland offered the example of a national system of education with which they were familiar. Legislation was needed: 'laissez faire' was a good principle in matters of trade, but not to be extended to education. Lord Brougham had introduced a bill to regulate national education in successive parliamentary sessions. His bill, among other proposals, advocated setting up a Board or Ministry of Education, and the possibility of levying rates to pay for board schools and non-sectarian education. Brougham's bill did not prosper but the defenders of the place of the Church in education could read the writing on the wall. They were not slow to mobilize their effectives to meet the pressure of those who wanted to make education a responsibility of the state. The year 1838 saw Wood and his friends becoming deeply involved in the affairs of the National Society.[13] Gilbert Farquhar Mathison, then Secretary of the Mint, played a decisive role in galvanizing his new Tractarian friends, and others, in an effort to re-awaken the flagging energies of the National Society as the educational arm of the Church of England. The National Society, in their opinion, was not in a fit condition to meet the challenge of the state: school expansion had lost its initial momentum, the running of the Society's business had fallen into a complacent routine, and those who ran it had been drawn into a false sense of security by the granting of state subsidies since 1833. However, in spite of the parlous condition of the National Society, Mathison and his friends thought that the way forward was to re-energize and develop it rather than creating a new organization.

Wood, in a letter to Newman, clearly described their aim: 'to forestall any Government or Abstract-Principle plan by an immediate, silent, and large extension of the funds and energy of the National Society'.[14] They wanted to steal a march on the government as far as the setting up of a system of national education was concerned. Their intention was to make state intervention unnecessary by creating a system of public instruction – from infant schools to university – essentially and intricately connected with the principles and ministers of the Church. Their approach to the National Society was successful, and they were incorporated into a newly formed Committee of Inquiry and Correspondence, whose aim was to study ways of carrying out their proposals. The consequent development of educational plans by the National Society was a remarkable one. It was to excite the concern of the then Whig Government, which set up the Committee of Council for Education as part of their effort to check the growth of the Church's school system. The years 1838 and 1839, in particular, were a time of incessant activity for Wood and his friends. Once their plans were approved by the Central Committee of the National Society, they carried out an intense campaign preparing circulars, fund-raising and trying to revive or set up new diocesan boards. Wood became a member of the General Council of the National Society, and of most of its relevant Committees, at a time when the activity generated by the new men involved a considerable increase in the workload of the society. Acland, in his 'Notice' after the death of his friend, would write that some of the most important documents produced by the National Society at the time had been written by Wood.[15]

His health suffered as a result of all those exertions, and in 1839 it would require the attention of the distinguished Dr Babington. Although Wood seemed to have regained strength as a result of his treatment, this decline in health marked the onset of tuberculosis which was to lead to his death in 1843. His debilitated condition did not, however, stop his efforts in the promotion of the causes he had at heart. Joshua Watson[16] came to rely more and more on him, to the point of having suggested that Wood should take over most of the running of the different societies in which he was engaged. Wood's health broke down again in 1841, and his father took him for a tour of the continent to help him recover strength. The remedy did not produce the desired effects. The deterioration of his physical condition was also accompanied by growing doubts about the Anglican Church. Wood's health broke down completely in late 1842 and early 1843. In spite of this he continued attending regularly the meetings of the General Committee of the National Society. The last meeting at which he was present took place on 8 March 1843.[17] His last letter to Manning was dated 7 April of the same year. It was written in pencil, and probably never sent. The doctor, he said in it, had diagnosed his case as hopeless. Wood felt that it was a sign of God's mercy 'that He seems to be taking a poor sinner away before he falls from Him again as he has so often done'.[18] He died on 22 April 1843.

The present book is divided into four chapters. The first examines the Movement's concept of *ethos*, its intellectual roots and the role it plays in the process of religious knowledge. It also tries to map out the contributions of different authors to the common theory (or at least to its written expression) in a broadly chronological sequence. The Tractarians never described clearly and systematically what they understood by *ethos* in any of their published works. Elements of their theory come to light here and there in their writings and correspondence at different times and in no particular logical order. Chapter II examines some concepts central to their theory of knowledge – like realizing and reserve – and the role Froude played as a Tractarian paradigm of the Oxford Movement's *ethos*. The third chapter explores some lines of thought within the Movement pointing in the direction of development, together with Wood's 1835 theory. Chapter IV pays particular attention to Newman's long progress towards his theory of doctrinal development, and the intellectual difficulties and tensions he had to resolve on the way. Wood's paper on development, and the letters that refer to it, are published as Appendix I; the narrative about the Oxford Movement can be found in Appendix II. The literature on the Oxford Movement is considerable and ever growing. Laurence N. Crumb's comprehensive bibliography of the Oxford Movement and its leaders[19] obviates in good measure the need for a lengthy bibliographical section in the present volume. The bibliographical references in the present work have therefore been confined to the notes.

Notes

1. Newman to J. D. Dalgairns, 10 January 1847, *LD*, XII, p. 5.
2. For more information on Francis Samuel Wood see J. Pereiro, *Ethos and The Oxford Movement. At the Heart of Tractarianism* (Oxford: Oxford University Press, 2008).
3. Newman to Wood, 23 March 1838, *LD*, VI, p. 221. While Newman was working on his book on justification he asked Manning for some papers of Wood on the subject (letter dated 30 January 1838, *LD*, VI, p. 195). Wood had sent them to Manning accompanying a letter of his, dated Passion Tuesday 1837, and had asked Manning to comment on them (Manning MSS Bod., c. 654, fos 452–3; see also Wood to Manning, 11 May 1833, ibid., fos 427–8).
4. Unfortunately Manning's and Newman's side of the correspondence is not extant. Wood left precise instructions in the album which contained his correspondence between August 1830 and February 1839 for the letters to be destroyed, unread, in the event of his death.
5. Wood to Manning, 29 January 1836, Manning MSS Bod., c. 654, fo. 449.
6. Thomas Dyke Acland (1809–98), Oxford contemporary of Wood, fellow of All Souls (1831–40), Conservative Member of Parliament (1837–41), served later as a Liberal (1865–86). He was to play a very important part in London Tractarian ventures in the years 1836–9; his marriage in early 1841 seems to have removed him from the centre of the action. He eventually returned to more mainstream Church positions.
7. Newman to T. D. Acland, 27 April 1836, *LD*, V, p. 290.
8. Frederic Rogers (1811–89), Baron Blachford; disciple of Newman at Oriel, and fellow (1840); barrister, Lincoln's Inn (1837); he distanced himself from Newman in the early 1840s; co-founder of the *Guardian* newspaper (1846); permanent under-secretary of state for the colonies (1860–71).
9. John William Bowden (1798–1844); contemporary and close friend of Newman at Trinity College (Oxford); Commissioner of Stamps (1826–40); died in 1844, after years of uncertain health.
10. F. Rogers to Newman, 2 July 1836, in *Letters of Frederic Lord Blachford*, ed. G. E. Martin (London: Murray, 1896), p. 30.
11. Newman to Rogers, 5 July 1836, *LD*, V, p. 319. See also Newman to H. Wilberforce, 16 July 1836, ibid., p. 326.
12. Willis to Newman, 9 May 1836, Box *Letters 1836*, BOA.
13. See J. Pereiro, 'Tractarians and National Education, 1838–1843', in S. Gilley, ed., *Victorian Churches and Churchmen* (Woodbridge: Boydell Press, 2005), pp. 249–78.
14. Wood to Newman, no date but before March 1838, Halifax Papers, A2.42.2, fo. 62R. The 'Abstract-Principle' mentioned seems to be a reference to the ideas of the small, but politically influential, liberal Central Society for Education founded in 1836.
15. [T. D. Acland], 'Notice of the Late S. F. Wood, Esq.', *The English Journal of Education*, I, no. 6 (June 1843), pp. 197–9.
16. Wine merchant. High Churchman and member of the Hackney Falanx; first treasurer of the newly founded National Society for the Education of the Poor (1811); acquired the *British Critic* (1811); active in the Society for the Promotion of Christian Knowledge and in the Society for the Propagation of the Gospel; co-founder of the Additional Curates' Society (1837).
17. Minutes *General Committee of the National Society*, vol. 4 (January 1838 – July 1847).
18. Manning MSS Bod., c. 654, fo. 528.

19. L. N. Crumb, *The Oxford Movement and its Leaders: A Bibliography of Secondary and Lesser Primary Sources* (Lanham: Scarecrow Press, 2009, 2nd ed.).

CHAPTER I

THE ETHOS OF THE OXFORD MOVEMENT

THE STUDENT OF THE OXFORD MOVEMENT soon becomes familiar with the word *ethos*; it appears frequently in the writings and correspondence of the Oxford Tractarians, particularly those of Keble, Froude and Newman. Keble, in Isaac Williams's words, 'in opposition to the Oriel or Whatelian [school], set *ethos* above intellect'.[1] Thomas Mozley would affirm in his *Reminiscences* that what 'Froude and others discovered continually was *ethos*, the dominant moral habit or proclivity'.[2] These and other testimonies suggest that the term encapsulated a concept of vital importance for Tractarianism. It comes, therefore, as a surprise that, given the amount of scholarly attention focused on the Oxford Movement, there should be such a dearth of studies on the subject. Most scholars pass over the concept of *ethos* as if it had little or nothing to contribute to the understanding of the Movement. The causes of this neglect may be varied, but there can be little doubt that John Taylor Coleridge's explanation of the idea of *ethos* in his *Memoir* of Keble made a considerable contribution to its trivialization. He considered that with Keble *ethos* 'imported certainly no intellectual quality, scarcely even any distinct moral one, but an habitual toning, or general colouring diffused over all man's moral qualities, giving the exercise of them a peculiar gentleness and grace'.[3] These were deceptive words and have misled many. Unfortunately, Keble himself contributed to trivialize the concept when, in his 1854 pamphlet against the admission of Dissenters to Oxford University, he blandly described the 'old Oxford feeling' (not *ethos*, although easily confused with it) as 'that indescribable mixture of something like innocent family pride, something like religious reverence, and something like a youth's playful fondness for an indulgent mother, mixed too often with just regrets . . . for opportunities thrown away'.[4] All this, he added, would be lost if the doors of the University were thrown open to Dissenters. Keble may not have intended it but his words contributed to obscure one of the fundamental insights of the Oxford Movement; one to which he had made an important contribution.

It is the contention of the present study that, in the language of the Tractarians, *ethos* is a concept rich in content and consequences, involving a complex theory of religious knowledge which deeply influenced the genesis and development of the Oxford Movement. The Tractarians would always maintain that it reflected the spirit of the University. Keble had forged the concept in Oxford, and two books in the University's syllabus – Aristotle's *Nicomachean Ethics* and Bishop Butler's *Analogy*[5] – provided the materials from which he fashioned it. Afterwards, the Oriel College tutors developed Keble's original idea in the interaction of the common room and with their students. Froude and Newman in particular, contributed significantly to enlarge the range of the theory and unfold its corollaries. Wood thought that anybody intent on gaining an understanding of the nature of the Oxford Movement should look into the cradle (intellectual as well as physical) in which it had been born. That is what he tried to do in his paper for Tholuck. He did not aim to list the Movement's doctrinal tenets. Pusey had already done that in his *Letter to the Bishop of Oxford* (1839), which he also sent to Tholuck. Wood considered that the Movement's distinctive feature was the spirit that inspired the Oxford men, and he tried to describe it in order to 'give some clue to their general scope and meaning'.[6] He placed the origin of the Movement in the Oxford intellectual revival of the 1820s, remarking that the renewal of the studies of Logic and Rhetoric in Oxford as the result of Whately's[7] works and influence had 'sharpened and disciplined the intellect', but they had done so 'without giving it matter to feed and rest upon'. They had served, however, as a 'remarkable preparation for what was to follow',[8] by which he meant the new direction given by Keble and the Oriel tutors – Newman, Froude and Robert Wilberforce – to the study of Aristotle and of Bishop Butler.

Bishop Butler and Oxford

Present-day studies on High Church doctrine and practical devotion in the late eighteenth and early nineteenth centuries have shown the long-established pedigree and the continuity of some Tractarian ideas and attitudes. This, however, should not lead us to underestimate the differences between the Oxford Movement and High Churchmanship.[9] Nowhere, perhaps, were these differences more obvious than in the *ethos* of the Movement, and Wood's paper has much to offer to the study of this subject. The particular interest of the paper is Wood's explicit desire to concentrate his attention on describing what the Tractarians conceived as *ethos* – although Wood himself did not use this term. They considered the *ethos* of the Oxford Movement as its distinctive and defining feature and it was to mark the parting of ways between the old High Churchmen who had initially supported the Movement and the men at the heart of it.

Keble had a deep sense of his pastoral calling, and soon after taking up his appointment as Oriel tutor, confessed to John Taylor Coleridge that he would not have undertaken that position had he not considered the tutorial office 'as a species of pastoral care'.[10] Although Keble soon retired from Oxford to a pastoral ministry in rural parishes, Froude, Newman and Robert Wilberforce would take up his mantle at Oriel. They bestowed on their pupils – especially those who were more able and endowed with better moral qualities – as much time and effort as was usually given by good private tutors, keeping a record not only of their intellectual but also of their spiritual progress. As a result, tutors and students were joined by bonds of mutual affection, and the former were rewarded by the enthusiastic following and devotion of their disciples.[11] It is true that, at the time, tutors in other colleges acted on a similar interpretation of the University statutes,[12] but it is doubtful whether they went as far or were as systematic in applying them as their Oriel counterparts. The University's Laudian Statutes of 1634–6 (Titulus III, par. 2) supported such a vision of the tutorial office, and they were quoted by Newman against Hawkins, when the Provost of Oriel objected to the praxis of the young College tutors. They claimed that the tutorship was a University, not a

College office, regulated by the Statutes.[13] The way the Oriel tutors applied the Statutes, however, amounted to a College revolution, and Hawkins perceived it to be such. His efforts to revert to the old system encountered the determined opposition of the tutors, who claimed that they were not able to exercise their tutorship under any other system. The negotiations reached deadlock. Hawkins could not countenance such a challenge to his authority, and, following Bishop Copleston's[14] advice, refused to assign any future students to them.

At the basis of their concept of the tutorial system was Keble's firm conviction that the search for truth could not be separated from the pursuit of goodness. Doing otherwise would lead to intellectual pride, an almost insurmountable obstacle to attain moral rectitude. Lack of moral rectitude, in its turn, would disturb the clear perception of truth, inclining the mind towards error. In essence, Keble's idea amounted to a reversal of the Enlightenment view of intellectual education as leading almost necessarily towards moral rectitude. As far as Keble was concerned, moral uprightness was a fundamental condition for clear intellectual perception; thus, intellectual training could not be dissociated from religious and moral formation. Wood described how Aristotle's *Nicomachean Ethics* – a text incorporated in the Oxford syllabus – acquired a particular importance within Keble's programme, and we have it on Isaac Williams's testimony that Keble made use of it 'as a foundation for instruction in religion and morals generally'.[15] Williams, Hurrell Froude and Robert Wilberforce had experienced Keble's methods in the reading parties they had attended at Southrop in the early 1820s. Some years later, Wilberforce and Froude, together with Newman, went on to use the *Ethics* in much the same way when they became tutors at Oriel. As Wood remarked in his paper, Aristotle's *Ethics* 'became in the hands of more than one College Lecturer the groundwork of a very constructive course of Ethical study. Not that this course was either very extensive or scientific, but it led to much useful reflexion on the formation of moral habits'.[16] The Oriel tutors had found the religious teaching of the day 'wanting in practical reality, in any discrimination of character or insight into motives and principles of action'. Wood thought that 'it was probably this which led them to make so religious a use of a Heathen treatise on morals, to dwell so largely on its details, and to make it as it were the ground work for an education bearing to a great degree a theological aspect. *They employed this indirect means for the inculcation of that which found no place in the explicit system.*'[17]

A later Tractarian, Frederick Oakeley, in his *Remarks on the Study of Aristotelian and Platonic Ethics* (1837), would describe the spirit in which the study of Aristotle should be undertaken. He started by pointing out the dangers of an education that led students to acquire the habit of viewing 'subjects essentially Practical in the light of mere theories' or as 'a mere way to Academical distinction'.[18] That involved a profanation of the discipline in question, and could lead to excessive self-confidence and arrogance. Oakeley maintained that the *Nicomachean Ethics* should be studied as a means to learn the grounds of obligation to right conduct. Aristotle's work was particularly valuable in this respect because of its agreement with Evangelical truth: 'both represent man's moral nature of advancing indefinitely towards its perfection'.[19] Years later he was to remark that Classical scholarship was not an end in itself but a 'means towards a certain habit of mind', and that the philosophical studies at Oxford tended to form great minds on a semi-Catholic type.[20]

Newman was a great believer in the existence of *genii locorum*, and considered that they had considerable influence in the modelling of the minds and hearts of those who dwelled and were formed, morally and intellectually, in particular places.[21] In the case of Oxford, this was the Catholic *ethos*, one in which holiness and learning met in continuous interplay; a moral temper poles apart from the utilitarian spirit prevalent at the time in both politics and religion. That Catholic *ethos* had often shown itself, at critical moments of the nation's history, in the University's attachment to right principles and in the defence of the just cause against all odds. Oxford's allegiance to King and Church against the usurpations of the Puritan Parliament; the defence of the established Church and of the privileges of the University during the reign of James II, and its later reluctant acceptance of his deposition, were clear exhibitions of that Catholic temper. Oxford had held its own, not accommodating herself to the temper of the hour, and she had survived.[22] The Tractarians were deeply convinced that they were now called to defend Church and country against the assaults of liberalism. The struggle had a national dimension. The University, as they saw it, was the depository and only stronghold of truth still standing in a land which had apostatized from right principles.[23]

It is interesting to compare their educational vision with the arguments used earlier by Edward Copleston in his spirited controversy with the *Edinburgh Review* about the study of Aristotle in Oxford. Copleston's main aim was to refute the *Review*'s contention that the study of Aristotle's philosophy, and in particular his logic, acted as a brake on the progress of scientific studies. His defence of Aristotelian ethics and rhetoric concentrated on their value for developing habits of discrimination and accuracy of thought, as well as a capacity for analysis and synthesis.[24] Copleston paid, however, little attention to their formal content; for him, ethics was part of religion, and, as such, should be inculcated from the pulpit.[25] Whether the Oxford pulpit in fact offered this instruction in the early nineteenth century was – then as now – a subject of debate.

It was more than a mere difference of approach; it involved radically different views of intellectual and university life. Two 'parties' were fighting for the soul of Oxford University. The first skirmishes had been fought within Oriel College, between the tutors and Provost Hawkins. Soon the contest acquired a University dimension. The controversy over subscription to the Thirty-Nine Articles gathered around the nucleuses of the Oriel Noetics and the early Tractarians those respectively in favour of or against the removal of subscription. Henry Wilberforce, in his letter to the Archbishop of Canterbury, marshalled the arguments against the proposals supported by men like Hawkins, Hampden, Arnold and Whately. The university, he wrote, was meant to be the nursery of the Church of England; from Oxford, men formed in the study of those disciplines which instil moral character, went forth ready to defend ancient religious truth. She had so far refused to give any prominent place in her course of studies to 'those elegant and scientific pursuits which in our day . . . have usurped almost exclusively possession of the title of philosophy'. But now a party in the university wanted to modify the system, moving it in a liberal direction, and making 'knowledge, rather than moral discipline the object of our studies, and to cultivate rather the habit of bold and irreverent inquiry, . . . [than] that humility and self-distrust which characterises the true philosopher, whatever be his subject'. Such an education would indeed produce scientists, patrons of commerce, and political economists but few men who had been accustomed to revere and pursue Truth. The proposal to abolish subscription was also made suspect by the intellectual character of its promoters. It had originated with Hampden, Arnold and others of similar stamp; men who were opposed to tests and creeds as conditions for religious communion, being of the opinion that in matters of faith truth is wholly indifferent.[26]

The course of studies followed in the university seemed to uphold Wilberforce's contention. The *Oxford University Calendar* for 1831 stipulated that the study of ancient authors should be illustrated from modern ones as part of the course of reading for Academic Honours. Bishop Butler's *Analogy of Religion*[27] had become by that date the authoritative modern text complementing the study of Aristotle's *Ethics*. For Butler, as for Aristotle, moral goodness facilitates the decision about what is right and wrong in particular circumstances; even more, it would be impossible to be practically wise in the choice of what is right without being virtuous at the same time: practical wisdom confers a sort of instinct for what is good.[28] Wood's 'Revival of Primitive Doctrine', when referring to the study of Aristotle and Butler, remarked on their fundamental agreement in respect of the doctrine about the formation of moral habits. At this point in the manuscript, an insertion – apparently in Newman's hand – added a sentence stressing the influence that habits have on the formation of opinions.[29] The connexions between virtue (or moral depravity) and opinions were very much in Newman's mind at the time, and his thinking on this subject found expression in his *Parochial and Plain Sermons* and later in his *University Sermons*.

In the *Analogy* Butler was primarily concerned with the defence of Christian revelation against objections levelled at it by the deists. These argued that if God had intended a revelation for the good of all men, it was inconceivable that he would have allowed most of humanity to remain in ignorance of it. Again, the argument went on, given the vital nature of that knowledge for man's salvation, it was unthinkable that God would have left his revelation to rest upon doubtful evidence. They contended that reason, on the other hand, was able to provide certain and universal knowledge about God and man's moral obligation, overcoming the conflicts between competing religions and confessions. Butler, in his response to their objections, drew the general lines of a philosophy of religious knowledge which was to have great influence among the Tractarians. He relied on the argument from analogy to respond to the critics of revelation, and started by defining the concept of the analogy of nature in words borrowed from Origen: he who believes Scripture to proceed from him who is also the author of nature, might well expect to find the same sort of difficulties in his knowledge of revelation as he encounters when approaching nature.[30] From that starting point, Butler argued that, as generally accepted, the order of nature vastly exceeds in its complexity our intellectual powers, and that, as a result, we are unable to see the multiple connexions which would offer explanation of natures and events which, although *a priori* might seem unreasonable to us, we are bound to accept as incontrovertible facts. The 'appearance of deficiencies and irregularities in nature is owing to its being a scheme but in part made known . . . Now we see no more reason why the frame and course of nature should be such a scheme, than why Christianity should. And that the former is such a scheme, renders it credible, that the latter, upon supposition of its truth, may be so too'.[31] In other words, Butler considered it unreasonable to demand higher standards of proof and evidence in matters of religion than in matters of science or in the practical ordering of human life. The imperfection of the human intellect forces man to admit that, in most cases, he will have to be satisfied – in his knowledge of both nature and revelation – with only probable knowledge, rather than certainty: 'probability is the very guide of life'.[32] Only the divine intellect, comprehending the whole of the natural and revealed dispensations, is able to have certain knowledge in every respect. Butler, applying again the analogy of nature, argued that the seeming lack of universality of revelation should not be an argument for incredulity: natural gifts are diversely distributed not only among different natures but even among individuals who share the same nature; therefore, there is no reason for wonder at the fact that revelation may have reached men in different degrees.

The vital question then was: how can man find his way to religious truth in a maze of probable arguments? In his answer Butler took as his starting point the Aristotelian concept of *phronesis* or practical wisdom, as described in the *Nicomachean Ethics*: that it is impossible to be practically wise – i.e., to discern the good to aim at and the means to achieve it – without also being good. Butler considered that God had granted man a perfectible nature, and that its potential for perfection is not confined to man's present earthly life: there is a future life which stands to this present one as adulthood does to youth. Man qualifies for that other life by developing his moral character in the practice of virtue: the improvement of one's human nature is achieved by the acquisition of sound habits resulting from the repetition of good actions. This is not a foregone conclusion. The present life is a state of discipline and probation, and man's resolve is tested by the disordered inclinations he experiences within himself, calling on him to deviate from right. Besides, part of that probation consists in the very fact that the distinction between good and evil is not always perceived with absolute clarity. Man, however, is not left unprovided, Butler affirmed with Aristotle that virtue already achieved is, in its own measure, also a 'security against the danger which finite creatures are in, from the very nature of propension, or particular affections'.[33] Virtue strengthens the will in its search for good, and facilitates the perception of the path that leads to it.

Butler next took the concept of practical wisdom or *phronesis* well beyond the confines Aristotle had set for it. In Butler's hands, without losing its ethical character, moral goodness acquired a more intellectual dimension. Doubtfulness in respect of the evidence of Christian revelation is, according to Butler, an element in man's probation; and he regarded probable knowledge as being perfectly adapted to the state of probation in which man has been established on this earth. In that respect, he even admitted the possibility that God, with that aim of probation in mind, might have withheld some truths which, had they been laid before us, might have facilitated our apprehension of revelation. In man's present condition, different moral tempers would behave differently in respect to the evidences of revelation. Neglect in examining them generally implies one form or another of depravity: lack of interest, a desire that those things may be proved not true, passion, prejudice, and so on. On the other hand, a virtuous moral temper would pay active and careful consideration to the evidences of revelation. It would be more inclined to give religion its assent and follow conviction by obedience to revealed precepts. For Butler, speculative difficulties play a role similar to moral temptations. Virtue is once again the reliable guide in doubt, helping the individual this time to weigh rightly the probability of divine revelation. A higher degree of virtue would be accompanied by a clearer perception of truth. Butler felt it to be 'a real imperfection in the moral character, not to be influenced in practice by a lower degree of evidence when discerned, as it is in the understanding, not to discern it'.[34]

Keble and the Formation of the Concept of *Ethos*

The reaction against the dry dictatorship of Rationalism took different philosophical forms in the eighteenth century, from idealism to empiricism, passing through Butler. In the religious sphere, as Brian Young has pointed out, 'far from being a rationalistic monopoly, religious debate in eighteenth-century England contained significant mystical, visionary and essentially biblical elements'.[35] Rationalism, philosophical and religious, still maintained, however, its intellectual hegemony for most of that period, although it might be said that its most outlandish claims had entered into terminal crisis towards the end of the century. By then it came to be generally admitted that reason, as already emphasized by the Cambridge Platonists or the Non-Juror William Law, had a considerable subjective dimension, not being able to escape the influence that moral habits and passions exerted upon it.

Butler's *Analogy of Religion* soon became a classic treatment of this question, and its influence was to prove long-lasting. It survived the eighteenth century, and was to reach the high-mark of its popularity during the first half of the following century. Keble and the Tractarians were particularly prominent among those who fell under Butler's sway. It was not, however, a purely High Church preserve. An Evangelical like Daniel Wilson, in a university sermon preached at Oxford in 1810, could affirm that the weight of the affections on the understanding was generally acknowledged; although, he added, 'few perhaps are sufficiently aware of the real extent of this influence in theological studies'.[36]

Butler had used the argument from analogy to defend Christianity against unbelief. Keble, for his part, would develop it further, applying the same argument to the maintenance of orthodoxy against heresy and to the practical guidance of individual consciences among the contrasting claims of the different denominations within Christianity or among parties and schools within a particular Church. Keble was conscious of marching into territory uncharted by Butler but he thought that Butler's doctrine had not closed the door to this particular use of the analogy.[37] Keble considered his ideas a timely development of the theory in the *Analogy*, given that intellectual temptation and doubt were more common in his day than previously.[38] Already in 1814, Keble had suggested the importance of criticism for discovering the laws of the human mind and, in particular, the connexions between the intellectual and moral faculties.[39] However, it is in his sermons of the early 1820s that we find the clearest and best developed expression of his new application of the analogy of nature. Butler had argued with the deist who rejected revelation, and therefore used arguments drawn from human reason. Keble spoke or wrote for those who accepted revelation, and, consequently, made use of the witness of Holy Scripture. And Scripture, to his mind, confirmed both Butler's theory and his own. Among the scriptural texts he quoted, two were particularly useful in support of his argument. One was taken from the Book of Psalms: 'I have more understanding than all my teachers; for Thy testimonies are my meditation. I understand more than the aged, for I keep Thy precepts' (Ps 119: 99–100). The other quoted words of Christ: 'a good will to do His Will shall know of the doctrine if it is from God' (Jn 7: 17).[40] From these and similar scriptural texts Keble concluded that moral rectitude, honest attention and thoughtfulness, with the assistance of the Holy Spirit, 'are not only necessary, but sufficient . . . to guide us into all truths really important to our final welfare; – not only to make us virtuous rather than vicious, but also to make us Christians rather than Infidels, orthodox Christians rather than Heretics, and conforming Christians rather than Schismatics'.[41] The inspired writers considered orthodox faith to be associated with sound morality. Truth and duty were unfailing tests of each other.[42] The Fathers put forward a similar message, and Newman could have read it in his beloved Athanasius, while working on the history of the Arian heresy.

As far as Keble was concerned, moral qualities were of greater importance than intellectual ones when analysing the truth of religious propositions. The reason was his conviction that, in matters of revealed truth, the moral sense can correct the errors of the intellect and supply its imperfections. A person experienced in the life of virtue and desirous to do good would have a sort of instinct for truth, making him or her more able to detect the bent of a particular doctrine.[43] This not only corresponded to the nature of things but also played a specific role within the plan of God's providence: 'it has been God's will to constitute uprightness, rather than ability, judge of the truth on the highest of all subjects',[44] as a means to put down spiritual pride. On the other hand, as St Paul had written to Timothy, 'evil men and seducers shall wax worse and worse, deceiving and being deceived' (2 Tm 3: 13). Keble thought that there is a sort of blinding power in moral disease, leading those affected along an inexorable descent from error into further error; a sliding into heterodoxy which could be arrested only by spiritual conversion.[45]

Keble went on to establish 'as a kind of canon of sacred criticism, that, in disputed cases, that interpretation of God's works and ways, which approves itself most entirely to the sober and devout spirit, stands in general a fairer chance of being the true interpretation, than what has the suffrage of minds ingenious and original but deficient in those moral requisites'.[46] If this criterion offered a guarantee on the part of the interpreter, Keble also provided a criterion – based on his concept of *ethos* – for judging the interpretations in themselves: the doctrinal view or interpretation of Scripture tending to deepen faith, and promote holiness, humility, etc., is safer than that which lowers the standard of morality, engenders spiritual pride and the like; the latter cannot be from

God.[47] He supplied further scriptural texts in support of these criteria, which he felt were much the same thing as the Aristotelian concept of *phronesis* or practical wisdom, although, with Butler, he had transferred Aristotle's *phronesis* to the realm of intellectual knowledge. Keble used the term *ethos* to refer to this moral disposition or character; and, in his early *Lectures on Poetry* (started in 1832), he described it as a stable disposition, not just a passing impulse; the result of a lifetime searching after virtue.[48]

Following Butler, Keble considered that man's knowledge is, for the most part, based on probable arguments. Within that scheme, he conceived moral rectitude as a light guiding man to find his way to truth through the maze of possible answers offered to him; the right moral temper would provide sure guidance to identify truth among conflicting arguments and probabilities.[49] This principle (already suggested by Butler) was not only suited to but also demanded by Keble's general theory, in order to give firmness and certitude to human knowledge of revealed truth. Thus, Keble, according to Newman, conferred on knowledge based on probability a degree of certainty that it did not have of itself: the firmness of assent to religious doctrines is derived not from mere probability but from the power of faith and love which serve as sure guides in determining where truth lies.[50] Keble saw the search for truth as an ascending spiral movement: moral rectitude influences discovery of truth; truth discovered should commit the person vitally; this commitment, in turn, would bring about a clearer perception of revealed truth, and so on. If Keble – as Isaac Williams had said – set *ethos* above intellect, he did so for intellect's sake.

Keble believed that the least of Christ's words and actions is charged with heavenly and mysterious meaning. This many-layered richness of revelation and Holy Scripture was well adapted to the ethical process of discovering truth. Within this process, the deepest meaning of the Gospel can be reached only by those who are in close communion with Christ. On this count, Keble defended a mystical interpretation of Holy Scripture against those who admitted only a literal one. He admitted that a mystical interpretation was not free from danger, but contended that the same was true of all ways of approaching revelation. The remedy was to strengthen the eyes of the intellect by means of repentance, devotion and self-denial, so as to make them able to stand the light of divine truth. The rules for mystical interpretation could not easily be defined and could not therefore be acquired as a mere technique. Only by regular exercise in the exposition of the Scriptures, and by practising the devout observances of the Fathers (the great models of scriptural interpretation), would the modern day exegete gain gradually their perceptive eye, enabling him to discern their first principles of interpretation. Intellectual acuteness and industry, if not accompanied by that moral training, would be equivalent to the blind leading the blind. Experience showed that pouring scorn on the Fathers' mystical interpretation of Scripture, and reducing interpretation to the merely critical and historical, had been in some well-known cases a step towards Arianism and other doctrinal errors. The poor and unlearned who feared God and led pure lives were for the most part better prepared to receive those divine lights than men of great learning and cultivation.[51]

It followed naturally that Keble saw the primary aim of education, in its broadest and truest sense, as the formation of a right *ethos*. He considered that poetry played a central role in this process. Indeed, writing in 1814, he described poetry's mission as 'the awakening of some moral or religious feeling, not by direct instruction (that is the office of morality or theology)', but by a process of imaginative associations.[52] He considered religion and poetry closely related, for God has used poetic language to communicate himself to man, employing symbolical associations – whether poetical, moral or mystical – to reveal a world beyond sense perception. Poetry and religion are meant to advance each other: poetry offers religion a means to express high realities otherwise inexpressible, while religion offers poetry a lofty field of sentiment to work upon.[53] The true poet, Keble thought, is the one who uses ideas and language calculated to raise religious and moral associations, presenting something absent, awakening longings, making man feel his own dignity and a desire to better something still imperfect, detaching him from earthly affections and lifting him nearer to what he once was.[54]

In this sense, the Tractarians would acknowledge the influence that poetry, and the Romantic poets in particular, had on the renewal of contemporary religious feeling. Keble, however, was critical of Wordsworth and Coleridge, although he recognized their contribution to the revival, and he had tried to distance himself publicly from Wordsworth as early as 1815 when reviewing two of his books. Keble admired the poet's talents, but he did not subscribe to all the tenets of his system. He criticized Wordsworth's 'theories and eccentricities', particularly his vision of poetic sensibility as giving access to a higher realm inaccessible to mere humans. He was also critical of Wordsworth's use of poetry to convey metaphysical ideas.[55] Keble's concept of *ethos* excluded the possibility of an innate faculty, independent from moral qualities, giving access to a higher realm of knowledge – especially religious knowledge. In later years, he was even doubtful about whether he should dedicate his lectures on poetry to Wordsworth, given the unorthodoxy of some of the poet's opinions. He considered, however, that Wordsworth, Coleridge and Scott had laboured under the disadvantages of the system in which they had been raised, and the prevailing tone of their time and place. Nevertheless, they had managed to rise above it by means of good sense and right instinct; their *ethos* was Catholic, and Keble could only wonder what their reaction would have been had the complete Catholic system been fully and fairly presented to their minds. He thought that they would have welcomed it.[56]

In the case of Coleridge, the fact that his theory of knowledge had arrived at conclusions that were similar to those reached independently by the Tractarians was, for Newman, a confirmation of the existence of a common underlying current, while the rapid spreading of their ideas manifested how attuned they were to the spiritual needs of the time. The poet had affirmed that scientific understanding, which organized sense perception, could not give a complete knowledge of reality, as some of its aspects escaped the senses; scientific information had to be complemented by knowledge attained by a higher faculty – 'reason', Coleridge called it – which provides access to truths beyond the reach of sense experience. Spiritual realities were the proper object of this faculty. This sort of knowledge, being moral in character, could not but be affected by the moral temper of the subject.[57] The similarities between Keble's and Coleridge's ideas are obvious, but the

Tractarian theory of religious knowledge did not depend upon the poet for its formation,[58] as its genesis preceded the publication of Coleridge's philosophical works. Coleridge's *Biographia Literaria* was published in 1817 and his *Aids to Reflection* did not appear in print till 1825. By then, Keble had already sketched some of the seminal future Tractarian ideas in his 1814 review of Copleston's *Praelectiones Academicae*.[59]

We also have from Newman's pen an indirect testimony to the independent formation of his own ideas: 'During this spring (1835) I for the first time read parts of Coleridge's works; and I am surprised how much I thought mine, is to be found there'.[60] Newman, while critical of Coleridge's doctrinal errors, felt that the poet had rendered great service to Catholic principles by preparing minds for something higher. Many, especially among the young men at Cambridge, were under his influence and could move in a Tractarian direction.[61] Maurice,[62] Newman thought, was one of them: a Coleridgean and a Platonist, not far from Catholic principles when compared with rationalists, but still some way off. The fundamental difference between the Tractarians and the Cambridge men consisted, Newman thought, in the fact that the latter believed sacred doctrines not because they had received them from authority, but because they could prove them from philosophy. They were distinct schools of thought. Nevertheless, the Oxford men would be naturally grateful for the additional confirmation and support offered by Coleridge's ideas. Some of those more or less closely associated with the Oxford Movement – men like Acland, Pattison and Manning – had at some stage or other been influenced by Coleridge.[63]

ETHOS: A FOUNDATION, A GUIDING PRINCIPLE AND AN END

Froude absorbed the concept of *ethos* from Keble, refined it further, and made it central to his vision of the intellectual and religious life, developing at length the relationship between character and opinions, especially in the religious sphere. In 1827 he had jotted down some of his thoughts about the connexion between right faith and right practice, claiming that opinions are essentially consistent with particular characters, and that in a double sense: a temper of mind or character would tend to generate a certain set of opinions, and, conversely, a given set of opinions would tend to shape mind and character in a particular way. This was by no means psychological determinism: men were not born Platonists or Aristotelians, heretical or orthodox believers. Character, for Froude, is defined morally, being in constant state of formation and flux; and the different moral phases of the individual manifest their corresponding effects on his opinions. Froude saw the development of character as controlled by a very sensitive tiller, holding or altering the course of moral progress at the touch of every moral decision. In summary, opinions are essentially homogeneous with particular characters: a man who is morally good will have a right faith, while heresy would be the intellectual fruit of a vicious *ethos*. Froude did not, however, apply the principle too strictly, and partly exonerated some of those in error, particularly those whose opinions – while they were engaged in the search for truth – were still in the process of formation.[64]

This theory helped Froude answer a question pressing upon him. He had been puzzled by the damnatory clauses of the Athanasian Creed: he could not understand how opinions, of themselves, could be the object of God's wrath.[65] He had also to contend with St Paul, who had clearly affirmed that errors of opinion, as well as of practice, make men unfit for the kingdom of Heaven. Keble's ideas about the influence of a particular *ethos* on the intellectual life offered Froude the elements of a solution. He rehearsed the argument *ab initio*. Men deserve reward or punishment on the basis of choices made in the exercise of their free will; they cannot be responsible for events or opinions over which they have no control. Therefore, if liberty of choice is implied in the idea of punishment or reward, the condemned opinion must involve something moral, either in its cause or in its effect. Froude concluded that, if men are to be punished or rewarded also for their beliefs (as the Athanasian Symbol professes), this could only be in so far as these are accepted and held under the influence of man's free will, and consequently the will's character cannot but play a decisive role in this process. Man is thus responsible for his faith to the degree that he is responsible for his character. This line of argument was not without its difficulties: it is a fact that man originally tends to accept religious truth – like natural truths – on the authority of those who instruct him, and, as a result, it may not be easy or even possible for some to rise above errors or prejudices inculcated in early life. Froude, however, thought that a moment arrives inevitably when one becomes responsible for adhering to error, and this implies that there must be some means by which truth is gradually presented to man. When confronted by it, he is called to make his decision: either to become responsible for the errors transmitted by his instructors, or to accept the truth now offered him.[66] Revealed truth does not impose itself on the mind. Froude, applying 'Pascal's wager', had suggested in 1835 an interesting corollary to the general theory. The safest course, in truth or in practice, is not always to be found in what is most probable: it may be safe to risk little if there is a small probability of a great gain; conversely it may not be safe to risk much – eternal life, for example – even when the probability of that happening is small.[67]

Man, unfortunately, does not start as a *tabula rasa*. As result of his sinfulness – beginning with original sin – he grows blind to God's revelations, and each individual needs to work in order to remove that blindness by persevering in good habits.[68] Froude would claim in one of his sermons that, without the discipline of loving and fearing God, man cannot even know him: it is by doing God's will that man gradually understands the doctrine God taught us about himself.[69] People assume that familiarity with the words necessarily implies familiarity with the ideas they contain, but this is not always the case. Froude distinguished between knowledge of facts and the knowledge that truly affects the life of a person to his or her advantage: the latter depends on the habitual religious convictions of the individual in question. A disposition to a life of pleasure will indispose the person to understand and welcome God's word, and he or she must remain in ignorance, although familiar with the words of revelation.[70] The liberal tradition of 'rational theology', even in its moderate form, set reason over faith, impeding access to the real meaning of a revelation that only opens itself to the humble. The Evangelicals on the other hand, stressing sentiment as the fundamental religious guide, made the revealed doctrines a secondary thing. Froude would see both positions as having much more in common that their respective partisans imagined: 'On the one hand we see [in the Liberals] a very strong and general disposition to divest Scripture of its apparent meaning, when such as our natural faculties cannot apprehend and verify [it]; and on the other [the Evangelicals] to invest man with supernatural faculties for the purpose of verifying it: thus, in both cases, Revelation and Experience are brought into accordance, though by processes the direct reverse of one another, and by persons for the most part diametrically opposed in all their habits of thought and feeling.'[71] In so doing, both Evangelicals and Liberals were neglecting fundamental dimensions of the Christian religion: the 'dogmatic principle' and the 'sacramental system'.[72]

Froude stressed the powerful 'influence of habit in moulding our opinions, and the consequent probability that every evil habit we may have contracted, consciously or unconsciously, from the day of our birth to the present hour, has in its degree perverted our judgement'.[73] It could be said, therefore, that there are as many different prejudices and opinions as there are different turns of mind and different moral histories. People, whether they are conscious of it or not, are likely to be prejudiced to some degree in the examination of evidence, inclined to underrate and neglect some while overrating and overemphasizing others. The fact that they may not be conscious of those prejudices only makes their influence more pervasive and determining.[74] On the basis of this theory, Froude criticized the Protestant principle of private judgement. He ridiculed those who thought that they would not be prejudiced in their interpretation of Scripture: 'Such people are under a great delusion. Let them try ever so much, they neither think for themselves nor interpret for themselves . . . Their notions, their feelings, their associations, are not their own. They have picked them up from others, or from opposing others . . . The views of their times and their society are most dogmatical commentators, and will intrude at every instant on unprejudiced thought, unperceived and unsuspected.'[75]

The opinions and prejudices of the times were to be the constant target of Tractarian criticism. Keble's *National Apostasy* sermon in 1833 did not merely denounce a particular measure – the suppression of some Irish bishoprics – being contemplated by

Parliament; his main criticism was aimed at the dominant national *ethos*. Its symptoms were: growing indifference; following the rule of public opinion rather than the rule of truth; impatience under pastoral authority. A nation led by this prevailing temper would go from bad to worse, abandoning the law of the Gospel through accommodations with evil, sometimes on the plea of toleration, at other times on that of state security or of sympathy with popular feeling.[76] Froude echoed Keble's words, and denounced the state of religious indifference in which the country found itself: indifference to sacred things amounting sometimes to contempt, accompanied by a veneer of empty artificial respect, and a clergy anxious to make the country appear Christian after it had ceased to be so.[77] The danger they dreaded was that the day might come when the state, without destroying the established Church, would corrupt it and, under the pretence of the usefulness of a profession of religion, would construct a national religion and use it for its own purposes.[78]

Newman continued building on foundations laid down by his friends. He acknowledged the influence that Butler had had on him, through the medium of Keble's mind,[79] and that Froude had also played an important role in the formation of his ideas about *ethos*. As he put it in 1828, he relied on Froude's authority 'for lowering the intellectual powers into handmaids of our moral nature'.[80] A subordination resulting from man's present fallen condition: the wounded and darkened intellect needs the guidance of right moral feeling or *ethos* to find its way. The fashion of the day was to consider the human mind as a machine, safely and surely producing the right results if operated properly, and education as the means to assure those proper workings. Against the ideas of the Enlightenment, and contemporary rationalism, the Tractarians insisted on the determining influence of the will on the intellectual process in general and, in particular, on religious thought.[81]

Samuel Wood saw Newman's first volume of *Parochial and Plain Sermons* (1834) as the exemplification of the moral temper which the Oriel tutors had tried to instil in the minds of the undergraduates assigned to them. In those sermons, Wood wrote, 'the fruits of that course of study to which I have adverted [Aristotle and Butler] became remarkably evident. This volume hardly contains a directly theological Sermon. The scope of the whole of it appears to be the production of a certain moral temper – a temper, for the most part, in strong contrast, with the prevalent one of the day.'[82] The first sermon, entitled 'Holiness necessary for future Blessedness', was emblematic of the whole content of the volume. Dean Church would remark many years later that the note struck by this sermon 'was never allowed to be out of mind', and he added that 'The movement was, above all, a moral one; it was nothing, allowed to be nothing, if it was not this'.[83] These words are true as far as they go; they underestimated, however, the connexion between truth and sanctity in Tractarian thought. The Tractarians considered sanctity the final end of man. But they saw truth as a necessary condition for attaining it, and sanctity as a sure and necessary guide for man in his search for truth.

They claimed that they wanted to generate an *ethos* rather than a system.[84] In their understanding, however, although *ethos* is not a system in itself, one of its proper fruits is to generate one. As Newman conceived it, the system by its very nature could never become a closed one; it would always be open to further perfection. In that progress towards perfection, *ethos* serves as a light to identify true principles and also as a guide in drawing the right conclusions or corollaries which follow from them. At another level, the Tractarians also pointed out that people might be better or worse than their principles. Newman even suggested that a good man under a defective religious system would joyfully and promptly accept a more perfect one when coming into contact with it, and that the process would continue until he made his own the perfect system of Christian orthodoxy. Progress along the path of truth depended on perseverance in virtue amidst trials. Religious truth was offered, not forced upon the intellect by syllogism or external evidences.[85]

The influence of the individual's moral temper upon his ideas was such that Newman could write: 'the difference between this and that system is *as nothing* compared with the effects of the human will upon them'.[86] As a matter of fact, different systems would produce similar results if acted upon by the same *ethos*. The right *ethos* would work as a corrective of the wrong ideas professed by the mind, pointing the persons concerned in the direction of truth, and inclining them to make it their own. The wrong *ethos*, on the other hand, would distort the perception of true concepts, and lead the intellect towards error. The theory went a step further. Ideas have their own proper *ethos*. It might happen that those holding a particular idea might personally be possessed of an *ethos* which is quite distinct from that of the idea they uphold and, as a result of this inner tension, the idea in question might be corrupted by the influence upon it of an unsympathetic *ethos*. It might also happen that a person's *ethos* could be progressively transformed by the pressure exerted on it by the idea's *ethos*. No department of the religious organism, whether at the individual or communitarian level, was isolated: 'the Church doctrine, the Church discipline, the Church ordinances, and the Church temper' – Oakeley would write – 'are all parts of a coherent whole, none of which can rightly or safely be separated from the rest'. A change in one of them would affect all the others sooner or later, with greater or lesser intensity. Only the Church system, particularly the Church *ethos*, guarantees the harmonic development of the whole Christian dispensation.[87]

It is obvious that the use of the term *ethos* always demands the presence of a context to determine its exact nature and direction. The Tractarians distinguished different types of *ethos* among Christians: Catholic, dissenting, heretical, and so on. Each of them reflects a different moral temper, resulting in a particular intellectual approach, leading to widely different conclusions and generating diverse systems of thought and action. While the right *ethos* directs man towards truth, a sinful one would direct him towards error and, in the religious sphere, towards heresy. Newman developed at length the connexion between particular *ethos* and the corresponding opinions. Especially revealing in this respect are his words in a letter to his brother Francis: 'I have been for some years preaching University Sermons, as I have had opportunity, on this one subject, that men judge in religion, and are meant to judge by antecedent probability much more than by external evidences, and that their view of antecedent probability depends upon their particular state of mind. I consider with you that "the alleged historical proof of miracles is unsatisfactory," separate from the knowledge of the moral character of the doctrine. Accordingly I think a Churchman is (abstractly speaking) a man of a certain *ethos* – and a Dissenter of another – And in like manner that, abstractedly, the Church has a tendency to produce in individuals a Church *ethos*, and Dissent a Dissenting *ethos*.'[88] The topic was an old one with him. In 1828 he had written to Blanco White that he felt like challenging Robert Wilberforce and Hurrell Froude, his fellow tutors at Oriel, to give him 'some account of the connexion (how far) of speculative error with bad *ethos* – e.g. *in what is a consistent Socinian a worse man than an orthodox believer*? I think him to be worse, but I wish my mind clear on the subject, which it is not at present.'[89] The subject was to occupy him for many years to come.

It is particularly in his 1839 *University Sermons*, when dealing with the nature of faith and its relations to reason, that Newman described in detail the essence of the Christian *ethos*, even though he barely used this term. Newman contrasted Faith and Reason as two different intellectual processes. In the same way as reason is a higher instrument of knowledge than merely sensual knowledge, 'so Faith rises above Reason in its subject-matter, more than it falls below it in the obscurity of the process. And it is, I say, but agreeable to analogy, that divine Truth should be attained by so subtle and indirect a method, a method less tangible than others, less open to analysis, reducible but partially to the forms of Reason, and the ready sport of objection and cavil'.[90] Divine truth is revealed for our probation. Absolute proof and certainty would not leave room for choice, and there would be no merit; the truth in question would impose itself on the mind, leaving no room for praise or blame in believing, no test of character.[91]

Newman characterized faith as an instrument of knowledge and action, which has 'its life in a certain moral temper'.[92] And he later described it along Froudeian lines: '*We can believe what we choose*. We are answerable for what we choose to believe.'[93] The acceptance or rejection of faith, he said, is dependent on two grounds: the credibility of the messenger, and the likelihood of the message. In both cases the mind has to judge not so much by facts but mostly on the basis of probabilities. Now, given that 'probabilities have no definite ascertained value, and are reducible to no scientific standard, what are such to each individual, depends on his moral temperament'.[94] A man of religious temper may be content with the evidence provided, while an irreligious mind will reject as unsatisfactory those same grounds. Their judgement is a test of moral character, and at the heart of this judgement is to be found an antecedent judgement or presumption. While one person judges on the basis of antecedent probability, another will base their judgement on antecedent improbability, assuming that presumptions on the side of belief have no substance, while presumptions on the side of unbelief have the nature of proof.[95]

Right faith, for Newman, is an intellectual act, an act of reasoning upon holy, devout and enlightened presumptions.[96] The believer judges the message to be probable because he feels that the truth offered him gives shape and supplies the spontaneous desires and presentiments of his mind. He has a keen sense of the intrinsic excellence of the message, of its desirability, of its likeness to what it seems to him God *would* reveal if he were to reveal anything; he feels the need of a Revelation, and its probability. When love is strong it supplies for the weakness of the testimony. On the other hand, if he is indisposed to believe, he may explain away even the strongest evidence.[97] Man's approach is influenced by his previous notions and prejudices, likes and dislikes, hopes and opinions; he is responsible for his faith in the measure in which he is responsible for his moral temper.[98] Newman kept repeating this central concept: 'Faith is the reasoning of a religious mind';[99] 'Right Faith is the faith of a right mind'.[100] He expressed his thoughts on the subject clearly and succinctly in the article 'Prospects of the Anglican Church' (1839): 'certain doctrines are the rightful property of certain minds, and true doctrines of true minds; that many minds are not true nor untrue, but in transition or intermediate state; moreover that true and untrue doctrines exert an influence upon all minds which admit them, whether of the formed or the unformed class'.[101] Newman considered that holiness, or love, was the eye of faith. A right heart keeps clear the vision of its object and acts as the safeguard of faith, preserving it from heresy or superstition; besides, the vision of faith is perfected not by intellectual but by moral cultivation helping the mind's progress along the path of truth. The words of an earlier sermon, though set in another context, describe well what he came to feel with increasing force in the late 1830s: 'in him who is faithful to his own divinely implanted nature, the faint light of Truth dawns continually brighter; the shadows which at first trouble it, the unreal shapes created by its own twilight-state, vanish'.[102]

Newman had mentioned the existence of a Catholic *ethos* and a Dissenting one. He went on to add that heresy is the fruit of an *ethos* marked by worldliness, intellectual pride or some other deficiency, however subtle or even unknown to the individual in question. Heresy has its own dynamism, impelling it forward to develop the seeds of error within itself till they grow to full stature. Even within heresy, different ethical characters generated different types of error.[103] The *ethos* of holiness, on the other hand, led man along the path of truth. One consequence of this outlook was Newman's reluctance to push liturgical reforms, or even projects of reunion, by looking for agreement on doctrinal matters; for him it was equivalent to beginning at the end. The first and fundamental aspect to promote was the raising of the moral tone of the Church: 'If we be holy, all will go well with us. External things are comparatively nothing; whatever be a religious body's reaction to the State – whatever its doctrines – whatever its worship – if it has but the life of holiness within it, the inward gift will, if I may so speak, take care of itself. It will turn all accidents into good, it will supply defects, and it will gain from above what is wanting.'[104] Sanctity is the great note of the Church, the one on which the others depend, the reason for its existence. Without this foundation no solid doctrinal edifice can be built. Truth and holiness are intimately interwoven: following the path of holiness would lead to the recovery of Catholic truths lost in previous centuries within the Church of England.

The Catholic or Apostolic *ethos*, besides being a safe guide in doctrinal matters, was also conceived by Newman and the other Tractarians as a guide in action. It did not just help distinguish right from wrong, truth from error; it also enabled an individual or group to detect the path intended by God's providence. The Tractarians were convinced that they were instruments God was employing to carry out his plans for the good of the Church of England. Their one concern was that they might be found faithful, and do the work God meant them to do. At the time of J. S.

Boone's resignation from the editorship of the *British Critic*, Newman wrote to Edward Churton a letter bursting with confidence in God's guidance. The Oxford men, Newman said, were ready to cooperate with the *British Critic* with a proviso: 'We want a Review *conducted*, i.e. morally conducted, on the Catholic temper – we want all subjects treated in one and the same principle or basis – . . . our Editor must be the principle, the internal idea of Catholicism itself, pouring itself outwards, not trimming and shaping from without.'[105]

The references to *ethos* appear in different contexts within Tractarian writings, and there is no single place where all its facets are brought together to define it conceptually or to describe all its implications. A further difficulty encountered when attempting to define the Tractarian concept of Catholic *ethos* is the development which it underwent in time. Nevertheless, there are enough elements in the already quoted texts (and others besides) to make it possible to attempt a description, if not a definition, of what the Tractarians understood by it. In its more developed expression, the Catholic *ethos* was conceived as a moral temper involving openness to God's action in the soul. At the human level, this openness to God rests on a humble temper of mind and heart – opposed to the self-sufficiency of Rationalism or the righteous confidence of private judgement – and on a generous spirit, capable of following a radical ideal. Those dispositions enable the individual to submit to God's guidance, manifested in light for the intellect to perceive truth, and grace to enable the soul to discover and follow the path presented to it. It may be said that, within this concept of *ethos*, there are no purely intellectual lights: every truth involves a certain giving of direction for present or future action. In addition, following the guidance of a Catholic *ethos* involves entering into God's plans for the individual and the community, and becoming a willing and knowing instrument of God's providence. Whatever their personal limitations, those possessed of that *ethos* were aware of having a root of truth in them which contained a blessing, which they would communicate to other hearts similarly disposed. The Catholic *ethos* was a source of power, for God granted those made the instruments of a divine providence the means to carry it out. The Tractarians had nothing to fear from Government (or even bishops): 'We have nothing to hope or fear', Newman wrote in 1837, 'from Whig or Conservative Governments . . . . We must trust our own *ethos.*' This was the source of their strength: 'that is, what is unseen, our unseen gifts and their unseen Author'.[106] How successful would the whole enterprise be? They could not tell, but neither should they worry about the issue. Newman would confess as much: 'the inward principle of truth will carry them on their tide of success to those bounds wider or straiter, which, in God's inscrutable providence, they are to reach and not to pass'.[107] The only thing they should concern themselves with was how to respond with generous faith, to aim at perfection, to have the courage to demand attention, and claim the submission of the world; they should offer the testimony of a true Christian people, living by that Catholic *ethos* which carries with it the evidence of the pure doctrine and the true Church. Having done that, they had 'to let matters take their course, and to trust God's good Providence for the issue'.[108] As Newman put it elsewhere, it was impossible 'to foretell *how* Providence will bring to an end what it begins'.[109] Following that rule of conduct, the Tractarians had left 'truth to fight its own battle', and 'their defence to time, or rather committed it to God'.[110] God measures success and failure by standards which are not those of this world.

The persons so guided would normally perceive only a part at a time of the divine plan; the light might perhaps show only the step immediately ahead. That was of no great concern to those possessed of the right *ethos*, for this involved trust in God's providence and the certainty that new light would be granted them at the appointed time to show the way ahead. Newman's poetical words in 1833 described that disposition well: 'Lead, Kindly Light, among the encircling gloom / . . . / Keep Thou my feet; I do not ask to see / The distant scene – one step enough for me.'[111] Faithfulness to the given light was a constant concern of the Tractarians; Newman, while delirious in Sicily, expressed this sentiment by repeating: 'I have not sinned against light'.[112] Of course, a man was only accountable for the light granted him, and no more; this represented his status in God's presence. Faithfulness to the light establishes a claim to further guidance and a clearer perception of truth. Were man to act otherwise, unfaithfulness to the light's guidance – if not promptly rectified – would eventually be followed by blindness. 'I have acted', Newman would write to Jelf in 1841, 'because others did not act, and have sacrificed a quiet which I prize. May God be with me in time to come, as He has been hitherto! And He will be, if I can but keep my hand clean and my heart pure'.[113] Were the Tractarians aware of the aim towards which divine providence was directing them? They thought they were. They regarded themselves as part of a divine intervention aimed at reviving the Catholic element in the Church of England, and faithfulness to their *ethos* was an absolute condition for effectiveness in bringing about such a revival.

Notes

1. I. Williams, *Autobiography of Isaac Williams*, ed. G. Prevost (London: Longman, Green, & Co, 1892), p. 46.
2. T. Mozley, *Reminiscences, Chiefly of Oriel College and the Oxford Movement*, I (London: Longman, Green, & Co, 1882, 2nd ed.), pp. 211–12. Mozley himself, on the occasion of his election as a Fellow of Oriel, was described by Newman as possessed of an admirable *ethos* (Newman to S. Rickards, 28 April 1829, *LD*, I. p. 139).
3. J. T. Coleridge, *A Memoir of the Rev. John Keble. Late Vicar of Hursley* (Oxford : James Parker and Co., 1870, 3rd ed.), p. 398. Coleridge, a friend of Keble at Oxford, was Justice of the King's Bench (1835–58), and sat in the Achilli vs Newman trial. Later biographies of Keble have tended to ignore or gloss over the idea of *ethos*; see for example W. Lock, *John Keble. A Biography* (London: Methuen, 1893), G. Battiscombe, *John Keble. A Study in Limitations* (London: Constable, 1963) and J. R. Griffin, *John Keble. Saint of Anglicanism* (Macon: Mercer University Press, 1987). The only scholar who has made a cursory incursion into the subject seems to have been W. A. Beek, in his *John Keble's Literary and Religious Contribution to the Oxford Movement* (Nijmegen: Centrale Drukkerij, 1959). Sheridan Gilley also referred to Keble giving currency to the word *ethos*, although he considered it fundamentally from a devotional point of view (S. Gilley, 'John Keble and the Victorian Churching of Romanticism', in J. R. Watson, ed., *An Infinite Complexity. Essays in Romanticism* (Edinburgh: Edinburgh University Press, 1983), p. 236).
4. J. Keble, *A Few Plain Thoughts on the Proposed Admission of Dissenters to the University of Oxford* (Oxford: Masson, 1854), p. 11.
5. Keble seems to have become familiar with the ideas of the *Analogy* during his earlier education at Fairford, well before his Oxford studies.
6. Wood, 'Revival of Primitive Doctrine', fo. 1. Pusey had not ignored this aspect; as he confessed to Harrison, his letter to the Bishop of Oxford had included many extracts from Newman in order 'to show *ethos*' (Pusey to Harrison, 22 February 1839, in H. P. Liddon, *Life of Edward Bouverie Pusey*, II (London: Longman, Green and Co., 1893, 3rd ed.), p. 76).
7. Richard Whately (1787–1863), fellow and tutor at Oriel College, Oxford; Archbishop of Dublin 1831–63. The *Lectures on the Church of England by an Episcopalian* (1826), attributed to him, and the treatises *Elements of Logic* (1826) and *Elements of Rhetoric* (1828) were very influential.
8. Wood, 'Revival of Primitive Doctrine', fo. 3. The general estimation of Whateley was that he knew logic and nothing more, his mind being an instrument rather than a receptacle (D. W. Rannie, *Oriel College* (London: Robinson, 1900), p. 176; see also A. H. D. Acland, *Memoir and Letters of the Right Honourable Sir Thomas Dyke Acland* (London: printed for private circulation, 1902), p. 26).
9. P. Nockles, 'Lost Causes and Impossible Loyalties', in *HOU*, VI, Part I, p. 201.
10. J. Keble to J. T. Coleridge, 29 January 1818, quoted in Coleridge, *Memoir of Keble*, p. 73.
11. Mozley, *Reminiscences*, I, pp. 180–1, 210, 229 etc.
12. M. G. Brock, 'The Oxford of Peel and Gladstone, 1800–1833', in *HOU*, VI, Part I, pp. 34 and 36.
13. J. H. Newman, *Autobiographical Writings*, ed. H. Tristam (London: Sheed and Ward, 1956), pp. 106–7; 90–6. Newman wrote that he had had this vision of the tutor's role from the first, and that, for a while, he had been unaware that Froude and Keble

held a similar theory of the tutorial office. Froude, on his part, confessed that he had received his idea about the tutor's role from Keble, from the way the latter exercised his tutorship (Froude to Hawkins, 15 April 1830, *LD*, II, 243). For the dispute between Hawkins and the tutors see their correspondence with Hawkins in *LD*, II, 207 ff. and 296 ff.; see also the correspondence between Froude and Hawkins quoted in P. Brendon, *Hurrel Froude and the Oxford Movement* (London: Paul Elek, 1974), pp. 97–9; K. C. Turpin, 'The Ascendancy of Oriel', in *HOU*, VI, Part I, pp. 188–90; and M. Pattison, *Memoirs* (London: Macmillan, 1885), pp. 85–7.

14. Edward Copleston (1776–1849); fellow of Oriel (1795), Provost (1814–27): he had great influence in establishing the intellectual pre-eminence that Oriel enjoyed in the first half of the nineteenth century; Bishop of Llandaff (1827) and Dean of St Paul's; supported Catholic Emancipation, the admission of dissenters to the University, and Dr Hampden's appointment.
15. Williams, *Autobiography*, p. 21.
16. Wood, 'Revival of Primitive Doctrine', fo. 3. The hero of Newman's *Loss and Gain*, Charles Reding, reflected on the impression made on him by Aristotle's teaching that 'habits are created by those very acts in which they manifest themselves when created' (J. H. Newman, *Loss and Gain. The Story of a Convert* (London: Longman, Green, & Co, 1898, 13th ed.), p. 26).
17. Wood, 'Revival of Primitive Doctrine', fo. 4 (my italics). The study of divinity had little room in the Arts syllabus. Extended theological studies were regarded as part of the clergyman's professional training, and, as such, unsuitable for a first-degree course (Brock, 'The Oxford of Peel and Gladstone', p. 10).
18. F. Oakeley, *Remarks on the Study of Aristotelian and Platonic Ethics as a Branch of the Oxford System of Education* (Oxford: Parker, 1837), pp. 14–15.
19. Ibid., p. 49.
20. F. Oakeley, *Historical Notes on the Tractarian Movement (A.D. 1833–1845)* (London: Longman, Green, Longman, Roberts, & Green, 1865), p. 18.
21. See for example Newman to S. Rickards, 14 April 1833, *LD*, III, p. 289.
22. Keble, *Plain Thoughts*, p. 5.
23. See for example the 'Letter of the Corpus Committee' against Dr Hampden's appointment (26 April 1836), probably written by Newman (*LD*, V, pp. 287 ff.).
24. E. Copleston, *A Reply to the Calumnies of the Edinburgh Review against Oxford. Containing an Account of Studies Pursued in the University* (Oxford: Parker, 1810), pp. 22 ff.
25. Ibid., pp. 177–8.
26. H. Wilberforce, *The Foundations of Faith Assailed in Oxford* (London: Rivington, 1835), pp. 5, 7–9, 13 ff.
27. Joseph Butler (1692–1752) conformed to the Church of England from Presbyterianism; Bishop of Bristol (1738) and then of Durham (1750). His *Analogy of Religion, Natural and Revealed, to the Constitution and Correct Course of Nature* (1736), exerted a considerable influence well into the nineteenth century. For the place occupied by Butler in the Oxford curriculum see J. Garnett, 'Bishop Butler and the Zeitgeist: Butler and the Development of Christian Moral Philosophy in Victorian Britain', in C. Cunliffe, ed., *Joseph Butler's Moral and Religious Thought* (Oxford: Clarendon Press, 1992), pp. 63–96.
28. *Nicomachean Ethics*, 1144–5a6. William Sewell also dwelt on this aspect in 1834 when defending the University against the threat of having to admit dissenters: a good heart is the best way to discover the right path to an end (W. Sewell, *Thoughts on the Admission of Dissenters to the University of Oxford* (Oxford: Talboys, 1834), pp. 9, 47 etc.). See also Pattison, *Memoirs*, pp. 134–5.
29. Wood, 'Revival of Primitive Doctrine', fo. 3.

30. J. Butler, *The Analogy of Religion Natural and Revealed to the Constitution and Course of Nature*, ed. W. E. Gladstone (Oxford: Clarendon Press, 1896), Introduction, §§ 8–9, pp. 9–11. The division in chapters and paragraphs is traditionally used in the references to this work.
31. Ibid., part II, ch. IV, § 6, pp. 248–9.
32. Ibid., Intro., §§ 4, 5, pp. 5–6.
33. Ibid., part I, ch. V, §24, p. 122.
34. Ibid., part II, ch. VI, § 15, p. 290.
35. B. Young, *Religion and Enlightenment in Eighteenth-Century England. Theological Debate from Locke to Burke* (Oxford: Oxford University Press, 1998), p. 121.
36. D. Wilson, *Obedience the Path to Religious Knowledge* (Oxford: printed for the author, 1810, 2nd ed.), p. 5. He based his arguments on Aristotle's *Nichomachean Ethics* and, in particular, on Jn 7: 16–17, a text much quoted in this respect by Keble and the other Tractarians.
37. J. Keble, *SAO*, Preface, pp. vi–viii.
38. Froude had expressed the same idea years before: 'These thoughts are indeed cast by Bishop Butler in a mould more immediately suited to the doubts of the Deist than a Christian: but by very slight alterations here and there of words obviously immaterial to the argument, it will be found that they apply with equal force, and carry equal satisfaction, to those who doubt how much they shall accept for revelation, as to those who doubt about accepting any at all'. (R. H. Froude, 'Essay on Rationalism as Shown in the Interpretation of Scripture' (1834), *Remains*, II–I, p. 83.
39. [J. Keble], 'Praelectiones Academicae Oxonii habitae ab Edwardo Copleston', *British Critic*, 1, new series (June 1814), p. 588.
40. These words of Scripture were a banner for the Tractarians. Frederick Oakeley used the same text of St John, and gave it a similar interpretation (F. Oakeley, *Sermons Preached Chiefly in the Royal Chapel at Whitehall* (Oxford: Parker, 1839), p. viii). Isaac Williams also quoted them in his tracts on reserve, adding: 'the secret senses of Scripture [are] revealed only to good men' ([I. Williams], *On Reserve in Communicating Religious Knowledge* (II), *Tracts for the Times*, 87 (London: Rivington, 1840), p. 37; see also his *On Reserve in Communicating Religious Knowledge* (I), *Tracts for the Times*, 80 (London: Rivington, 1838), p. 36.
41. Keble, 'Favour Shewn to Implicit Faith' (1822), *SAO*, p. 4.
42. Keble, 'Implicit Faith Reconciled with Free Enquiry' (1822 or 1823), *SAO*, pp. 44–5.
43. Keble, *SAO*, Preface, p. xvii; see also 'Implicit Faith Reconciled with Free Enquiry', p. 64.
44. Keble, 'Implicit Faith Recognised by Reason' (n.d.), *SAO*, p. 42.
45. Keble, 'Iniquity Abounding' (6 March 1823), *SAO*, p. 102.
46. Keble, 'Favour Shewn to Implicit Faith', *SAO*, p. 14; see also p. 21.
47. Keble, 'Implicit Faith Reconciled with Free Enquiry', *SAO*, pp. 62–3.
48. J. Keble, *Lectures on Poetry*, I (Oxford: Clarendon Press, 1912), pp. 75 ff. He thought that right *ethos* was a fundamental characteristic of true poetry. Froude had already mentioned to Newman Keble's intention of connecting in his lectures high *ethos* with poetical feeling (Froude to Newman, 1 August 1830, *LD*, I, p. 260).
49. Keble, Preface, *SAO*, p. xvi.
50. J. H. Newman, *Apologia pro Vita Sua. Being a History of his Religious Opinions* (London: Longman, Green and Co., 1913, new impression), p. 19. Newman considered Keble's concept deficient as a general theory of knowledge: Keble achieved no more than a 'loving guess', no more than a 'practical certainty'.
51. [J. Keble], *On the Mysticism Attributed to the Early Fathers of the Church, Tracts for the Times*, 89 (London: Rivington, 1841), pp. 40, 134–6.

52. [Keble], 'Praelectiones', p. 579.
53. Keble, *Lectures on Poetry*, II, pp. 478–84.
54. [Keble], 'Praelectiones', pp. 581 and 585. Poetry in general, and sacred poetry in particular, to be successful should be the expression of the general tone and feeling of the poet ([J. Keble], 'Sacred Poetry', *Quarterly Review*, LXII (June 1825), pp. 217, 219, 220).
55. [J. Keble], '*Poems* by William Wordsworth', *Quarterly Review*, XXVII (October 1815), p. 225. In Keble's view, poetry is not an adequate vehicle for instruction: the poet teaches by association, using sign and gesture not to impart religious doctrine but to describe the effect that those doctrines have upon the human heart and mind ([Keble], 'Praelectiones', pp. 579, 586, etc.; see also 'Sacred Poetry', p. 221). In a similar way, Keble did not share Coleridge's concept of the secondary or poetic imagination (ref. poetic imagination: see for example J. S. Hill, ed., *Imagination in Coleridge* (London: Macmillan, 1978).
56. [Keble], 'Memoirs of Scott', pp. 474 ff. Froude, reading Walter Scott's novels in 1834, would also remark on Scott's liberalism, which he thought was affected, while his *ethos* was sound (Froude to Keble, October 1834, in Froude, *Remains*, I–I, p. 379).
57. Coleridge in 1817 had made a distinction between abstract science and morality/religion: the evidence of the latter's doctrines could not, like the truths of abstract science, be wholly independent of the will (S. T. Coleridge, *Biographia Literaria*, ed. G. Watson (London: Dent, 1975), p.111); see also B. Reardon, *From Coleridge to Gore: A Century of Religious Thought in Britain* (London: Longman, 1971), pp. 72, 114, etc.
58. Stephen Prickett considers that Butler reinforced in Keble ideas which he had received first from the Lake Poets, Wordsworth and Coleridge (S. Prickett, *Romanticism and Religion: The Tradition of Coleridge and Wordsworth* (Cambridge: Cambridge University Press, 1976), p. 108). He and others have tried to superimpose German dialectic philosophical categories on Tractarian thought, particularly on Keble and Newman (ibid., p. 97 ff.). There is, however, little evidence of direct or indirect German influence on their thought. The results of the present study suggest rather that Wordsworth and Coleridge reinforced ideas which Keble had already elaborated from his reading of Butler.
59. [Keble], 'Praelectiones', pp. 577–88.
60. J. H. Newman, 'Chronological Notes', in *Letters and Correspondence of John Henry Newman*, ed. A. Mozley, II (London: Longman, Green, & Co, 1908), p. 35.
61. Newman to S. Rickards, 9 February 1835, *LD*, V, p. 27.
62. John Frederick Denison Maurice (1805–72), studied at Cambridge but moved to Oxford in 1830 to take Anglican orders; chaplain at Guy's Hospital, London (1836–46), while lecturing on moral philosophy; professor of English literature and history, King's College, London (1840–53). His theological evolution from Unitarianism into Anglicanism approached briefly Tractarian positions; he was later accused of heterodox opinions.
63. Manning confessed that Coleridge had done for his mind in theology what Bacon had done to the philosophy of nature (Manning to J. Hare, 1840, Manning MSS Bod., c. 653, fo. 22). Acland was also struck by Coleridge's philosophy; Newman was amused at Acland's reference to his 'metaphysical views' agreeing with those of Coleridge (Acland to Newman, 11 May 1834, *LD*, IV, p. 256; and Newman to R. F. Wilson, 3 July 1834, ibid., p. 289). Mark Pattison also mentioned how he had been deeply influenced by Coleridge (Pattison, *Memoirs*, p. 164).
64. R. H. Froude, 'Occasional Thoughts': 'On the Connexion between a Right Faith and Right Practice; on the *Ethos* of Heresy' (16 July 1827), *Remains*, I–I, pp. 114–17.

65. Newman would formulate the same principle in the *Development*: 'opinions in religion are not matters of indifference, but have a definitive bearing on the position of their holders in the Divine Sight' (J. H. Newman, *An Essay on the Development of Christian Doctrine* (London: Toovey, 1845), p. 339).
66. Froude, 'Connexion between Right Faith and Right Practice', pp. 114–17; 'On the Anathemas in the Athanasian Creed' (16 July 1827), pp. 117–18 (both in *Remains*, I–I); 'Essay on Rationalism', p. 107.
67. Froude, 'Remarks upon the Principles to be Observed in Interpreting Scripture' (November 1835), *Remains*, II–I, pp. 378–80.
68. Froude, 'Occasional Thoughts' (26 November 1826), *Remains*, I–I, p. 86.
69. Froude, 'Knowledge of God Attainable Only by First Acting on It' (written around 1830), *Remains*, I–II, p. 93.
70. Froude, 'Knowledge useless except for the Serious Minded' (Easter Monday 1830), *Remains*, I–II, p. 49.
71. Froude, 'Essay on Rationalism', p. 2.
72. A. Härdelin, *The Tractarian Understanding of the Eucharist* (Uppsala: University Press, 1965), pp. 28–31, 87 ff.
73. Froude, 'Principles to be Observed in Interpreting Scripture', p. 359.
74. Froude, 'Essay on Rationalism', pp. 34–5.
75. Ibid., p. 88.
76. J. Keble, *National Apostasy Considered in a Sermon Preached in St. Mary's, Oxford, before Her Majesty's Judges of Assize, on July 14, 1833* (Oxford: Parker, 1833). The theme of a national apostasy had been taken up before by millennialists like Irving and Drummond: the chosen British people had rejected God's plan for them, and were ripe for punishment (W. H. Oliver, *Prophets and Millennialists. The Uses of Biblical Prophecy in England from the 1790s to the 1840s* (Auckland: Auckland University Press, 1978), pp. 108 ff.). Some of the 'Oxford seceders' used similar language (H. Borlase, *Reasons for Withdrawing from the Ministry of the Church of England* (Plymouth: Rowe, 1833), p. 32).
77. Froude, 'Remarks on Church Discipline', *Remains*, II–I, pp. 273–4; see also 'Religious Indifference', ibid., I–II, pp. 186–7.
78. W. J. Copeland, 'A Narrative of the Oxford Movement', notebook II, p. 18. Copeland Papers, Pusey House, Oxford.
79. Newman, *Apologia*, pp. 18–20. Newman had started reading Butler in 1825 (Diary, 25 June 1825, *LD*, I, p. 238).
80. Newman to J. Blanco White, 1 March 1828, *LD*, II, p. 60. Vincent Blehl reckoned that Froude had introduced Newman to a concept of religious *ethos* previously unknown to him (V. Blehl, *Pilgrim Journey. John Henry Newman 1801–1845* (London: Burns & Oates, 2001), p. 179). At that time he had come to the realization that he 'was beginning to prefer intellectual excellence to moral' (*Apologia*, p. 14). David Newsome pointed out Newman's new use of the concept of *phronesis* but he did not consider the previous developments of the concept at the hands of Butler, Keble and Froude, neither the influence they had on Newman (D. Newsome, *The Parting of Friends* (London: Murray 1966) pp. 88–90; see also his *Two Classes of Men. Platonism and English Romantic Thought* (London: Murray, 1974), pp. 62 ff.).
81. Newman to Wood, 4 September 1832, *LD*, III, p. 91.
82. Wood, 'Revival of Primitive Doctrine', fo. 9; see also ibid., fo. 10.
83. R. W. Church, *The Oxford Movement. 1833–1845* (London: Macmillan and Co., 1891), p. 167.
84. Newman to Pusey, 13 Aug. 1838, *LD*, VI, 283; see also Pusey to Newman, 21 August 1838, in Liddon, *Pusey*, II, p. 39. Oakeley conceived the Tractarian Movement as consisting 'not in certain doctrines only, but in a great ethical system, by which

the whole character was to be leavened, and not merely the reason convinced' (Oakeley, *Historical Notes*, p. 22).
85. Newman, 'Memorandum on Revelation', 2 January 1831, *LD*, II, p. 282.
86. Newman to Wood, 4 September 1832, ibid., III, pp. 90–1.
87. Oakeley, *Sermons Preached in the Royal Chapel*, p. iv; see also p. liii n.
88. J. H. Newman to F. Newman, 10 November 1840, *LD*, VII, p. 438; see also J. H. Newman to C. Newman, 24 March and 14 April 1825, ibid., I, pp. 219, 227–8.
89. Newman to B. White, 1 March 1828, ibid., II, p. 60.
90. J. H. Newman, 'The Nature of Faith in Relation to Reason' (13 January 1839), *US*, p. 209.
91. Newman, 'Faith and Reason, Contrasted as Habits of Mind' (6 January 1839), *US*, p. 184.
92. Newman, 'Faith and Reason', p. 171.
93. Newman to Mrs W. Froude , 27 June 1848, *LD*, XII, p. 228.
94. Newman, 'Faith and Reason', pp. 182–3.
95. Newman, 'Love the Safeguard of Faith against Superstition' (21 May 1839), *US*, pp. 222 and 224.
96. Newman, 'Love Safeguard of Faith', ibid., p. 232.
97. Ibid., pp. 219–20; and Newman, 'Nature of Faith', p. 196.
98. Newman, 'Faith and Reason', p. 184.
99. Newman, 'Nature of Faith', p. 195.
100. Ibid., p. 232.
101. J. H. Newman, 'Prospects of the Anglican Church', in *Essays Critical and Historical*, I (London: Longman, Green and Co., 1897, new ed.), p. 278.
102. Newman, 'Personal Influence, the Means of Propagating the Truth' (22 January 1832), *US*, p. 66.
103. S. Thomas, *Newman and Heresy. The Anglican Years* (Cambridge: Cambridge University Press, 1991) studies at length Newman's ideas on the connexion between particular *ethos* and specific heresies.
104. J. H. Newman, *A Letter to the Right Reverend Father in God, Richard, Lord Bishop of Oxford, on Occasion of No. 90 in the Series Called The Tracts for the Times* (Oxford: Parker; London: Rivington 1841), pp. 44–5.
105. Newman to E. Churton, 21 November 1837, *LD*, VI, pp. 169–70.
106. Newman to M. R. Giberne, 3 December 1837, ibid., VI, p. 174; see also Newman to E. Newman, 9 August 1835, ibid., V, p. 121.
107. J. H. Newman, *A Letter to the Rev. Godfrey Faussett, D.D., Margaret Professor of Divinity, on Certain Points of Faith and Practice* (Oxford: Parker, 1838), p. 4.
108. Ibid., p. 98.
109. Newman, 'Prospects', p. 293. Newman, however, had tried in 1835 to predict the future progress of the Oxford Movement: he thought that it would take some fifteen to twenty years for its fruits to manifest themselves (Newman to Froude, 9 Aug. 1835, *LD*, V, p. 120).
110. [J. H. Newman], *Letter to a Magazine on the Subject of Dr Pusey's Tract on Baptism, Tracts for the Times*, 82 (London: Rivington, 1837), p. xi.
111. J. H. Newman, *Verses on Various Occasions* (London: Longman, Green, & Co., 1896), p. 156.
112. Newman to H. Wilberforce, 16 July 1833, *LD*, IV, p. 8.
113. J. H. Newman, *A Letter Addressed to the Rev. R. W. Jelf, D.D., Canon of Christ Church, in Explanation of n. 90 in the Series Called the Tracts for the Times* (Oxford and London: Parker and Rivington, 1841), p. 47.

CHAPTER II

'Realizing Divine Truth'

Newman's concept of 'realizing'

Following God's guidance presupposes an openness to receive and make one's own that kindly light of which Newman spoke about. There was, however, no single answer to the question about how the individual is supposed to perceive this illumination exposing new depths of truth or presenting new fields of action. Newman described different forms or paths of what he called the process of 'realizing' in the later volumes of his *Parochial and Plain Sermons*, and specially in his *University Sermons*. He did not feel it necessary to define or explain in detail what he meant when using the word 'realizing': 'we all understand the word enough for my present purpose', he said.[1] He provided, however, enough dispersed elements to form a clear idea of his thinking on the subject. And it soon becomes apparent that the process of 'realizing' is practically and conceptually closely intertwined with the idea of *ethos*.

Newman started by pointing out that men might sometimes assent to a proposition without feeling, thinking, speaking or acting as if it were true. They may hear the truth daily, but they do not 'realize' what they are so ready to proclaim. There is no full impression in the soul, the heart or the mind of what has been received by reason; the imagination has not been kindled, nor the heart inflamed, nor has conduct being reshaped by that knowledge.[2] As a result, the proposition itself is for them little more than mere words. As early as 1825, Newman had considered how men might think that 'because they are familiar with the words they understand the ideas they stand for', while not being fully conscious of their real meaning or the corollaries which follow from them. If this may be true in the case of natural knowledge, it is particularly so in respect to divine truth: 'they think they understand terms used in morals and religion, because such are common words, and have been used by them all their lives'.[3] In fact, men have a special difficulty in realizing divine things. This want of apprehension arises from man's intellectual and moral frailty. He is bound by nature to a slow and progressive realization of himself and of the world; besides, as a result of his sinfulness, man's perception of spiritual realities is blunted in proportion as he has been seduced into worldliness: natural man understands not the things of the spirit (1 Co 2: 9, 14).[4] In such a condition, he needs to undergo a process of preparation and purification in order to attain a gradual real apprehension of revealed truth. Humility and the obedience of faith to the divine will open the path leading to the 'realizing' of divine truth. 'Our duties to God and man are not only duties done to Him, but they are means of enlightening our eyes and making our faith apprehensive . . . We humbly trust that as we cleanse ourselves from this world, our eyes will be enlightened to see the things which are only spiritually discerned. We hope that to us will be fulfilled in due measure the words of the beatitude, "Blessed are the pure in heart, for they shall see God" (Mt 5: 8).'[5]

This sort of perception is not merely the result of a process of reasoning and investigation; it is a gift from God. Manning, theorizing on the subject, wrote in 1844 that it is 'a gift passively received, to which we bring nothing but the simple capacity and consciousness of perceiving'.[6] This passivity, however, does not imply a lifeless and inert condition, but just the opposite; it requires a disposition involving the active presence of the virtues of faith, hope and love. Divine truth, Newman had said, cannot be summoned at will; it cannot be hurried. He who read the Scripture or studied Christian doctrine merely in order to seek proof in critical argumentation would be left in darkness. Nor would mere mental acuteness and reasoning powers, of themselves, make man progress in religious wisdom. A different approach was required to gain access to the treasures of revelation: 'Faith and humility are the only spells which conjure up the image of heavenly things in the letter of inspiration . . . Faith and obedience are the main things; believe and do, and pray to God for light, and you will reason well without knowing it.' And, paradoxically, 'looking back, we shall find we have proved what we did not set out to prove'.[7] In this continuous process of 'realizing' men are being guided by Christ's wisdom and his Spirit, by means of an 'inward incommunicable perception of truth and duty'. As Charles Reding put it in the novel *Loss and Gain*: 'Conviction is the eyesight of the mind, not a conclusion from premises; God works it, and His works are slow.'[8] The individual can do little about it except trying to move in what he perceives as God's way; a higher power must overtake him and carry him forward. It is a radically personal process, adjusted to the particular spiritual condition of the individual, and corresponding also to his place in the plans of God's providence. Once light has been shown and guidance given, men must respond with a persevering obedience, making God's will the rule of their reason, affections, wishes, tastes and all that is in them.[9] In this way God leads men forward 'to the one perfect knowledge and obedience of Christ', passing from 'one state of knowledge to another'. They are 'introduced into a higher region from a lower, by listening to Christ's call and obeying it'.[10]

God gives with measure and in season. Man must begin at the beginning. The steps in that process of 'realizing' depend on man's response to the light already granted him. Were man to act upon that light, he would be carried on by God, never knowing exactly how far or in which direction he would be taken.[11] Those who are faithful are led gradually along the path of divine truth. Like most processes of growth, this is barely perceptible while it is taking place. In Newman words: 'For the most part we have gained truth, and made progress from truth to truth, without knowing it. We cannot tell when we first held this, or first held that doctrine.' God leads men on, 'and they do not know it themselves. They are gradually modifying and changing their opinions, while they think they remain stationary.'[12] In *Loss and Gain*, Newman described the manner of this development when portraying the religious evolution of his main character, Charles Reding. Charles had turned his thoughts away from religious controversy but, unknown to himself, his religious views had continued progressing all the while: the slow spontaneous action of the mind had helped ideas take shape, find their place and establish connexions with previously held notions, putting forth new shoots.[13] Along that process it sometimes happened that, all of a sudden, a new view opened for the pilgrim, revealing an unsuspected horizon. Newman described this moment in one of his sermons: those who 'are living religiously, have from time to time truths they did not know before, or had no need to consider, brought before them forcibly; truths which involve duties, which are in fact precepts, and claim obedience'.[14] The sudden and unexpected moment of realizing involves the coming into consciousness and the outward expression of a long process of maturing of principles already held. It entails a deep and vital appropriation of a particular truth, involving the opening of the heart to the knowledge. Only then can it bear fruit.

This realizing, the perception of that guiding light, might be granted directly by God's illumination; it might take place while meditating or reading the Scriptures, when, its sense suddenly breaks upon the reader as it had never done before; it might be mediated through a person, introducing another to truths he did not know or helping him understand previously half-understood ones; it might result from the application of principles to particular circumstances or problems.[15] The list is not an exhaustive one. God might choose other avenues to bring about the process of realizing. In any of those ways, the individual in question comes to perceive at the appropriate time, and according to his personal dispositions, new dimensions of already held principles, corollaries of known truths, the path he is to follow, and so on. In 1843, Newman described to Manning one such moment of 'realizing': the exchange of letters, in which Newman had been trying to explain his present condition to Manning, had helped him 'realize my own views to myself'; they had become more clearly defined, and he could also see for the first time how God's providential hand had been at work, guiding him.[16]

The moment of 'realizing', therefore, may also cast a light upon the past, enabling the person in question to perceive the development of his previous opinions into the ones he now holds. He may become conscious of the changes he has undergone, and perceive that there is a connexion between his former opinions and his later ones. He may discover that the new truths just perceived had perhaps been with him long, barely hidden under the surface of his consciousness or the principles he held. Past events are now seen under a new light: some of those not considered relevant at the time may now be perceived as having had a determining influence in leading the person to his present notions; particular decisions which did not seem specially significant when taken now appear as having had momentous consequences.[17] The hand of God, previously unseen, may now be discerned steering man along the way.

As Tractarians conceived it, the very nature of religious knowledge scorns barren erudition of divine things; such knowledge would not only be divorced from action, but would also prevent the existence and growth of proper learning in religious matters. The scriptural knowledge of many a pharisee and scribe, divorced from true religious feeling, prevented them from welcoming Christ's revelation. Newman would speak in the *Apologia* of his dislike for 'paper logic', and declared that 'all the logic in the world' would not have made him move faster towards Rome than he did. 'Paper logic' could only be the record of what had already taken place: the logical account or analysis of what had been a process of implicit (non-logical) reasoning, complete in itself and independent. Newman could even say that Faith is not 'compatible' with those logical processes; these cannot not bring about the 'realizing' which characterizes the act of true faith.[18] On the other hand, 'When men realize a truth, it becomes an influential principle within them, and leads to a number of consequences both in opinion and in conduct'.[19] The truth becomes alive intellectually, opening fresh views into its depths, revealing connexions with other truths or developing new corollaries; in practical terms, it directs man's steps, and presents new fields of action. It also expresses itself in devotional feeling. Genuine religious feeling, Oakeley would say, is 'the consequence of vividly *realizing* its truths'; the Catholic system would enliven feeling beyond any other, in a deep rather than impetuous way.[20]

After what has been said, one might be tempted to dismiss notional knowledge as of little relevance. This would be a serious mistake, never intended by Newman. As far as he was concerned, notional knowledge plays an important role in man's process of knowing. The first contact of the human mind with a particular truth is, in many cases, an act of notional apprehension. This is especially the case with revealed religious truth. Religious or catechetical instruction ordinarily communicates the truths of faith notionally at first; only at a latter stage – depending on the moral dispositions of the individual – that knowledge is progressively realized. Newman considered that notional knowledge advances the *range* of known truth, while real knowledge increases the *depth* of apprehension.[21] He was, however, conscious of the fact that, by their very nature, no divinely revealed religious truth could ever be fully realized.

Ethos also had an ecclesiological dimension. Newman saw it as a constituent element of the life of the Church, guiding her to achieve a further perfection on the foundation of the truth and holiness already attained. The progress or decay of the Church would always be dependent on its faithfulness or unfaithfulness to its Catholic *ethos*. Individuals played an important part in this process. In the normal course of events, the seeds of a particular development were first planted in an individual mind, and grew out of the person's response to divine grace. Then, 'as time went on what was at first spontaneous and the *ethos* of the individual became imprinted on the Church'.[22]

The principle of reserve

The ideas about the concept and role of *ethos* were developed by the Tractarians before they had explicitly formulated another notion closely related to it and dear to them: the principle of reserve. Newman seems to have been the first among the Tractarians to write, albeit briefly, on the subject. In his readings of the Alexandrian Fathers he had found that the early Church had applied the principle of reserve or economy in the communication of truth. He touched upon the subject in his *Arians of the Fourth Century* (1833). It was obvious to Newman that different doctrines are suited to the neophyte and the confirmed Christian. St Paul had referred to this fact, using the simile of the different foods appropriate to the very young and to those who have already reached adulthood. The variations in communicating or publishing doctrine arose, therefore, 'not from the arbitrary will of the Dispenser, but from the necessity of the case, the more sublime truths of Revelation affording no nourishment to the souls of the unbelieving or unstable'.[23] The early Church had translated reserve into a system to be followed in the instruction of those who wanted to become Catholics or in disputation with the pagans: the *Disciplina Arcani*. This caution was not only aimed at keeping Christ's injunction not to cast pearls before swine, but also as a charitable consideration for the recipients of doctrine, who would otherwise have been perplexed rather than converted by the sudden exhibition of the whole evangelical scheme.[24] The Christian teacher was to unfold the revealed doctrines in due order and within their proper context, so as not expose beginners prematurely to doctrines for which they were unprepared. The economical method and the *Disciplina Arcani* were, therefore, an 'accommodation to the feelings and prejudices of the hearer, in leading him to the reception of a novel or unacceptable doctrine'. It was founded in the actual necessity of the case: 'because those who are strangers to the tone of thought and principles of the speaker, cannot at once be initiated into his system'.[25] Reserve was concerned not so much with withholding the truth as with setting it out to advantage.

Newman felt that the *Disciplina Arcani* could not have been preserved for very long, as Christian doctrines quickly passed into the stock of public knowledge: they were promulgated in the form of Symbols to make profession of the faith or to refute heretics, the Apologists divulged them in order to correct pagan misinterpretations, apostates publicized them, and so on.[26] He considered, however, that the principle was still a valid one in the communication of doctrine. This should always be done with discrimination and sensitivity, taking into consideration the mental and moral dispositions of those receiving instruction. The Evangelicals, in Tractarian eyes, were perceived as serious offenders in this respect, for they presented solemn religious truths in public without consideration for the fact that they were to be attained slowly by the sober and watchful, following the light granted them. For the same reason, Newman was even doubtful about using books for religious instruction: books are not able to discriminate the subtle differences of mind and temper required for each kind of knowledge.

James Rose was not entirely happy with Newman's account of the case, and asked John Kaye,[27] Bishop of Lincoln, to read the *Arians* and give his opinion on the matter. The bishop felt that Newman had overstated the antiquity of the *Disciplina Arcani* in the Church. This was the view expressed in the review published by Rose's *British Magazine*: the reviewer could not agree with Newman that the *disciplina* was so early and so widely diffused as Newman made it; the authorities quoted in the *Arians* to support his case seemed to refer to the third or fourth century, not to an early age.[28] This negative response offered Newman the opportunity to make a reference to *ethos* in connexion with reserve. The *disciplina* was not strictly a rule; it existed originally, and had been practised, as a principle or feeling, as a religious instinct. As time went on, this spontaneous *ethos* became imprinted on the Church: the principle became a rule, as the result of a process of self-reflection. Therefore, the existence of the rule, clearly attested in the fourth century, was evidence of the existence of the principle in the first. The high Catholic *ethos*, Newman concluded, always tends to the *Disciplina Arcani*, whether in Antiquity or in the present day.[29] This he was always to maintain. In his edition of Athanasius's historical tracts he remarked in a note on the need for reserve in those times when Christianity was acknowledged by the state but not embraced by the people, and added that England had now returned to the state of religion in the fourth century.[30]

Isaac Williams developed more fully than Newman the doctrine of reserve, and his *Tract 80* is the most systematic and complete formulation of the principle within the Oxford Movement.[31] He illustrated the connexion between *ethos* and reserve by quoting not only the Scriptures and the Fathers, but also the doctrines of Aristotle and Butler, whom he had read under the guidance of Keble in the reading parties at Southrop. In the tract, Williams stressed the fact that God's infinite desire to communicate the knowledge of himself without any limit or measure is hampered by the unfitness of mankind to receive divine truth. The principle of reserve represents an accommodation on God's part to the nature of the recipient, and the Scriptures clearly showed how God had employed it in revealing himself to man. Withholding knowledge is, paradoxically, an act of divine mercy, given that this knowledge would be injurious to those who were not in possession of a certain disposition to receive it.[32]

Newman had already pointed out that the allegorical method used by the Scriptures was the chief means by which God used reserve in the act of self-revelation, as Jesus's recourse to parables clearly showed.[33] In choosing this method, Williams affirmed, God used those forms of style that man himself spontaneously selects for the expression of sublime truths or thoughts. Besides, the allegorical method of the Scriptures, and the allegorical interpretation demanded by it, is the most appropriate means to communicate different levels of truth to different people; the more spiritual and heavenly truths were left with a veil over them, hiding them from the worldly, while manifesting themselves to the earnest and thoughtful believer.[34] The mystical meaning of God's word is disclosed only unto the faithful.[35] God communicates light to help and direct man, but in such a measure as not to overwhelm him, lest man in his weakness be overcome by God's greatness or crushed under the weight of his full obligation toward his Creator. Knowledge involves a responsibility, and ignorance in those who might not be ready to act according to that knowledge diminishes culpability for wrongdoing: 'Father, forgive them, they do not know what they are doing.' The open disclosure of Our Lord's divinity, a signal blessing and an occasion of improvement for some, would have involved a proportional danger for those not ready to welcome it, leaving them in worse condition than before.[36] Accordingly, God first draws man to himself by cords of love until he is able to reveal himself more fully. In summary, it might be said that God uses reserve to disclose himself better.

Revelation, as explicitly shown by Jesus at the time of Peter's confession, is a divine gift. God reveals himself according to the state of each man's heart, disclosing his nature and will to those who are earnestly desirous of obtaining that knowledge and ready to order their lives in accordance with it. A fervent piety is the key to the stores of God's knowledge, and he leads man progressively onto higher levels of it as man becomes ready for them. For Williams, 'this hidden wisdom [the knowledge of God] is entirely of a moral nature, and independent of any mere cultivation of the intellect. Indeed the latter of itself would appear to be a hindrance to it, – for such "knowledge puffeth up" . . . [We find] passages of Scripture which are only understood in the day of visitation; and in the new and pregnant meanings, which the illiterate perceive in Scripture when religiously excited, and the more devout and thoughtful at all times. This depth and infinity of comprehensiveness seems thus to disclose itself by a continual new adaptation to circumstances all in a *moral* way . . . [Our] blessed SAVIOUR appears to be disclosing Himself to those who are earnest desirous to obtain the knowledge of Him in order to obey Him.'[37] Actions of self-denial dispose the heart to prayer, prayer to the love of God, and the love of God to the knowledge of Him.

On the other hand, God hides from those who approach sacred truth with a mere speculative mind, out of curiosity. Knowledge is withheld from these, and God punishes their attempts with a blindness which will lead them further and further along the path of error.[38] He 'appear[s] to be hiding Himself from those who venture to approach Him with another mind. For, in perfect harmony or analogy to all that has been before observed, we find that we are in a striking way hedged in by ignorance respecting great truths, which we endeavour to gain the knowledge of by any way but that of practical obedience'.[39] These are riches that are given to men in possession of certain qualities, not cast loosely on the world. Williams here made the explicit connexion between the doctrine of reserve and Butler's *Analogy*, concluding that the 'only mode, therefore, of arriving at the truth was by means of that moral inference, under the influence of GOD's good Spirit, which arises from that probable evidence, which He has given us as the guide of life'.[40] Our present state of probation may be one of increasing moral light, accompanying growth in virtue, or of increasing darkness, following on evil conduct.

Aristotle had pointed out the state of moral darkness brought about by a vicious life; Williams transferred Aristotle's *phronesis* from the moral to the doctrinal sphere, as Butler and Keble had done. In a sense, he also tried to answer the question, posed by the deists, which had exercised Butler: why is divine truth not set before mankind so clearly as to make it perfectly open and unequivocal for all to see? Williams gave a twofold answer to this question. On the one hand, he said, God's mercy governs the economy of his self-communication, adapting himself to human infirmity; man cannot see clearly divine truth in his present condition, without the adequate moral growth resulting from divine grace and obedience. Secondly, he affirmed with Butler that probability is a law of human life even at the supernatural level. The moral sense serves as sure guide to help the believer to judge rightly, and to distinguish saving truth from heretical error. Williams concluded that, following God's example in communicating divine truth, reserve is required when speaking about sacred things. Bearing testimony to God's truth is a Christian duty, but it should be done only in so far as it would leave all persons who hear that testimony the better for it. Not observing proper reserve when speaking on sacred subjects might be a source of great harm; it might eventually coarsen the heart, leading men to trample sacred things under foot.[41] The Tractarians felt that the reverential reserve of the early Church with regard to holy things, was 'of all its characteristics apparently the most unaccountable to the spirit of the present age'.[42]

It is interesting to note that for the Tractarians, as for the early Church, reserve had been at first simply a way of being and living, before becoming a clearly defined rule. Williams confessed in *Tract 87* that his opinions on the subject were not 'at first formed from a knowledge of any system of the kind in sacred antiquity, nor from observing that the principle was so fully maintained throughout the whole of the Holy Scriptures as he has since found it to be, much less from any speculative theory adopted in the study; but from his own dealings with mankind in the care of a parish, and his observation of the conduct of others who, he thought, had more experience and good sense and singleness of heart in winning men to the truth'.[43] It was in them, as it has been in the early Church, something almost instinctive. Copeland thought that Keble, following Aristotle and Butler, considered that true poetry and religious feeling shared common sentiments of shyness, veiling the poet's self or the exhibition of religious experience, and showing a sense of reverence in the utterance of things too high and holy.[44] Newman, on his part, would point out how foreign to his nature was, from the first, the emotional and feverish devotion so common among Evangelicals; he felt a deep inner reluctance – an almost physical inability – for the expression of enthusiasm.[45]

For the Tractarians, the discovery in the early Church of a principle of reserve that was already theirs by force of their human tone and religious temper was a reassuring sign. It was a guarantee and confirmation that they shared in the *ethos* of Antiquity, the foundation and spring of religious orthodoxy and right practice. Once again, as in the days of old, life and experience had preceded the formulation of principles and rules: similar *ethoi* brought forth similar principles and generated similar doctrines. Reserve corrected irreverence in handling religious truths. It was a state of thought and feeling, Williams continued, totally at variance with the system '(improperly) called Evangelical, or the cold and barren (equally miscalled) orthodoxy of the last age; so as to show an entire and essential difference in tone and spirit'.[46] The Evangelicals, however, were the worst offenders in this respect, and the evil results of their mode of conduct were visible to all.[47]

Froude as the paradigm of Catholic ethos

Wood considered that Froude had played a definitive and defining role in the formation of the Movement's *ethos*, and felt that it was 'difficult to estimate too highly the personal influence which he exercised over those contemporaries who thought and acted with him'.[48] He exerted his influence on his friends through his words, but in a very special way by personifying the Tractarian *ethos*. Froude's radical search for holiness, his persevering effort to achieve it, and his readiness to follow God's guidance wherever it took him, would have given him an intuitive grasp of the fundamental principles which inspired the Oxford Movement and of the corollaries that followed from them. That is how the authors of the Preface to the second part of the *Remains* saw him: Froude's papers, and particularly his Journal, presented the preparatory spiritual training necessary for the clear perception of primitive Catholic doctrine and practice.[49] It was this that justified in Newman's eyes the publication of the *Remains*. As their correspondence during 1837 shows, both Keble and Newman were aware of the potentially disturbing content of some of Froude's thoughts and of his way of expressing them. Still, in spite of their attachment to the doctrine of reserve, they felt that the benefits which might follow from publication would outstrip the negative effects.

Wood was in favour of publishing the *Remains*, and he was involved in negotiations with Rivington about their publication.[50] His initial enthusiasm, however, was tempered by later reflexion, and he suggested to Newman the possibility of applying the principle of reserve in the presentation of Froude's materials. He was not the only one. Rogers also thought that people should not be let behind the scenes too soon.[51] Wood, however, shared Newman's opinion of Froude's intellect and ideas, and he thought that the Catholic principles which others had to acquire by means of books and study were Froude's 'as it were by instinct'.[52] He seemed to have perceived those principles not only 'as regards their general scope and meaning, but also to have rehearsed in his own mind their application to matters of detail and conduct, in such a manner as to be able to give directions on these points which afterwards proved to be in accordance with Catholic usage'.[53] This was an opinion widely shared. Henry Wilberforce reported to Newman in 1836 how, in a conversation in which George Chandler (Dean of Chichester) and Samuel Wilberforce[54] had taken part, it had been said that Froude had run on ten years in advance of the Church.[55] The Preface to the second part of Froude's *Remains* (1839) stressed this point: 'events have been continually happening, which have tended in a remarkable manner to illustrate the Author's remarks and confirm his prognostications'; 'His sagacity, it begins to be found, did but anticipate the lessons of our experience'; 'his judgement, both of persons and things, has been remarkably verified'.[56] Even Richard W. Church, who judged Froude hasty in his conclusions, thought however that much of what he said looked 'like clear foresight of what has since come to be recognized'.[57] Frederick Oakeley would be even more explicit: although Froude was the youngest of the Triumvirate, he had been 'the first who took a comprehensive view of the character and bearings of the movement'.[58]

The authors of the Preface to the second part of the *Remains* considered, however, that the revival of Primitive Doctrine did not depend on the efforts of any particular individual; rather it was something in the air, going on in all places at once, developing in spite of any efforts to prevent it from doing so. While some might consider it a fruit of the spirit of the age, others would see in it the work of the Holy Spirit, carrying out the plans of divine providence. Still, they said, it was remarkable how that process had been 'anticipated and rehearsed in a single mind; a mind of itself inclined to rationalism'. The pride of rationalism, however, had been checked in Froude by submission to the Church, and such submission had been rewarded by an extraordinary insight into the true nature and claims of the Universal Church, and into 'the means of improving to the utmost our high privilege of being yet in her Communion'.[59]

Froude had proved himself fearless in the pursuit of first principles to their ultimate conclusions, neither sparing personal sacrifice nor being delayed by utilitarian considerations. Once the great principle of Catholicism – universal consent – was rooted in his mind he did not flinch from its results, 'convinced that the only safe way for the Church is, to go back to the times of universal consent, so far as that is possible, inasmuch as such universal consent is no doubtful indication of His will'.[60] The *Remains*, Newman wrote to Bowden, brought out, 'in a most natural way, an *ethos* as different from what is now set up as perfection as the East from the West'. He guessed that different people would react in different ways when reading the *Remains*: that was to be expected, and had a positive aspect. They would serve as a test to separate the wheat from the chaff: 'All persons of unhacknied feelings and youthful minds must be taken by them – others will think them romantic, scrupulous, over refined, etc.'[61]

As Sheridan Gilley has pointed out, Newman felt that in religion, moral and religious truth is communicated by the power of 'a personal presence'; an abstraction is too cold to move the heart. Any programme, political or moral, needs the force of a leader, an individual, who embodies its message and proclaims it to others.[62] Newman, in this respect, spoke of a 'method of personation'.[63] Christ is its supreme example. There is, in this respect, an important difference between Christian religion and natural religion or philosophy. 'The philosopher aspires towards a divine *principle*; the Christian towards a Divine *Agent*. Now, dedication of our energies to the service of a person is the occasion of the highest and most noble virtues, – disinterested attachment, self-devotion, loyalty. It also implies habitual humility, from the knowledge that there must ever be one that is above us. On the other hand, in whatever degree we approximate towards a mere standard of excellence, we do not really advance towards it, but bring it to us; the excellence we venerate becomes part of ourselves – we become a god to ourselves'.[64]

Truth is preserved and communicated 'not by books, not by argument, nor by temporal power, but by personal influence of such men as have already been described, who are at once the teachers and the patterns of it'.[65] Froude was providentially called to fill that role. The Oxford Movement, Newman thought, must be enthusiastic: 'now here is a character fitted above all others to kindle enthusiasm'.[66] He probably saw in the publication of the *Remains* the fulfilment of his own prophecy, when he had written to Froude in 1834: 'It is quite impossible that in some way or other you are not destined to be an instrument of God's purposes – Tho' I saw the earth cleave and you fall in, or heaven open and a chariot appear, I should say just the same – God has ten thousand posts of service, you might be of use in the central elemental fire, you might be of use in the depths of the sea.'[67]

Wood, for his part, considered that in this consisted the permanent value of the *Remains*. The doctrinal points on which Froude dwelt were already widely accepted, but the *Remains* presented an ideal, an *ethos*, which was always in need of being kept alive. 'External tastes and opinion are fluctuating things', he wrote, 'but the laws of belief, the deep wants and universal tendencies of the human mind cannot but continue [being] matters of enduring interest, and it is these with which Mr. Froude deals, and that with all the freshness and vigour of reality.'[68] The *Remains* would contribute to keep alive the spirit which animated the revival, and would help it forward towards a more Catholic doctrine and practice.

It was Froude, Wood added, who had also inspired the Movement with the uncompromising Catholic principle. He 'had first directed their minds to the study of Catholic antiquity, with a view of bringing its principles to bear on the actual state of the Church around'.[69] The authors of the Preface to the *Remains* considered that those who shared that Apostolic *ethos* would pay allegiance to no human establishment, but only to the Church Catholic and to the great principle of Catholicism: the universal consent of the primitive and true Church, the certain witness of God's divine truth and will. Their minds would be uncompromising in their Catholicity, feeling deeply that ancient consent bound them to 'all doctrines, interpretations, and usages, for which it can be truly alleged'.[70] The Church had fallen into decay and had to be raised up again from its very foundations. Catholic Antiquity was the perfection from which the Church had declined after its divisions, and that was the condition to which the Church should be restored. Antiquity should be followed in all those points confirmed as generally held and practised by the Ancient Church.

It might be objected – as it was at the time – that this appeal to Antiquity and the Fathers was a new form of private judgement. The voluminous nature of their writings would make it difficult to determine what constituted their 'consent': how many Fathers, how many instances should be adduced in order to establish the Fathers' consent to a particular doctrine or practice? The question did not trouble Newman. As a matter of fact, that state of affairs served as confirmation of the general theory: Vincent of Lerins's rule is not of a precise mathematical nature, it is moral. Indeed, this fact recommended it to the disciples of Butler. It required a judgement based on probabilities, in which only the right *ethos* could serve as a sure guide.[71]

All this was not mere antiquarianism, a return to the exact external forms of antiquity; neither did it stop at the recovery of long neglected doctrines. The early Church was the home of what the Tractarians called the Catholic or Apostolic *ethos*, and that was a fundamental reason for the return to Antiquity. This was one of the main elements of the universal consent: the religious temper to be found 'everywhere, always and in all' Christian Antiquity. It represented the very heart of the Primitive Church.[72] The Apostolic *ethos* did include well-defined moral qualities, these were '*less tangible and definite* though *not less real*' than doctrines or liturgical uses.[73] It was an *ethos* in direct opposition to the one then predominant in England, and Keble would cite the school of Warburton as an example of disregard for Antiquity.[74]

The Tractarians, as we have seen, left no definition of the Apostolic *ethos*, but perhaps the words of the Preface to Froude's *Remains* could be used to describe it in an ecclesiological key: this Catholic character or temper is none other than the mind of Jesus Christ, which 'by the secret inspiration of His Spirit [is] communicated to His whole mystical Body, informing, guiding, moving it, as He will'.[75] Manning developed a similar argument, adding that in the early Christian centuries, the mind of Christ had prevailed over the diversities of individual wills and characters; as a result, there was within the Church an invisible unity of will which knitted all its members together. It was then that the Church enjoyed the fullness of those powers granted to her by Christ, when the expansive energy of the Gospel could not be stemmed by the might of the Roman Empire.[76] Froude affirmed that the present-day Church, and the individual believer, had to conform themselves to that cast of mind of the Primitive Church, 'its way of judging, behaving, expressing itself, on practical matters, great and small'.[77] Only then would the Church recover from its current prostration and regain its hold on human minds and hearts.

The Tractarians caught glimpses of that moral temper in the lives of particular individuals. Newman's words in the *Apologia* described the spiritual temper of a person (Froude) inspired by that Apostolic *ethos:* an individual possessed by it would have a 'vivid appreciation of the idea of sanctity, its possibilities and its heights', he would embrace the principle of penance and mortification, and have a deep devotion to the Real Presence.[78] Froude, for his part, had that Catholic *ethos* in mind when he depicted the character of Thomas Becket. The Archbishop was not free from defects. His ardour, the eagerness and fiery zeal with which he defended the cause of the Church were not always free from blame, but Froude thought that an 'excess of zeal in the cause of God, is indefinitely less culpable than lukewarmness'.[79]

Froude's influence on the men of the Oxford Movement was, however, a delicate issue. Wood's paper spoke of him as having had an indirect effect on the Movement as a whole by giving 'a tone and direction to those writings the influence of which has been widely felt by the public'.[80] Pusey objected to this sentence, and this is one of the two passages marked in the text by a vertical line and an interrogation mark. A marginal note to Newman, in Pusey's own hand, questioned the extent of Froude's influence: 'How far did he influence the writers of the Tracts? This is a point upon which people would be very jealous and suspicious, if they thought that the tone and direction of yours and Keble's writings had been given by Fr[oude]'. Newman's marginalia answer, probably intended for Wood's eyes only, was to add simply: 'But it has been. JHN'.[81] Newman did not agree with Pusey's objections to Wood's manuscript. However, for the sake of peace, he would write to Wood: 'you speak of Froude's views as influencing the writers of the Tracts. Now Pusey of course ought to be excluded – but as to the *anonymous* writers it is quite true – and I could not consent to its not being said.'[82]

Pusey had little contact with Froude, and was not aware of having been influenced by him. It is true that his intellectual development was atypical among the Tractarians, and there were also notable differences between him and his friends even after his joining the Movement. Pusey had spent a considerable part of the years 1825 to 1830, the most formative years of the Oxford Movement, either away from Oxford or away from Oriel, involved in a very different course of reading and study from those which had occupied the circle around Keble. David Forrester pointed out that Pusey seems not to have started reading the Caroline divines – at Newman's instigation – until 1829, and that it is possible that it was Newman also who introduced Pusey to the reading of the Fathers and the importance of the early Church around 1834.[83] Copeland affirmed in his 'Narrative' that Pusey was not a Butlerian like the others, and he thought that this went a long way to explain his differences with them.[84] Pusey had obviously read Butler, and had been influenced by him in respect of the theory of probability, as his 1827 correspondence with his future wife clearly shows.[85] But Copeland was right in so far as the theory of *ethos* was concerned; it had mostly bypassed Pusey, and he would never make it fully his own, even though he would refer to some aspects of it in his sermons and elsewhere. Oakeley corroborated Copeland's judgement: he thought that Newman and Keble were considerably in advance of Pusey in their opinions, 'as well as materially different from him in *ethos*'.[86] Although, after Newman's departure, Pusey came to be considered as the personification of the Oxford Movement, it is open to question how much he was identified with its core principles. In 1841 he would confess that he did not know what Newman thought about the Reformers; neither had he read the preface to the second part of Froude's *Remains*, a truly programmatic text of the Movement. Had he read the actual *Remains*? Probably not. All this, make it difficult to determine how Pusey's stood in respect to some central tenets of Tractarianism. Still, there is little doubt that Froude's influence was too pervasive and active in Keble and Newman for Pusey to escape it entirely.

The strength of the reaction against Froude's *Remains* appears to have taken Newman and his friends by surprise. Once they recovered sufficiently from the first shock, the Tractarians tried to rationalize the negative response. Pusey thought the publication would result in a temporary check, but considered that it would help people to think more deeply of the principles they had espoused.[87] That was over-optimistic. High Churchmen began to distance themselves from the Oxford Movement, and some who had previously been neutral before declared themselves against them. This, and the attacks in the newspapers, made some Tractarians rather doubtful about the Movement's prospects. Newman, however, was unrepentant about publication. No harm could come from those quarters. Their hope was, as it always had been, the young: 'I do not see what they can do, unless they manage to seduce our brethren or children from us – can they do that, when souls have once tasted of immortal truth? R[ogers] says our hope [is] in the younger – that the elder are wedded to Newspapers – so it is'.[88] The young were capable of enthusiasm and of perceiving the greatness of the Catholic *ethos*. The publication of the *Remains* had them in mind.[89] Wood felt, however, that their publication had not had the desired effect. The principles put forward in Froude's writings had long been generally accepted (he seems to contradict himself here), and men were moving on to 'the knowledge of the things themselves, and are engaged in explaining the records of Christian antiquity',[90] while some of the more personal aspects depicted by the *Remains* had 'tended to repel rather than to win over'.[91]

Notes

1. J. H. Newman, 'Subjection of the Reason and Feelings to the Divine Word' (16 December 1841), *PPS*, VII, p. 263. For a study of the concept of 'realizing' see B. Trocholepczy, 'Newman's Concept of "Realizing"', in A. McClelland, ed., *By Whose Authority? Newman, Manning and the Magisterium* (Bath: Downside, 1996), pp. 136–48). For the later distinction between 'notional' and 'real' apprehension–assent see J. H. Newman, *An Essay in Aid of a Grammar of Assent*, ed. I. Ker (Oxford: Oxford University Press, 1985), Introduction; T. Merrigan, *Clear Heads and Holy Hearts. The Religious and Theological Ideal of John Henry Newman* (Louvain: Peeters Press, 1991), pp. 176 ff.; and L. Richardson, *Newman's Approach to Knowledge* (Leominster: Gracewing, 2007), pp. 50 ff. These works concentrate their attention on Newman's *Grammar of Assent*, and do not investigate the Tractarian sources of Newman's ideas.
2. Newman, 'Difficulty of Realizing Sacred Privileges' (31 March 1839), *PPS*, VI. pp. 94–5; see also 'Subjection of the Reason and Feeling to the Revealed Word', ibid., p. 263, and *An Essay in Aid of a Grammar of Assent* (London: Longman, Green, & Co., 1898, new ed.), p. 126. It is difficult to escape the impression that Newman's distinction between 'notional' and 'real knowledge' owed a certain debt to the Evangelical distinction between 'nominal' and 'real' Christians.
3. Newman, 'Secret Faults'(12 June 1825), *PPS*, I, p. 42.
4. Newman, 'Difficulty of Realizing', *PPS*, VI, p. 97.
5. *PPS*, VI, p. 100.
6. H. E. Manning, 'The Gift of Illumination' (Trinity Sunday 1844), *Sermons Preached before the University of Oxford* (Oxford: Parker, 1845, 2nd ed.), p. 158. For a detailed study of Manning's ideas on the subject see P. Erb, *A Question of Sovereignty: The Politics of Manning's Conversion* (Atlanta: Emory University Press, 1996).
7. Newman, 'Faith without Demonstration' (21 May 1836), *PPS*, VI, pp. 340–1; see also 'Truth hidden when not sought after' (17 October 1830), ibid., VIII, p. 198.
8. J. H. Newman, *Loss and Gain. The Story of a Convert* (London: Longman, Green, & Co, 1898, 13th), p. 294.
9. Newman, 'Subjection of Reason', p. 267.
10. Newman, 'Divine Calls' (27 October 1839), *PPS*, VIII, pp. 27–8. These notions were not exclusively Tractarian. The Evangelical D. Wilson, commenting on the stories of Cornelius and the Ethiopian eunuch, had written in 1810: 'following with sincerity what they knew of the *will of God*, attained to a full discovery of his *doctrine*' (D. Wilson, *Obedience the Path for Religious Knowledge* (Oxford: printed for the author, 1810, 2nd ed.), p. 13).
11. Newman, 'Truth Hidden', *PPS*, VIII, pp. 195–6.
12. Newman, 'Difficulty of Realizing', pp. 101–2.
13. Newman, *Loss and Gain*, p. 202.
14. Newman, 'Divine Calls', p. 24; see also p. 25.
15. Ibid., pp. 24–5, 28–30, etc.; see also *Grammar of Assent*, pp. 78 ff. and 314.
16. Newman to Manning, 14 and 25 October 1843, Manning MSS Bod., c. 654, fos 52–3. In *Loss and Gain* Newman drew a similar picture: Charles Reding 'might not realize his own belief till questions had been put to him; but a single discussion with a friend . . . would bring out what he really did hold to his own apprehension – would ascertain for him the limits of each opinion as he held it, and the inter-relations of opinion with opinion' (Newman, *Loss and Gain*, p. 202).
17. Newman, 'Divine Calls', 25–7; see also 'Truth Hidden', p. 195.

18. J. H. Newman, *Apologia pro Vita Sua. Being a History of his Religious Opinions* (London: Longman, Green and Co., 1913, new impression), p. 169; also 'Explicit and Implicit Reason' (1840), *US*, pp. 258 ff.
19. Newman, 'Subjection of Reason', p. 263. D. Wilson described the need for 'realizing', without calling it by that name: a man may have an outline of true doctrinal in his mind, 'but not having received it into his heart, he shall not *know of the doctrine* [. . .] his notions remain barren and unproductive' (Wilson, *Obedience*, p. 57).
20. F. Oakeley, *Sermons Preached Chiefly in the Royal Chapel at Whitehall* (Oxford: Parker, 1839), pp. xxxviii–xxxix.
21. See for example Newman, *Grammar of Assent*, pp. 34–5.
22. Newman to T. Falconer, around 26 January 1834, *LD*, IV, p. 180.
23. J. H. Newman, *The Arians of the Fourth Century* (London: Rivington, 1833), p. 48.
24. Ibid, p. 52.
25. Ibid., p. 79.
26. Ibid., pp. 58 ff.
27. John Kaye (1783–1853) had been regius professor of divinity at Cambridge, publishing on the ecclesiastical history of the early centuries of Christianity; bishop of Bristol (1820) and then of Lincoln (1827); his letters in the *British Magazine* as 'Philalethes Cantabrigiensis' attracted considerable attention.
28. *British Magazine*, V (1 January 1834), p. 68.
29. Newman, 'Memorandum' (10 Janury 1834) and Newman to T. Falconer, 26 January 1834, *LD*, IV, p. 169 n. and p. 180.
30. Athanasisus, 'Apologia contra Arianos' (18), in *Historical Tracts*, ed. J. H. Newman (Oxford: Parker, 1843), p. 28 n. h.
31. Pusey thought Williams's *Tract 80* the most valuable one of the whole collection (Pusey to Hook, February and 12/11 August 1838, Pusey House, *LBV* 95 (transcript). It is interesting to notice that Selby did not even mention Williams's Tract in his study on Newman and Reserve (R. Selby, *The Principle of Reserve in the Writings of John Henry Cardinal Newman* (Oxford: Oxford University Press, 1975).
32. [I. Williams], *On Reserve in Communicating Religious Knowledge, Tracts for the Times*, 80 (London: Rivington, 1838), pp. 3, 11 etc.
33. Newman, *Arians*, pp. 62 ff.
34. [Williams], *Tract 80*, p. 10.
35. [I. Williams], *On Reserve in Communicating Religious Knowledge, Tracts for the Times*, 87 (London: Rivington, 1840), pp. 6 and 21.
36. [Williams], *Tract 80*, pp. 14–17 and 47. Newman, in this same respect, was concerned about people in the Movement not keeping together: a person might anticipate a truth towards which others were advancing but for which they were not yet prepared; this anticipation could throw them back (Newman to Wood, 29 September 1839, *LD*, VII, p. 156).
37. [Williams], *Tract 80*, pp. 40, 44, 45.
38. Ibid., pp. 40 and 45.
39. Ibid., p. 45.
40. Ibid., p. 23.
41. Ibid., pp. 8 ff.; also *Tract 87*, pp. 7 ff.
42. Froude, *Remains*, II–I, Preface, pp. xiv–xv.
43. [Williams], *Tract 87*, p. 4. He, no doubt, thought of the two Kebles, Thomas and John. He also quoted Hurrell Froude as an example of reserve (ibid., p.141, and *Tract 80*, p. 51), disguising the seriousness of his utterances under exaggerated language.
44. W. J. Copeland, 'Narrative of the Oxford Movement', notebook I, pp.18–19.

45. John Henry Newman, *Autobiographical Writings*, ed. H. Tristam (London: Sheed and Ward, 1956), p. 82. Selby's study on Newman's principle of reserve dedicates a whole chapter to establishing the connexion between the principle of reserve and Newman's character (Selby, *Principle of Reserve*, pp. 96–105).
46. [Williams], *Tract 87*, p. 7. Brilioth also considered that reserve involved an important difference of *ethos* between the Evangelical and the Oxford Movements (Y. T. Brilioth, *Three Lectures on Evangelicalism and the Oxford Movement, together with a Lecture on the Theological Aspect of the Oxford Movement, and a Sermon Preached in Fairford Church on 11 July 1933* (London: Oxford University Press, 1934), p. 41).
47. Hook, who praised Williams's Tract, thought that the way to deal with the problem of irreverence was not 'by avoiding all allusion to them [truths abused], but by speaking of them with increased reverence' (Hook to Pusey, 9 June 1840, Pusey House, *LBV* 94 (transcript); see also E. B. Pusey, *A Letter to His Grace the Archbishop of Canterbury, on Some Circumstances Connected with the Present Crisis in the English Church* (Oxford: Parker, 1842), p. 77.
48. Wood, 'Revival of Primitive Doctrine', fo. 15. According to Oakeley, Newman had called Froude the real author of the Movement (F. Oakeley, *Historical Notes on the Tractarian Movement (A.D. 1833–1845)*. (London: Longman, Green, Longman, Roberts, & Green, 1865), p. 4). In 1850, Newman referred to Froude as the 'one, who if any, is the author of the movement altogether' (J. H. Newman, *Certain Difficulties felt by Anglicans in Catholic Teaching Considered in Twelve Lectures Addressed in 1850 to the Party of the Religious Movement of 1833*, I (London: Longman, Green and Co, 1897, new ed.), p. 41. In 1864, however, he would speak of Keble as the 'true and primary author' of the Movement (Newman, *Apologia*, p. 41).
49. Froude, *Remains*, II–I, Preface, pp. xxxv–xxxvi.
50. *LD*, VI, 75 n.; and Newman to Wood, 2 June 1837, ibid., pp. 77–8.
51. Rogers to Newman, 31 May 1837, *LD*, VI, p. 75 n., and Wood to Newman, 22 July 1837, ibid., p. 100 n. See also Rose to Newman, 7 July 1838, and Newman to Rose, 18 July 1838, ibid., p. 263.
52. Wood, 'Revival of Primitive Doctrine', fo. 15. Newman remarked on how Froude had a keen insight into abstract truth, and a strong hold on first principles, together with a keen perception of their value (*Apologia*, pp. 24 and 38). And he maintained that Froude, 'if any one, gained his views from his own mind' (J. H. Newman, 'Prospects of the Anglican Church', in *Essays Critical and Historical*, I (London: Longman, Green and Co., 1897, new ed.), p. 273).
53. Wood, 'Revival of Primitive Doctrine', fos 15–16.
54. Samuel Wilberforce (1802–75), third son of William Wilberforce. Raised as an Evangelical he became a High Churchman at Oxford; Archdeacon of Surrey (1839); Bishop of Oxford (1845–69) and Bishop of Winchester (1869). He soon distanced himself from the Tractarians, after an early and vague connexion with them.
55. H. Wilberforce to Newman, 22 November 1836, *LD*, V, p. 384.
56. Froude, *Remains*, II–I, Preface, pp. vii, vii–viii and ix–x.
57. R. W. Church, *The Oxford Movement. 1833–1845* (London: Macmillan and Co., 1891), p. 39; see also p. 49 where he compares Froude to Pascal.
58. Oakeley, *Historical Notes*, p. 5.
59. Froude, *Remains*, II–I, Preface, p. x.
60. Ibid., pp. xi–xii.
61. Newman to J. W. Bowden, 6 October 1837, *LD*, VI, p. 145.
62. S. Gilley, *Newman and his Times* (London: Darton, Longman and Todd, 1990), p. 83.
63. Newman saw it as part of God's plan for Revelation and also for the Church; in this last respect, he adduced the institution of bishops: 'a centre of action and a living

witness against all heretical or disorderly proceedings' (Newman, 'The Influence of Natural and Revealed Religion respectively' (13 April 1830), *US*, p. 32).

64. Newman, 'Natural and Revealed Religion', pp. 29–30.
65. J. H. Newman, 'Personal Influence', *US*, p.77; see also p. 80.
66. Newman to Keble, 16 July 1837, *LD*, VI, p. 97. Brendon suggested that for Newman the *Remains* were also a means to overcome the limitations of memory, preventing Froude's image in Newman from becoming fainter (P. Brendon, 'Newman, Keble and Froude's *Remains*', *English Historical Review*, CCCXLV (October 1972), pp. 708–10).
67. Newman to Froude, 12 November 1834, *LD*, IV, p. 362.
68. Wood, 'Revival of Primitive Doctrine', fo. 18.
69. Ibid., fo. 15. The primitive *ethos* would introduce some particular practices, like saints' feast days and fasting, and discountenance others then in use, like marriage of the clergy (Newman to Froude, 17 January-1 February 1836, *LD*, V, pp. 221–2).
70. Froude, *Remains*, II–I, Preface, p. xiii.
71. J. H. Newman, *Lectures on the Prophetical Office of the Church Viewed Relatively to Romanism and Popular Protestantism* (London: Rivington, 1837), pp. 68–9.
72. [J. H. Newman], *Letter to a Magazine on the Subject of Dr Pusey's Tract on Baptism, Tracts for the Times*, 82 (London: Rivington, 1838), p. xx.
73. Froude, *Remains*, II–I, Preface, p. xiii.
74. [J. Keble], *On the Mysticism Attributed to the Early Fathers of the Church, Tracts for the Times*, 89 (London: Rivington, 1841), pp. 7–10; see also [J. Keble], 'Unpublished Papers of Bishop Warburton', *British Critic* 29/58 (April 1841), pp. 432 ff. William Warburton's Whig latitudinarianism propounded a rationalist theology, and was thus inimical to the concept that the ideal of the Church, or pure Christian doctrine, were to be looked for in Primitive Christianity; he expected that his time would bring about as considerable an advance in the knowledge of God as that which was taking place in the discovery of his natural works. Warburton's erastianism was particularly distasteful to the Tractarians.
75. Froude, *Remains*, II–I, Preface, p. xiii.
76. H. E. Manning, *The Mind of Christ the Perfection and Bond of the Church* (Chichester: W. H. Mason, 1841), pp. 7–13.
77. Froude, *Remains*, I–I, Preface, p. xiii.
78. Newman, *Apologia*, p. 24.
79. Froude, 'History of the Contest between Thomas à Becket, Archbishop of Canterbury, and Henry II, King of England', *Remains*, II–II, p. 24.
80. Wood, 'Revival of Primitive Doctrine', fo. 16.
81. Ibid. Newman spoke of Froude's as a 'pupil of Keble's formed by him, and in turn reacting upon him' (*Apologia* , p. 23). Newman, speaking of himself, could say: 'I cannot describe what I owe to him as regards the intellectual principles of religion and morals' (Newman to Bowden, 2 March 1836, *LD*, V, p. 249; see also *Apologia*, p. 25). Froude was aware of the interplay of influences at work between him and Keble (Froude to Newman, 17 November 1833, *LD*, IV, p. 112).
82. Newman to Wood, 6 September1840, *LD*, VII, p. 389.
83. D. Forrester, *Young Doctor Pusey* (London: Mowbray, 1989), pp. 85–8. In Forrester's opinion, these and similar facts demolish any idea that Pusey had been brought up in the High Church tradition of the Caroline divines: Pusey, in 1829, at least, might be considered the living embodiment or representative of the 'forgetful generation' mentioned by Newman.
84. Copeland, 'Narrative', notebook I, p. 65.
85. Forrester, *Young Doctor Pusey*, pp. 59–60.
86. Oakeley, *Historical Notes*, p. 8.

87. Pusey to B. Harrison, 13 August 1838, *LD*, VI, p. 282 n. Harrison who, to the delight of the Tractarians, had recently been appointed Chaplain to the Archbishop of Canterbury soon grew less sympathetic towards the Movement. The Archbishop's displeasure over the *Remains* may have had something to do with it (see ibid., p. 299 n.). Wood, somewhat optimistically, hoped that the publication of Palmer's treatise on the Church could serve as a plaster for the broken head the *Remains* had given Anglicanism (Wood to Manning, 23 March 1838, Manning MSS Bod., c. 655, fo. 465).
88. Newman to H. Wilberforce, 22 January 1839, *LD*, VII, p. 17.
89. Newman's euphoria and confidence did not survive the year 1839 intact. He became worried by the possibility of a split within the Church of England along the fracture lines between Puritans and the Apostolic or Catholic party, and Wiseman's article in the *Dublin Review*, added a personal dimension to his unsettlement.
90. Wood, 'Revival of Primitive Doctrine', fo. 17.
91. Ibid., fo. 17.

CHAPTER III

Ethos, Heresy and Development

Newman and the Ethos of Heresy

Newman considered that the acquisition of doctrines depends upon a judgement based on antecedent probability, and the evaluation of antecedent probability, in its turn, depends on the individual's state of mind, considered in its moral dimension or character: an orthodox believer is a man of a certain *ethos*, a dissenter of another. He, like Froude, found in history confirmation of the general theory. His studies of early Christian heresies showed him that heresy was the mature and natural fruit of an *ethos* characterized by intellectual pride, worldliness or other moral deficiencies; within heresy, different ethical characters generated different types of error.[1] The noble traits of character in an individual might be mixed with some miserable feelings and principles. These latter might exist at first only in seed but, if not checked by obedience, they would grow up and corrupt the integrity of the faith.[2] A progressive decline into heresy would follow inexorably. The person in question would then be carried off by heresy's own dynamism, impelling him forward to develop the seeds of error within it until they grew to full stature. It could even happen that an apologist for orthodox truth against heresy, because of some personal moral deficiency, would stray from the truth while trying to defend it. In some cases, he might be tainted by the heresy he was combating; in others, he might be inclined to fall into the opposite error. The *ethos* of holiness, on the other hand, led man safely along the path of truth.[3]

Newman's vigorous depiction of the personalities involved in the events connected with the Arian heresy served to illustrate the connexion between their characters and the particular positions they adopted in the doctrinal disputes of the time. Arius had been motivated by private ends; Eusebius of Nicomedia and his namesake of Caesarea, were political men, with the virtues and vices of men of letters: an attraction for the comforts of literary life and a lack of a deep hold on truth. Their intellectual deviations from orthodoxy were the result of moral flaws.[4] After his work on the Arian controversy, Newman studied other ancient Christian heresies, such as Sabellianism, Apollinarism and Monophysitism. He came to see Apollinarism and Sabellianism as intellectual forerunners of Arianism – earlier forms of the more fully developed doctrinal error – even though, chronologically speaking, Apollinarism came after the heresy of Arius. Newman thought that research into the topic was able to establish the subtle connexions existing among them, helping to explain their convergence at certain points of their development and in their final end. As a matter of fact, he considered that all heresies sprang from a common principle. They were particular forms of an original and originating error: an underlying rationalism rooted in a moral deficiency. As a result, all heresies ran into one, even when they had started from very diverse and even contradictory presuppositions. Their common *ethos* – a better guide than doctrine to detect their drift – led them in the same direction, and they would reach the same terminus, infidelity. Heresy, being dead, could not but develop into dissolution.[5] Blanco White's personal history – his passage from Catholicism to Unitarianism, with an intermediate sojourn in the Anglican Church – reflected this general tendency.[6] Newman would band him with Arnold: they were wrong, yet sincere. Newman felt that he could put his finger on this or that defect in their characters, and say: here was the fault.[7] It was paradoxical that men who had yielded to the superstitions of their own age might come to countenance old errors which had long been extinct.[8]

In striving to articulate the essence of all heresy and to structure heresies within a systematic pattern, Newman employed a method which resembled his later theory of development: he went beyond the consideration of merely terminological development to accept a doctrinal – albeit heretical – development. Indeed Newman considered that heresy manifests its true nature in its development, and he mapped in detail the path of that development for several cases, establishing continuities where others had found only discontinuity. This was not a mere process of terminological clarification but the progressive and necessary unfolding of a principle, a concept or an idea into its proper corollaries. It was a development determined not only by the pressures of logical inference, spurred at times by criticism levelled at heresy by orthodoxy, but also by vicious moral dispositions. Among these, pride might be singled out as particularly injurious, inclining man to rationalism.[9] The Tractarians also considered the vagaries of deformed religiosity, based on exaltation of feeling and sentiment, a possible path towards doctrinal error. Exposing without due discrimination and reverence the high mysteries of the Christian faith to the gaze of those not spiritually prepared for them was not exempt from risk; it could open the door to unforeseen doctrinal deviations. In this respect, the Tractarians viewed the principle of reserve as a bulwark against heresy.

A DEVELOPMENT OF ORTHODOXY?

All this might have suggested to Newman the possibility of a parallel development of doctrinal orthodoxy. But that did not happen. The evidence suggests that, for most of the 1830s, Newman repeatedly opposed the existence, and even the possibility, of doctrinal development in orthodoxy; only error seemed to be capable of real development. The Tractarians admitted that there was progress within orthodoxy, powered and guided by the Catholic *ethos*, but they perceived it as aimed at the gradual recovery of the full Catholic orthodoxy of the Ancient Church. Froude, however, seems to have contemplated the development of the Apostolic *ethos* as reaching beyond the task of recovering the lost inheritance of Catholic doctrine and practice, writing in 1834: 'We cannot know about any seemingly indifferent practice of the Church of Rome that is not a development of the apostolic ethos.'[10] The *ethos* would legitimize the developments, even in cases where there was no evidence of their existence in patristic times. Later, in the same spirit, he would complain against the epithets – unscriptural, blasphemous, monstrous, and so on – Newman applied to Roman doctrines: 'How mistaken we may ourselves be on many points that are only gradually opening on us.'[11] Newman had spoken about 'expansions' in credal doctrines. 'What is to be the end of expansions? . . . what are the Nicene and Athanasian Creeds but expansions?' Roman Catholics could claim that their whole dogmatic system was an expansion of the truths in the Apostles' Creed.[12]

There were many obstacles preventing Newman from extending his view of the development of error to the development of orthodoxy. The Tractarian theory of *ethos* seemed to suggest development, either by favouring a deeper perception of revealed truth in those possessed by the right *ethos*, or by diverting the mind towards heresy in the case of those in thrall of a vicious one, and thereby generating new erroneous doctrines. But in other respects their idea of *ethos* appeared to preclude development. As the Tractarians saw it, a desire for new doctrines – for knowledge beyond that of the great Fathers and Doctors – betrayed a proud spirit, and this could not but set man on the path to error. Their theory of religious knowledge led Newman and the other Tractarians to distrust an over-intellectual approach to revelation divorced from spiritual advancement. Warburton, and even Butler, had considered that the development of theological knowledge would follow the logical combination of the truths contained in revelation, and that new scientific and historical discoveries would contribute to this process. Newman and Keble did not feel comfortable with those views; they shared a dislike for 'paper logic', and were suspicious of attempts at forming a systematic theology. Such systematizing usually involved an effort on the part of the human mind to impose its law on revealed truths, and this opened the door to proud reason aiming at sovereignty in the realm of religion. And, as the Tractarians repeated tirelessly, access to religious truth is barred to the proud intellect that seeks to control God's truth, while it is open to the humble. In this respect, Keble considered that the purely critical and historical discussions of the eighteenth century had led many into serious doctrinal errors.[13]

Newman's study of ancient heresy seemed to suggest that heretics were generally to be found in the camp of those trying to systematize revealed doctrine, while those who defended orthodox truth tended to be found mostly among the uneducated men of faith.[14] As he put it in his *Arians*, the minds of speculative men are 'impatient of ignorance, and loath to confess that the laws of truth and falsehood, which their experience of this world furnished, could not at once be applied to measure and determine the facts of another'.[15] He was afraid of the risks involved in the effort to structure revealed truths and to establish connexions between them, when those connexions had not been explicitly revealed.[16] Keble, for his part, would maintain that it was a fundamental mistake to regard theology as a science, given that the substance of revelation is beyond man's intellectual powers, and our knowledge cannot indefinitely progress by mere syllogism. The Roman system offered a clear example of the dangers involved in any attempt to arrange revealed truth into an organic scheme. Roman efforts in that direction had been further compromised by the doctrine of the infallibility of the Church, which Newman considered another manifestation of human pride, involving a claim to omniscience: 'To know some things infallibly [in any subject], implies to know all things.'[17] As a result, Rome was forced to profess a complete theology, to know more than had been given to man. She determined the relative importance of doctrines, established their mutual connexions, and so forth; in a word, she subjected divine truth to the intellect. She shared this tendency with other modern systems, like Rationalism and Protestantism, proving once more to Newman's satisfaction that all religious errors, however diverse, have a similar origin and a common end.[18]

Newman went further. He had confessed in the *Arians* his belief 'that freedom from symbols and articles, is abstractedly the highest state of Christian communion and the peculiar privilege of the primitive Church'. He considered this to be the case not through sympathy towards latitudinarian laxity 'but first, because technicality and formalism are, in their degree, inevitable results of public confessions of faith; and next, because when confessions do not exist, the mysteries of divine truth, instead of being exposed to the gaze of the profane and uninstructed, are kept hidden in the bosom of the Church'.[19] The truths of revelation could then be dispensed in due measure and season to those who were prepared to profit by them, as they progressed along the successive stages of faith and obedience. With its *Disciplina Arcani* the Church also forestalled the 'vanity of men, who think that they can explain the sublime doctrines and exuberant promises of the Gospel, before they have yet learned to know themselves, and to discern the holiness of God, under the preparatory discipline of the Law and of Natural Religion'.[20] As a result, the 'rulers of the Church were dilatory in applying a remedy, which nevertheless the circumstances of the times imperatively required. They were loath to confess, that the Church had grown too old to enjoy the free unsuspicious teaching with which her childhood was blest'.[21]

Was this a Golden Age irremediably lost to the Church? Was the new development imposed on the Church because of man's corruption? The Newman of the *Arians* and of the middle 1830s considered the systematization of revelation a necessary evil that followed from a weakening of the vigorous faith of the early Church and from the contemporary assertion of reason aiming at sovereignty in the province of religion.[22] There seems, however, to have been a certain lack of consistency in Newman at this point. When defending freedom from precise conceptual expression of revealed truth as the highest state of Christianity, he appears to have had in mind a religion more adapted to the intellectual nature of angelic creatures, or to man's beatific vision, than one suited to the present human condition. He was forced to admit, albeit reluctantly, the need for the Church to express its faith in formulas and definitions, creating a progressively more precise theological language. And this, he said, was necessary not only because heretical error attempted to contaminate the message of the Gospel, but also because the nature of the human intellect demanded it: 'we cannot restrain the rovings of the intellect, or silence its clamorous demand for a formal statement concerning the Object of our worship'. And, although 'rovings' suggested intellectual restlessness, Newman appeared to admit that those formal statements were demanded by man's nature, rather than by man's fallen condition after original sin. The cultivation of the religious affections demands the intellectual expression of theological truth. In this way, it 'directly assists the acts of religious worship and obedience.'[23] Ten years later, in 1843, he would express the same idea in more vigorous terms: the first impulse of faith consists in trying to express itself about the great vision granted it; the mind naturally turns 'with a *devout curiosity* to the contemplation of the Object of its adoration, and begins to form statements concerning it before it knows whither, or how far, it will be carried'.[24] The Tractarian general theory of religious knowledge would add here that only a theologian with special gifts of piety and holiness would be able to find the most appropriate words to describe the mystery and give it precise conceptual expression. Right *ethos* would provide not only a proper grasp of revealed truth but also confer a particular assistance – lower than that of inspiration, but no doubt of divine origin – to facilitate the selection of the terms used when giving it verbal expression.[25]

Newman's main objection to a development of doctrine in the late 1830s resulted, however, from his attachment to the Vincentian Canon or Rule of Faith, the foundation of the *via media* between Protestantism and Rome: that is to be received as Apostolic which has been taught always, everywhere, and by all.[26] His understanding of Vincent's Rule was soon to be tested in his controversy with the Abbé Jager in 1834–5. Their correspondence revolved, most of the time in circles, around the interpretation of the Vincentian Rule of Faith, which both the Roman Church and the Church of England claimed as their own. The exchange of letters – intended for publication – had been initiated by Benjamin Harrison, who expected Newman to take up the correspondence, which he eventually did. The letters were published in *L'Univers* and *Le Moniteur religieux*. The whole episode had considerable influence on Newman's theological development. His *Prophetical Office* (1837) was to reproduce, in a more developed form, the arguments of the letters, without moving far from the positions maintained against Jager or the terminology used in the correspondence. As it happened on other occasions, controversy had an energizing effect on Newman. Ideas maturing slowly in his mind were forced into shape by the pressure of argument and counter-argument, and new concepts were forged in the heat of controversy to respond to the reasons of his opponent. It was also under this sort of pressure that he entered some of the intellectual and theological cul-de-sacs from which he would later find it difficult and time-consuming to extricate himself.

In Newman's interpretation, the *quod semper, quod ubique, quod ab omnibus* referred believers to the time before divisions in the Church started to appear. Catholicity, Antiquity and the consent of the Fathers are the proper evidence of the fidelity or Apostolicity of a professed Tradition.[27] This was traditional Anglican doctrine and terminology. Harrison had himself used it, although he spoke of the first six centuries of Christianity while Newman restricted the time of unity to the first five. In addition, Newman's strict interpretation of the Vincentian canon ruled out any development in doctrine not only beyond the Patristic era but also after the passing of the Apostles. It was a difficult position from which to argue, and Newman, in spite of his often dismissive treatment of his opponent, felt the restricted nature of the platform on which he had taken his stand. The abbé, as a Catholic, did not admit that the unity of the Church had ever been or could be broken, not even in the limited way recognized by those who upheld the theory of the Three Branches of the Church. This was not the only difference between them. They were also at variance about development, and the concept and role of Tradition. The main question in this last respect concerned the role of Tradition once the Scriptures had been written. What was the status of doctrines contained in Tradition but not explicitly in Scripture? Both admitted that Tradition was prior to Scripture, as the first rule of faith for individuals and the Church. Newman, however, thought that once the writings of the New Testament were completed, Scripture became the first authority, and Tradition came to have a secondary and subordinate role: the Bible contains the whole of Divine Revelation; Holy Scripture contains all things necessary to salvation; the 'very *need* of Tradition arises only from the obscurity of Scripture, and is terminated with the interpretation of it'.[28] Tradition teaches, and Scripture provides verification of the doctrine.

During the correspondence, Newman introduced a classical distinction in Anglican theology between fundamental and non-fundamental doctrines. The distinction had long been in use, but Newman surprised both Jager and his own friends by the way in which he applied it. Fundamental doctrines were those revealed truths necessary for Church communion, and Newman considered that the Creeds contained the complete catalogue of them.[29] The Church had no power over fundamental doctrines, either to add new ones or to subtract from those already established. He admitted, however, that the Church might explain and 'develop' the fundamentals, although he did not clearly define the actual extent and character of that 'development'. Newman went on to point out that although Tradition contained and communicated fundamental truths it also witnessed to other non-fundamental doctrines – which included among them a good number of so-called articles of faith 'necessary for salvation'.[30] He was following closely the Thirty-Nine Articles, particularly the Sixth Article. Newman paraphrased it when he wrote: 'As then I may impose nothing to be believed as terms of communion but the Creed, so I may impose nothing to be believed in order to Salvation, but what is founded on Scripture. And the proof I say, of each proposition is of an historical character, the authority of the early Church, that church which is a sufficient [guide?], first as coming close after the Apostles, next as being unanimous in its teaching'.[31] The doctrines necessary for salvation were those both contained in Tradition and provable from Scripture. Newman maintained that, beside fundamental doctrines and those necessary for salvation, there were other doctrines witnessed to by Tradition but which found no corroboration in Holy Scripture, and which the Church could not impose as necessary for salvation. At this point, Newman clearly stated his case against Rome: she had added to the fundamentals, and she had declared as necessary for salvation doctrines founded on the sole authority of Tradition.[32]

Newman found opposition to those distinctions even within his own camp. Harrison, for one, objected to the narrow radius of Newman's fundamental doctrines.[33] Jager, for his part, thought that these distinctions had no Scriptural basis, and that traditionally 'fundamental articles' and 'articles necessary for salvation' had meant one and the same thing. A Christian was bound to believe the whole divine revelation, as proposed by the Church. He also disputed Newman's view of the general authority of Tradition. At this point, Newman's fertile mind introduced into the controversy a novel distinction between what he called Apostolical or Episcopal Tradition and Prophetical Tradition. The Apostles' Creed, he affirmed, 'does not come to us by the same tradition as the corpus of theology which contains its development'. The first was Newman's Apostolical or Episcopal Tradition. In the Church, however, besides Apostles there are also prophets. They are 'the interpreters of the divine law, they unfold and define its mysteries, they illuminate its documents, they harmonize its contents, they apply its promises'. Their teaching constitutes a vast system, a body of truth 'part written, and part unwritten, partly the interpretation, partly the supplement of Scripture; partly preserved in intellectual expressions, partly latent in the spirit and temper of Christians'.[34] In so far as Tradition is interpreting Holy Scripture, the Church may declare those doctrines necessary for salvation, although Newman thought that the power to do so ended when the original unity of the Church was broken. The Prophetical Tradition, however, continued growing beyond the Patristic period up to the present day. These later developments are not immune from the contagion of error, being particularly open to corruption after the Church fell prey to schisms.

Froude, from the sidelines of the controversy, raised the most powerful argument against Newman's distinctions, and – as was often the case – he went straight to the very heart of the issue in question. Froude felt that Newman had taken some retrograde steps, particularly in respect to the concept of Tradition. Newman, in the *Arians*, had accepted 'as a general truth, that the doctrines in question [the Creed] have never been learned merely from Scripture. Surely the sacred volume was never intended, and is not adapted to *teach* us our creed.'[35] For Newman it was inconceivable that the Apostles would have not taken care to arrange revealed doctrines more systematically. They must have done so 'as soon as their converts became exposed to the attacks and misrepresentations of heretics; unless they were forbidden so to do, a supposition which cannot be maintained'. He did not stop there but went on to affirm that the 'recollections of apostolical teaching would evidently be binding on the faith of those who were instructed in them; unless it can be supposed, that, though coming from inspired teachers, they were not of divine origin'.[36] These words left open the possibility that a doctrine might be fundamental or necessary for salvation if it came from the Apostles, and was considered such by Tradition, even if not contained in

Scripture. In his correspondence with Jager, however, he seemed to have retreated to a more conservative and easily defensible position. Froude probably had Newman's earlier words in mind when accusing him of drawing in his horns during his controversy with Jager by re-drawing too narrowly the boundaries of the fundamentals of the faith and of the truths necessary for salvation.

Froude had little respect for 'fundamentals' – 'I nauseate the word'[37] – or for 'doctrines necessary for salvation'. And he asked Newman to define the criteria for considering a doctrine fundamental: is it fundamental because it can be proved from Scripture or is it so because the early Christians held it as such? Would Newman accept a doctrine considered fundamental by Antiquity even when it could not be proved from Scripture?[38] Implicit in these questions was an important argument: Vincent had not listed the fact of being found in the Scripture among the conditions making up his rule. Newman found himself in a tight corner. If he were to answer that it was the Scriptural character of a doctrine that identify it as fundamental or necessary for salvation, there would be little reason for denying the same character to other doctrines also contained in Scripture. On the other hand, were Tradition to be made the defining criterion, there would be no reason to deny that some doctrines not contained in Scripture but attested by Tradition might be fundamental or necessary for salvation. Newman's answer was rather lame: 'in that case [Antiquity considering fundamental a doctrine not contained in Scripture] I should admit that it was fundamental, but you cannot show it'.[39] This was not the only question in Froude's mind. Article Six also came under scrutiny in a later letter: 'what does the Article mean by 'doctrines necessary to salvation'? No doctrine is necessary to salvation to those who have not neglected it wilfully, and every true doctrine is necessary to salvation to those who if they reject it must reject wilfully'. He could only accept the existence of 'doctrines necessary to salvation' if these were understood as terms of communion. Froude added that 'if the Fathers maintain that "nothing not deducible from Scripture ought to be insisted on as terms of communion," I have nothing more to say'.[40] He had broken the shackles of the Thirty-Nine Articles.

Froude did not add much more, and let the argument run into

the sand and disappear. He may have grown tired of it because of the advance of his illness or, more likely, he dropped it because he knew his friend too well. Newman, as a dialectician, could defend an almost hopeless position with an impressive array of weapons, and overwhelm his opponent with a superabundance of arguments. He was, however, too honest a thinker not to see eventually the flaws in his own line of reasoning and the force of his opponent's ideas, which he might have dismissed in the heat of controversy. Any neglected or badly answered question, any misjudged reason, would eventually return to haunt him until it was properly laid to rest. This was one of those occasions. Newman would claim at the time that he had beaten Froude in the argument, but even then he had the suspicion that things were not as simple as he had made them, and he asked his friend to keep the letter: 'that I may think it over; and help me out of any puzzle, I may have got into'.[41] His letters to Froude later that year clearly show that he was still pondering the question.

A few months after his controversy with Jager, when Newman published *Tract 71*, he did not speak about fundamentals, even though he still referred to them under the name of 'high theological doctrines'; that is, those contained in the Creed. More significant than this terminological change is the fact that Newman now affirmed that we have the certainty of possessing the entire truth about these doctrines 'by an argument which supersedes the necessity of arguing from Scripture against those who oppose them. It is quite impossible that all countries should have agreed to that which was not Apostolic'. He hurried to add that this 'majestic evidence, however, does not extend to any but to the articles of the Creed, specially those relating to the Trinity and Incarnation'.[42] Froude might well have smiled while reading the tract, had he been able to do so. He died on 28 February 1836, the month of its publication.

Among the neglected and unexploded shells abandoned in the battlefield of the controversy were Jager's assertions about development and the infallibility of the Church. Jager accepted the distinction between Apostolic and Prophetic traditions. But he denied that developing truth meant inevitably changing it: prophets and doctors could comment and develop the mysteries of religion while preserving the same doctrine, the same sense, and the same judgement – the signs of true development, as indicated by Vincent of Lerins. In so doing they could give more force and greater scope to Apostolic Tradition. This was what the Fathers had done in their time, and the Church continued doing so at present.[43] Newman would use Vincent of Lerins, and to the same purpose, in his *Development of Christian Doctrine*.[44]

S. F. Wood: An Early Theory of Doctrinal Development in the Oxford Movement

As we have seen, it was up to one of the younger members of the Oxford Movement to make the connexions which had not yet taken form in Newman's mind. Wood was the first to sketch out what was to become – in Newman's hands – one of the most enduring contributions of the Oxford Movement: a theory of doctrinal development. Wood, when speaking of his theory, called it a 'presumptio'; Newman would describe his own as a 'hypothesis'. But these terms were not intended to imply a lack of solid foundation in the premises or uncertainty as to the conclusions. Wood and Newman seem to have viewed their respective theories within the context of Butler's doctrine of probabilities: most knowledge, even scientific, rests on probabilities rather than on absolute proof, and both Wood and Newman accounted probabilities high in support of their ideas. As Newman put it, a hypothesis has no claim on our time and attention until the facts are adduced on which it is built or for which it accounts.[45] Both Wood and Newman felt that their theories rested upon facts as well as accounting for them, offering a solution to a commonly experienced difficulty.

Wood's letter to Manning of 19 November 1835 was accompanied by his paper on development, and they form the most complete statement of his ideas. He wrote three more letters, and also maintained some long conversations with Newman on the subject. Wood put his theory on the anvil, under the hammers of Newman and Manning objections, and objections rained down on it, forcing Wood, in answer to their criticisms, to develop or define more clearly some aspects of the theory, while keeping intact the substance of his first enunciation. He considered that he was addressing a real problem, one he felt very deeply: how to reconcile the doctrines held by the early Church and those which, although not found in antiquity, were held by Christians in the nineteenth century. Among them were 'doctrines which to many holy men have appeared most surely founded on God's word, and the preaching of which have[,] to say the least[,] been outwardly eminently blest'. He was loath to have them wrested from him. He was not concerned with whether he, as an individual, could maintain those doctrines – that went without saying – but with whether the Church could grant them the hallmark of revealed truth and impose them authoritatively. As he put it, 'I should be ashamed of myself if I wanted any practical reassurance of truths to which my heart and conscience bear testimony. But on what theory are they to be defended?'[46] An over-strict interpretation of Vincent of Lerins's rule seemed to rule out those doctrinal propositions which could not be found in early Christianity. Wood thought he had found a poor hint of a solution; it was as yet only a 'presumptio', but he felt it had a solid basis and answered an obvious need.

In the paper accompanying the letter to Manning of 19 November 1835, Wood described first his conception of the role of Tradition. He also referred to it in the letter, which has been preserved only in part. Manning used his scissors freely when going over his correspondence, excising those parts he did not want others to see. In this case, the clean cut at the bottom part of the page may indicate that Manning was more interested in removing some of his own comments on the same letter rather than in excising Wood's words. What remains seems to imply that Wood did not consider Tradition's role to be confined to the interpretation of Scripture, as was the received High Church doctrine. Edward Hawkins had offered an escape route from that constraining vision of Tradition in his *Dissertation upon Unauthoritative Tradition* (1819), where he had addressed a question troubling many minds at the time: why are many of the most important articles of the faith implied, rather than directly or systematically taught in the Scriptures?[47] Hawkins considered that it was part of a divine design for Tradition to supply the arrangement and carry down the system of divine truth, from the initial moments of the life of the Church until the end of time;

Scripture's role was to furnish the proofs of Christian doctrines.[48] Apostolic or authoritative Tradition would have already been a systematic body of doctrine before the Scriptures were written. That previous oral Apostolic teaching had an authority equivalent to that of the Scriptures themselves; the latter had been written 'to enforce and establish what has been taught before'.[49] However important and influential these ideas were to be, it was another of Hawkins's expressions that exerted even a greater influence upon some of the Tractarians. It read: 'The historical Scriptures indeed not even contain all the doctrines of the Christian faith'.[50] Jeremy Taylor and William Laud might have spoken of the Apostles not having committed some oral traditions to writing, but Hawkins's words – apparently without intending it, as he would later claim – seemed to go a step further, almost to the point of suggesting that Tradition was an alternative source of revealed doctrine not found in Scripture. Some Tractarians, Wood among them,[51] seem to have taken those words at face value; Newman, without going as far as Wood, later acknowledged how Hawkins's ideas on this subject had left their mark on him, and proved very serviceable weapons in the fight against the principle of *sola Scriptura*.[52]

Wood had read Newman's *Arians*, and agreed with its general lines. He shared ideas common among the Tractarians: the importance of Vincent of Lerins's *Commonitorium* in defining the rule of faith; the Tractarian theory of religious knowledge; Apostolic succession; the sacramental system; the present state of the Church, fallen from the purity of primitive Christianity; and many others. On these bases, he thought that his ideas on development were in tune with those of his friends, and, at the time of writing his paper, he seems to have expected their general concurrence in his hypothesis. He was, therefore, surprised by their negative response to some of his ideas, and particularly so by Newman's reaction when discussing the topic in their January 1836 meetings. He came to believe – as Froude had done – that Newman's position had shifted during his controversy with Jager.

Wood presented his 'presumptio' of development with confidence, even (at least on one occasion) carelessly. The paper contained six numbered propositions, accompanied by some explanatory notes. The first two put forward his understanding of the relationships between Holy Scripture and Tradition, Tradition and Faith.

> 1. Under the direction of the Holy Spirit, and pursuant to Christ's commands, the Apostles committed to the charge of the Church a formal system of doctrines ordinances discipline etc. And this orally, their writings imply or presuppose, but do not contain, it.
>
> 2. It is therefore only incidentally that the obligation to receive doctrines arises from their being found in Scripture; primarily, it results from them being of ascertained Apostolical Tradition.[53]

Hawkins would have recognized these ideas, even though Wood asserted with greater force the divine plan with respect to Tradition, and left the door open to the possibility that Scripture does not record the whole teaching of the Apostles. The obligation to preserve and transmit that Tradition had not been overridden by the writing of the New Testament books; the divine plan includes a role for Tradition which far exceeds its being merely an interpreter of Holy Scripture. Wood used two arguments to support his case. He thought that, as a matter of fact (and ignoring the vagaries of private judgement), there were very few points 'on which candid minds differ in Scripture interpretation'. Besides, he added, these were 'for the most part of a kind not within the scope of Apostolic Tradition',[54] since differences had arisen in post-apostolic times, and were concerned with topics the Fathers had not dwelt upon. If the role of Tradition was a merely interpretative one, there seemed little if anything left for it to do. This, in his view, did not correspond to the place and importance that Tradition had been given in the Anglican Rule of Faith.

In Wood's view, the system orally transmitted by the Apostles to the Church, following the divine command, had a life independent of, and previous to, the writings of the New Testament. He used two classic scriptural quotations as proofs of the pre-existence of this tradition, and of its authoritative character. The first was 2 Th 2: 14: 'So then, brethren, stand firm and hold to the traditions you were taught by us, either by word of mouth or by letter'. The fact that the epistles to the Thessalonians were among the first writings of the New Testament only strengthened the case: Paul affirms there the existence of a system of Christian beliefs and practices which precedes the written word of the New Testament. The other scriptural quotation was taken from 2 Tm 1: 13, and it insists on the importance of the spoken word: 'Follow the pattern of the sound words which you have heard from me, in the faith and the love which are in Christ Jesus.'[55] There was faith before Holy Scripture was written. The Apostles had committed to the care of the Church a system of doctrines and discipline, which later found no systematic or complete exposition in Scripture.

Wood's second proposition followed from the first. The authoritative and obligatory character of a particular doctrine was dependent on whether it had been taught by the Apostles, rather than on its Scriptural title deeds. This was the essential test: the fact of being of '*ascertained* apostolical Tradition'; a term he understood more broadly than Newman. It was in this respect that inclusion in Holy Scripture was *incidental*. The primary teaching authority – the 'fundamental' authority, we might call it – is that of Apostolic Tradition. In Wood's mind, Scripture's main role was to witness to Apostolic Tradition. Scripture is a holy and infallible witness, but not the only one. As far as Wood was concerned, there were truths the Christian should believe, and practices he should follow, beyond those recorded in the Scriptures, provided they could be ascertained as part of apostolic Tradition. And this – a historical fact – is to be determined by means of the canon proposed by Vincent of Lerins and St Augustine: what has been confessed always and everywhere by the universal Church cannot but be considered as handed down by the Apostles.[56] Although Wood did not have any intention of going beyond the limits imposed by the Articles of the Anglican Church, he was none the less beginning to step over the line.

The first two propositions were not discordant with those maintained by Manning and Keble, and even Newman, at about the same time. Manning's letter in response to Wood's paper satisfied Wood enough for him to write back on 18 December: 'Your paper on Tradition, and your general concurrence in my view gave me very sincere delight'.[57] Manning's paper has not been preserved. The nearest contemporary evidence of his opinions on the subject is to be found in his sermon *The Rule of Faith* (1838), and it confirms Wood's contention about their general agreement on antecedent Tradition. 'The writing of Scripture', Manning wrote in it, 'pre-supposes the foundation of Churches, and the foundation of Churches the delivering of the faith on which they were built'.[58] Thus, the oral teaching of the Apostles was the sole rule of faith before Holy Scripture was written; that meant, for Manning, that it remained the sole rule until all the books were not only written, but also collected and dispersed among the churches (as not every book contains all divine truth); a process which lasted, according to him, till the end of the second or the beginning of the third century. Furthermore, the Scriptures, once they had been written, were interpreted within the Tradition the Churches already possessed. Tradition was not seen merely as the interpretation of the Scripture; the written word was interpreted within the previous Tradition of faith.[59]

Keble and Newman were proposing similar ideas at about the same time, but their opinions seemed to ebb and flow, their steps forward to be followed by steps back. This was the result of their efforts to combine principles which were in tension, if not in contradiction. The *quod semper* led them to accept those doctrines and practices witnessed by Antiquity. On the other hand, the Thirty-Nine Articles, especially the Sixth, cast a chastening shadow over their thoughts: only those doctrines found in Scripture could be imposed as of necessary faith. Tractarian principle found itself straining at Anglican formularies. Urged on by what some have called their 'patristic fundamentalism', they sometimes took bold steps forward when speaking about Tradition, only to find themselves sharply jolted back by the Anglican formularies; then, they would retreat, confessing their adherence to the formularies while not retracting their previous statements. Their effort to combine Antiquity and Articles was riddled with internal contradictions.

During the Jager controversy, Newman had affirmed that under the umbrella of Tradition, and with all the guarantees of the Vincentian Rule, could be found doctrinal teachings and religious practices of different character, demanding different types of assent. Tradition, he wrote in his first letter, 'tells us all that Scripture tells and much besides'. Within it might be distinguished '1. a tradition interpretative of Scripture. 2. a tradition of doctrine not in Scripture. 3. a tradition of discipline, ceremonies, historical facts, &c. &c. extending to a variety of matters'.[60] In *Tract 85* (1838) he admitted that the Apostles did not say in the Scriptures all they had to say – as indeed they themselves affirmed. The story of their composition, and their internal structure, seemed to tell against their being a complete depository of the divine revelation. As a matter of fact, Newman continued, the early Church did not tell us that Scripture contained all divine truth; it taught that Scripture contains all that is necessary for salvation.[61]

Keble, for his part, had affirmed in *Primitive Tradition* that if any portion of the unwritten word of God 'can anyhow be authenticated, [it] must necessarily demand the same reverence from us [as the written word]; and for exactly the same reason: *because it is his word* [Christ's]',[62] and he thought that the agreement of the Fathers was a probable index of Apostolic tradition.[63] That was to say much, as probability rated high with the Tractarians in matters of faith. At this stage, Keble seems not to have been fully aware of the corollaries that followed from his own statements. All the same, the door had been unlocked and left ajar; others would push it open. Newman in 1837 seemed to have been moving along similar lines. In his *Prophetical Office*, when speaking about the Creed, he wrote: 'independently of this written evidence in its favour, we may observe that a Tradition, thus formally and statedly enunciated and delivered from hand to hand, is of the nature of a written document, and has an evidence of its Apostolic origin the same in kind with that [adducible] for the Scriptures'.[64] Later he added that whatever 'doctrine the primitive ages unanimously attest, whether by consent of Fathers, or by Councils, or by the events of history, or by controversies, or in whatever way, whatever may fairly and reasonably be considered to be the universal belief of those ages, is to be received as coming from the Apostles',[65] faithful and infallible witness to the teaching of Christ. The Apostolic origin of non-Scriptural traditional doctrine may be proved historically; it is a matter of fact. Both Keble and Newman seemed to maintain that pre-Scriptural Apostolic Tradition contained God's word, and that this was compulsory on the believers to whom it had been communicated. Did the obligatory character of the Apostolic Tradition end with the writing of the New Testament books? The fact of inclusion or not in Holy Scripture would not, presumably, change the status of those apostolic doctrines or practices not contained in it. As we have seen earlier, Keble suggested that if any portion of God's unwritten word reached us through Tradition, and could be authenticated as apostolic, it should demand the same reverence as the written word of God. Newman had stopped short of that conclusion, but his words in the *Arians*, and in the Tracts, seem to point in that direction.

Manning's and Newman's principles, however, refused to jump over the fence of the Sixth Article on the sufficiency of Holy Scripture. Froude would have taken that fence boldly: he had already disqualified the Reformers as religious teachers, and that undermined for him the authority of the Articles they had framed. He had no doubts on the subject. He professed that the Apostolic Church was infallible, its judgements and interpretations – even when not committed to writing – 'as binding on men's conscience as the written word itself; and that, if a portion of them has been preserved faithfully to the present day, it is still binding, for the same reason and to the same extent'. Froude thought that what had been traditionally held from the very first 'derived ultimately from the Apostles', and could not be regarded as less than infallible.[66] This was what constituted authoritative teaching. He considered, with Butler, that it was antecedently possible that God might have revealed, and left his revelation to be handed down only by Tradition, without an inspired Scripture; consequently, 'the supposition, that He may have left some parts of it [his revelation] to be thus handed down, cannot be inconsistent with anything we know of them'.[67] The editors of the *Remains*, still constrained by the Thirty-Nine Articles, hastened to add a note at this point saying that, although antecedently this was possible, in fact God had not left any doctrine necessary for salvation in that condition. If that was the case, the Preface to the second part of the *Remains* may have said more than they intended when it affirmed: 'Ancient Consent binds the person admitting it alike to all doctrines, interpretations, and usages, for which it can be truly alleged.'[68] This was an absolute claim, with no reference to the need for these doctrines, interpretations and usages to find corroboration in Scripture. And, given that ancient consent was the rule of faith of the Catholic Church (not just of the Anglican), those truths possessing the hallmark of ancient consent must bind the individual and the Church.

Newman tried to find a solution to the apparent contradiction presented by Article Six, and sought to determine the status of the doctrines not contained in Scripture but found in Tradition. In *Tract 85* he seemed to suggest at one point that Holy Scripture had overruled them. But, in the same treatise, Newman would also speak of the imperative character of revealed truths *per se*: there is no excuse for not admitting them; revelation is imperative on our faith *because* it is revealed.[69] Did this mean that the strict connexion between fundamental and necessary doctrines with Scripture would no longer be applicable? Not necessarily. Newman also seemed to be admitting a third type of truths to be believed when, at about the same time, he wrote: by '*necessary* faith, is not meant all that must be believed, but all that must be *immediately* believed, what must be professed *on* coming for admittance into the Church, what must be proclaimed as the condition of salvation'.[70] There were doctrines, which were delivered as part of the tradition sanctioned by the Fathers but not as part of *the Faith*. What were these other degrees of belief and necessity beyond those of 'fundamentals' or 'necessary for salvation'?

Newman and Manning seem not to have objected to the general drift of Wood's first two propositions. There were differences not only of emphasis but also of substance between Wood and his friends in these questions, but Manning's and Newman's own ambiguities made it possible for them to accept Wood's ideas as compatible with their own. Wood's third and fourth propositions, however, would not find such a sympathetic hearing; they were a clear step into unknown and uncharted territory, far beyond the more or less shifting borders of Keble's, Manning's or Newman's thoughts at the time. The third proposition read as follows:

> 3. In common with other societies the Church has the inherent power of expanding or modifying her organisation, of bringing her ideas of Truth into more distinct consciousness, or of developing the Truth itself more fully.[71]

Wood used a pure Butlerian argument to make his case. He found the basis for this 'presumptio' in the 'general analogy of

God's dealings with us'. Salvation history reveals to man not only particular truths and injunctions but also the mode of God's operations and the paths of his wisdom. That discernible divine way of doing things, although not determining all God's possible actions *ad unum*, provides support to the presumption that those general laws of divine operation also inform similar divine acts. It is a fact that God has revealed himself to man in a progressive manner: the long process of revelation is recorded in the Old and New Testaments. God's truth is gradually presented to man, until revelation reaches its summit in the Incarnation. One revealed truth is followed in time by a new revelation, and this latter one by another; the old truths prepare the understanding and facilitate the reception of the newly revealed ones, while these react in their turn upon previously known truths. The earlier truths become more distinct, and better known, with the unfolding of God's revelation.

Wood acknowledged that the cycle of divine revelation was complete with Our Lord's departure from this earth, but contended that analogy suggested that to the progressive unfolding of God's revelation in the past, there now corresponds a progressive development in the understanding of the truth revealed. He considered that the analogy warranting this 'presumptio' had a considerable argumentative force. Within a Butlerian-Tractarian approach, the force of his argument and the degree of probability of his theory rested on the strength of fact supporting it and on the validity of the analogy; his 'presumptio' could not be dismissed except by making the opposite case on the basis of irrefutable facts or by the compelling force of a contrary analogy. Wood felt that facts and analogy supported his case. He could claim that his view 'assumes indeed that the full body and perfection of divine truth could not be *ecclesiastically exhibited* at once, in a moment, without a violation of the ordinary course of the divine dealings with us'.[72] He felt that even common sense seemed to stand on his side. There was, however, an exception to that general process. Wood, with other Tractarians, considered that at the beginning, to 'the divinely instructed minds of the Apostles, glancing to and fro' over the whole range of Christian doctrine, the whole body and perfection of truth was indeed ever present'.[73] This was one of the special gifts attached to their mission as foundations of the Church, but it was not preserved in the Church after their departure from this earth.

Doctrinal development was thus part of the divine plan: 'it was intended that there should be a "profectus religionis" in the Church'.[74] Or, in other words, that God's design implied 'that the Church should gradually and carefully, taking the divine word for her guide, and proceeding in the course which is natural to the mind . . . , evolve, comment on, and exhibit the whole counsel of God'.[75] This process of gradual understanding of revealed truth, like that of revealing it, necessarily involved God's providential guidance. Wood seems to have taken for granted that the Holy Spirit would lead individuals and the Church in their step-by-step discovery of the truths explicitly or implicitly contained in revelation. His first proposition referred to the providential role of the Holy Spirit in the transmission and preservation of Christ's revelation; it followed that, if the Spirit was to guide the Church in transmitting and preserving revelation, his assistance would be particularly required when it came to its development.

The guidance of God was one of the agents of that progress in the understanding of religious truth and in the development of the virtualities contained in revelation; it was not, however, the only one. The pace and direction of that development would be determined by the conjunction of God's guidance and man's will and mind, by the interaction between the positive act of God and man's degree of openness to divine action; an openness determined by his *ethos*. Wood added another human element to this equation, what he called the 'natural course' of the human mind. He considered that God, who had created human nature, could not but take into consideration the structure and psychological laws of the human mind when devising his providential plan of self-revelation. Development involves the gradual understanding of revelation, and, consequently, is affected by the general constitution of the human mind receiving it and by the general psychological laws governing human thought. Wood reckoned that, once her infallible guides had disappeared, the Church would '*dwell* on those *parts* of the scheme to which the mind is naturally first directed, however completely she might be *informed* in *all* truth'.[76]

He thought that the natural course of the human mind leads man to regard first those things which are external to himself, turning later towards introspection. When translating this process to the understanding of the faith, Wood concluded that 'the external objects of faith' (the Trinity, the Incarnation, and so on) would first attract man's notice; he would next turn his attention towards the effects of Redemption and grace in himself, to the study of the influence grace has on man's soul and on its operations.[77] He thought that the process just described would follow the same steps in both the heretical and the orthodox believer. The history of the Church showed that process at work, and seemed to prove his assertion. Questions about the Trinity and about Church Order had first attracted the attention of believers, and the early Church had collected and arranged the Scripture notices of the Trinity, building thereupon the doctrines of the Hypostatic Union. These had then been exposed in her symbols to 'satisfy the requirements of the intellect and to discover heresy'.[78] As a result, these doctrines had been developed more fully in the early Church than the rest of the truths contained in Divine Revelation. From them, Wood thought, the Church had moved to other doctrines, until it reached those related to the inner sanctification of man: grace and predestination, or the more recent doctrines on justification.

Newman and Manning gathered the full import of Wood's theory from his third proposition (completed by the fifth), and they drew here the line they were not ready to cross. Their reaction was unequivocal: doctrinal development was not possible. Wood had approached his friends at a particularly unfavourable time to get a sympathetic hearing for his theory. Newman, as a result of his controversy with the Abbé Jager, seems to have entrenched himself in a firm rejection of whatever might imply the acceptance of developments in doctrine, and Wood found it impossible to break through his arguments. He summarized the tone of their conversations when telling Manning that he had 'tried each joint of his [Newman's] intellectual panoply, but its hard and polished temper glances off all my arrows'.[79] However, both Newman and Manning, while rejecting the idea of development, took notice of Wood's theory and would later refer to the concept of development (mostly the Roman one) in the books they published in the following years. They considered Christ alone to be the author and finisher of the faith, and that the faith had been perfected *uno afflatu* by the inspiration of the Apostles. The only development which had taken place since apostolic times had been a verbal and explicative one, rather than a conceptual or ideal development.[80] Manning, in his *Rule of Faith*, thought that the idea of doctrinal development in religious knowledge resulted from 'an insatiate lust of ever-progressing discovery', a result of the rapid advances taking place in all branches of human knowledge during the nineteenth century. It was assumed that all knowledge, religious knowledge included, 'is, or ought to be, ever on the move'.[81] But it was otherwise in religious knowledge: 'the rule of faith is retrospective altogether'.[82] It looked at what was believed at the beginning, and progress meant recovering and restoring lost or neglected ancient truth and practice.

Newman also seems to have objected that Wood's theory of doctrinal development showed disrespect towards the Fathers. He might have employed the same argument he was to use in 1837: those maintaining the idea of development would 'profess to know better than the Fathers; that they . . . consider questions to be determinable on which the early Fathers were ignorant'.[83] Even more, men like Petavius,[84] in order to defend Roman developments, had dared to charge the ante-Nicene Fathers with sharing the sentiments of Arius. Newman rounded off his diatribe in highly rhetorical fashion, quoting Bull: 'The Divine oracles themselves are to be convicted of undue obscurity, the most holy Doctors, Bishops and Martyrs of the primitive Church are to be charged with heresy; so that in one way or other the credit and authority of the degenerate Roman Church may be patched up and made good'.[85] Much was at stake. The Unitarians, and not a few Anglicans, rejected the doctrine of the Trinity on Scriptural grounds. Petavius had then 'pretended' to show the lack of clear Trinitarian theological vocabulary in the pre-Nicene Fathers. In both cases, the central truth of New Testament revelation seemed not pass the test of the Vincentian Rule of Faith: that a doctrine be believed and clearly taught always, everywhere and by all. Wood's ideas threatened ancient consent. He was sensitive to this criticism and strenuously denied that his theory implied disparagement of the Fathers or of the early Church. On the contrary, rather than diminishing the stature of the Fathers, his theory ascribed 'to the early Church the praise of having alone borne Her share of that "profectus" which has been more or less neglected ever since'.[86] The early Church could do no more, and she was required to do no more. He went further when writing to Manning on 18 December, adding that his 'presumptio' was fully in agreement with what Vincent of Lerins says in his *Commonitorium* chapters 28, 29, 30 and 32.[87] The *Commonitorium* did not condemn all novelties, but only the 'profane ones', those undermining Tradition or contrary to it.

Wood, at this point, asked: is the process terminated with the passing away of the Primitive Church? 'Is the structure to be arrested at this stage?'[88] He answered in the negative. In God's plan, the early system of truths – rearranged, collected and developed by the early Church – was to serve as 'the basis of the ecclesiastical Traditive structure'. The first patristic development 'ought to have been but the foundation (and a most precious one) of the *doctrinal Ecclesiastical Structure*. If the Church in after times had fulfilled her office as well as the early Church did, she would have proceeded to arrange and expand (excusare et dilatare, Vinc[entius]:) other doctrines, in the same manner.'[89] The objections of his friends led him to exclaim: 'are we to be deprived of the benefit of a great truth clearly deducible from Scripture, merely because the constitution of the human mind was not entirely changed in the case of the early Church, and made capable of at once conceiving and exposing a stupendous system?'[90] Wood, responding to the criticisms raised by his friends, maintained the possibility of deducing new truths from Scripture, as Article 6 suggested: doctrines necessary for salvation are those read in Scripture or *proved* from it. Newman was the one out of step with the Articles.

Wood's fourth proposition was intended to follow logically from the third. He might have had clear in his mind what he wanted to say but was not very precise in its formulation.

> 4. It follows then that doctrines may be true, though not traceable to the Apostles.[91]

Manning seems to have perceived, and pointed out, the obvious flaw in this assertion, because Wood qualified it in his next letter, suggesting that the fourth proposition could be reformulated as follows: 'doctrines may be true, though not apparent in the teaching of the primitive Church'.[92] He foresaw the possibility that a doctrinal development might have reached a point where it would require considerable effort and study to discern the path connecting primitive teaching and modern doctrine. And he went on further to qualify this statement with a nod in the direction of the Articles: 'Of course if doctrines are provable from Scripture they *must* be "*traceable* to the Apostles".'[93] The sentence seems to have been imposed on Wood by the need to square his theory with Article 6; it did nevertheless sit uneasily with what he had previously said about Tradition.

Wood had originally quoted Newman in support of his contention that the late rise of a particular doctrine (e.g., predestination) was not conclusive against its being true. In his letter to Manning of 18 December, he tried to illustrate further his theory using another example: the doctrine of justification by faith. He thought that Manning would not dispute its orthodoxy. It was obvious to Wood that this great doctrine 'lay hid (latitaverit Vinc[entius]: 29) in the bosom of the Church for a considerable time, and perhaps was not evolved in her teaching before Luther'.[94] Like this one, other doctrines might make a late appearance in the horizon of the Church. It therefore came as a surprise to Wood when Newman, during their conversations towards the end of January 1836, dismissed this appeal to the doctrine of justification by laying the axe at the root of it. Newman, Wood reported to Manning, held 'that before the Reformation the Church never *deduced* any doctrine from Scripture'.[95] Newman had used similar words in a letter to Froude a few weeks before.[96] He kept repeating that Christ alone 'is the Author and Finisher of Faith in all its senses; His servants do but witness it, and their statements are, then, only valuable when they are testimonies, not deductions or conjectures'.[97]A strict reading of the Vincentian canon ruled out the possibility of the Church adding to the truths to be believed as they were deduced from Scripture. The Sixth Article of the Anglican Church, however, did seem to suggest something different: 'whatsoever is not read therein, nor may be proved thereby, is not to be required of any man'. In 1837 Newman seems to have been forced by it to contradict what he had previously said to Wood and Froude. In the *Prophetical Office*, published that year, he wrote: 'Holy Scripture contains all things necessary to salvation; that is, either as being read therein or *deducible* therefrom.'[98] There is no indication that he tried to explain the apparent contradiction. As a matter of fact, he went on to add in the same work that councils – even truly Ecumenical ones – did not have a mandate either to deduce new doctrines from Scripture. Councils were trustworthy, and to be followed, in so far as 'they speak one and all the same doctrine, without constraint, and bear witness to their having received it from their Fathers, having never heard of any other doctrine, and verily believing it to be Apostolic'. When, on the other hand, they 'do not profess to bear witness to a fact, but merely to deduce from Scripture for themselves, besides or beyond what they had received from their Fathers, whatever deference is due to them, it is not of that peculiar kind which is contemplated by the Rule of Vincentius':[99] such a doctrine is not to be received as of necessary faith. The Fathers and the Councils are simply witnesses to Apostolical Tradition. Newman found it difficult to marry Vincent's Rule with the Sixth Article of the Anglican Church. The Rule was chronologically narrower than the article; in another respect, however, it was less restrictive, as it did not demand that the doctrines under the umbrella of the *quod semper* should also be found in Holy Scripture.

Wood could not accept Newman's arguments. After their conversations in January, he wrote a forthright letter to Manning, showing that he had not surrendered any element of his theory. He went on to make a far-reaching statement: it did not tell against a doctrine that the Fathers had not systematically held it. He claimed that the character of the appeal to the Fathers had been misinterpreted: 'we have no business to look to the Fathers about it further than to be satisfied that their general thinking was not contrariant to it'.[100] The same might be said, *mutatis mutandis*, of the appeal to Holy Scripture. Although Wood did not explicitly say so, the analogy suggests that the recourse to Scripture serves similar purposes: either to show that a doctrine was scriptural or to demonstrate that it was not in contradiction to Scripture teaching.[101]

Newman's attitude towards the Reformers had been one of

the reasons for their disagreement in the London conversations. Wood told Manning that he had discovered in his friend a 'violent repugnance' towards the doctrines of the Reformers. He felt that, to justify this repugnance, Newman had adopted a series of principles that were clearly unsound; so much so that 'they open one's eyes to their unsoundness'.[102] And Wood seemed to include among them Newman's rejection of doctrinal developments. He had not been aware of the development of his friend's thought in respect to the Reformers; by this time, Newman had already started to make Froude's contempt for the Reformers his own on the basis of their corrupt ethos.[103] More fundamentally, Wood seems not to have not realized that behind Newman's stand was his attachment to a strict interpretation of the Vincentian Rule. To Newman's mind ancient consent limited Tradition chronologically, while Scripture defined Tradition's boundaries as to the doctrines it contained by determining which truths were fundamental or necessary to salvation. Doctrines not found in Antiquity and Scripture are doctrines of men, and cannot be super-added to the doctrines of faith. Bishop Fisher's acknowledgement that the doctrines of Purgatory and of indulgences were not mentioned by the early Christian writers was enough to disqualify them in Newman's eyes.[104] It is true that some doctrines of faith were not openly propounded from the beginning; this, according to Newman, was not because they were unknown but rather because these articles had been kept secret. They would have been part of the *Disciplina arcani*: the rule of secrecy practised in the early Church that forbade the publication of the more sacred articles of faith to the world at large (or even to those Christians who were not in a condition to understand some of them properly). The power to propound articles of faith, explaining and clarifying the doctrines of the creed, would have been suspended from the time the Church had ceased to be one and lost as a result some of the powers granted her by God.[105]

Wood thought that the result of his friend's principles was 'not merely to *refer* us to antiquity but to *shut us up* in it, and to deprive, not only individuals but the Church of all those doctrines of Scripture not fully commented on by the Fathers'.[106] He felt that this did not correspond to God's ways of dealing with man or to the experience and tradition of the Church; nor did it match the workings and needs of the human intellect. Besides, Wood thought, if the process just described had not been intended by God (or if it had stopped with the early Church), then the Church would have been deprived of almost all weapons of defence against error, and she would be powerless to counteract the heresies bound to spring up in her later history. The rebuttal of errors concerning doctrines not clearly contained in Holy Scripture or commented upon by the Fathers could not be made without a corresponding affirmative and authoritative teaching of the present day Church about revelation's true meaning. He considered that the teaching role of the Church was not merely concerned with the faithful transmission of a series of truths, always the same in number and reach. The new truths acquired in a process of doctrinal development might be 'ecclesiastically exhibited' and proposed to the belief of the faithful, as his fifth proposition stated:

> 5. And further, that the Church retains the right of authoritatively exhibiting them, subject only to the condition – arising from the withdrawal of her inspired guides and from her fallibility – of their being true.[107]

The adverb 'authoritatively' holds the key to this proposition. It could be given different meanings, and Tractarians used it in different contexts. Froude considered that nowadays the only authoritative teaching for proposing doctrines to be believed was that of the Bible and Tradition, and criticized Keble for assuming in *Tract 52* that the clergy could teach authoritatively. Wood's use of the term here implied that today's Church might propose for the belief of the faithful doctrines which had been formulated at any stage of the doctrinal development, even when they had not been explicitly known to the Primitive Church. Both Newman and Manning clearly understood the development propounded by Wood as a doctrinal or dogmatic development, not a merely theological one. Newman's idea of a Prophetical Tradition admitted the existence, and even the convenience, of theological development. A doctrinal development was something very different: it would add to the truths the Christian believer should receive by faith. In this case, a doctrine which was not Catholic dogma in the first ages – though it could have been more or less clearly stated by individual Fathers, or hinted at in Scripture – must later be considered as part of the doctrines to be believed by the faithful as necessary for salvation. The fifth proposition could not but draw Manning's and Newman's combined fire.

Manning's own fourth proposition, as recorded in Wood's letter of December 1835, put it in no uncertain terms: 'the Church has no warrant to promulgate new truths'.[108] A note in Manning's *Rule of Faith* may give us an idea of the ground for his objections. Anglican and Catholic controversialists had clashed over the interpretation of Ga 1: 8: 'Sed licet nos aut Angelus de coelo evangelizet vobis praeterquam quod evangelizabimus vobis, anathema sit' (But even if we, or an angel from heaven should preach to you a gospel contrary/different to that which we preached to you, let him be accursed/condemned). In his note Manning quoted Thorndike's rejection of Bellarmine's interpretation of *praeterquam* as 'against'; Thorndike and Bishop Taylor maintained, on their part, that it was to be understood as 'beyond'.[109] Newman also objected to Wood's proposition on similar grounds. Wood reported to Manning what Newman had said in that respect: 'from the time the Church ceased to be one, the right of any part of it to propound *Articles of Faith*, as such, is suspended, all that remains to them is to impose terms of communion, articles of peace etc'.[110] Did Newman say more than he intended? There seems to be a certain contradiction between these words, as reported by Wood, and Newman's strict interpretation of the Vincentian Rule, given that a future re-united Church would presumably be in a position to propound articles of faith beyond what had been included under the rule. In any case, it is quite likely that Newman might have also complained, as he did in his *Prophetical Office*, against making the Church 'so absolutely the author of our faith, that what the Fathers did not believe, we must believe under pain of forfeiting heaven'.[111] The door was firmly closed on Wood's suggestion that the Church might present doctrinal developments to be believed by the faithful.

Wood, early in this triangular exchange, was still unfamiliar with Newman's general doctrine on the subject, and seems not to have been aware of the distinction between 'fundamental truths' and 'truths necessary to salvation' made in the Second Letter to Jager. Newman furnished him with information on the above subjects either in November or December. Wood's letter of 1 January seems to suggest that Newman had read Wood's paper, and sent him his comments on it, together with Newman's own paper on Tradition. Wood quotes literally from Newman's unpublished Third Letter to Jager, the one probably read at the meeting of the Theological Society of 20 November. On the basis of that paper and of Manning's answer, Wood rather optimistically considered that there was only an apparent divergence of opinions between him and his friends. In a previous letter to Manning he had said that he was concerned with determining the authentic records from which the whole body of divine truth is derived, and this 'when ascertained may well be called the "rule of faith," in as much as it is the duty of every Christian to receive truths so warranted'.[112] He now added that Newman and Manning were using, the term 'rule of faith' in a different sense from his own. 'You intend by it', he writes to Newman, 'the measure of "things necessary to salvation", of "the terms of communion", while I employed it so as to comprehend what you call "doctrines additional to those which are emphatically called the Faith".' Wood seems to have considered that the declaration by the Church of 'fundamental doctrines', 'truths necessary for salvation', and the like responded to a need to establish the terms of communion. He appears to have emptied the terms of their absolute value, reducing them to purely terminological (even 'arbitrary') distinctions, conditioned by historical circumstances. As far as he was concerned, the virtue of faith had as its object all truths revealed by God. In short, he considered the rule of faith 'as "that which so warrants any doctrine to a Catholic Churchman as to make it his duty to receive it"'.[113] He did not intend to determine whether those truths were 'necessary for salvation' or not; these distinctions had only a relative value, insofar as the individual's membership of a Church at any given time was concerned.

Besides, Wood considered that, in fixing the terms of communion and the truths necessary for salvation, the Reformers had not entered into abstract reasoning 'as to what the terms of communion ought to be, but took those of the Primitive Church as an *historical fact*'.[114] Desperate times required desperate remedies. At the time of the Reformation crisis, in order to avoid the complexities of the question, they settled for the terms of communion of the Primitive Church as offering sufficient guarantees. In so doing, they ignored the doctrinal developments which, under God's guidance, had taken place during the intervening centuries. Theirs was not a definitive or absolute standard, and it could (or should) be revised in quieter times. There was another reason, Wood thought, for that revision of the Reformation doctrinal and disciplinary settlement: the Articles had been drawn up to refute Popish errors, and, in rejecting error, they had gone further than they ought in the opposite direction. The Reformers, he thought, had not intended to condemn Catholic doctrine, and this consideration justified him in not following their injunctions too closely; the door had been left open for other times and circumstances, not marked by the same strife and insecurity, to settle differently the question of the 'fundamentals' of the faith and of truths 'necessary for salvation'. He answered Newman's difficulty about the Church's divisions by saying that in that unhappy state in which the Church found itself there was still a possibility of development. Its present situation had 'left Her divided members to complete the Ecclesiastical structure each for itself'.[115] As a result of their separate developments, the three branches of the Church might arrive at the same doctrine, and this would give the doctrine in question the authority of ecumenical consent. There would be other doctrines (e.g.: justification by faith) developed by one part of the Church but not recognized by others. These teachings would obviously lack the authority given to a doctrine by ecumenical consent, but this would not detract from their legitimacy or prevent the particular Church from exhibiting them 'authoritatively'.

The teaching authority of the Church was a fundamental tenet of the Tractarians, although they found it difficult to establish the actual status and force of this teaching in the contemporary Church. Newman clearly identified the deficiency in *Tract 90*: the Articles say 'that all necessary faith must be proved from Scripture, but do not say *who* is to prove it. They say that the Church has authority in controversies; they do not say *what* authority. They say that it may enforce nothing beyond Scripture, but do not say *where* the remedy lies when it does'. He had no answer to this problem, and at the beginning of the Tract he had already expressed his intention of avoiding the subject: 'The other question, about the ultimate judge of the interpretation of Scripture, shall not be entered upon.'[116] Wood had perceived the problem in 1835: the Church as teacher of doctrine can be trusted only to a very limited extent. His sixth proposition did try to answer the main question raised: how do we know the doctrines exhibited authoritatively by the Church to be true; truth being their only claim to our acceptance?

> 6. But the only mode of proving this [the truth of a particular doctrines] is by showing their accordance with Scripture. So that while the Church has ever been our sole expositrix, we have now two co-ordinate tests of doctrine – Apostolical Tradition and Scripture.[117]

In the present state of division in the Universal Church, the task of testing against Scripture and Tradition the truth of the propositions proposed by one of the Church's Three Branches seems to be left to the individual Christian. Wood felt obliged to affirm this, and he did so under duress: 'Rather than exult, we should feel pained at being obliged – a caution imposed by the sad experience of past errors – to *test* what the Church may propound to us by Scripture, instead of yielding an implicit confidence to our holy Mother.'[118] But as Manning was later to point out, to leave Scripture and Tradition to the individual was as much private judgement as to leave him Scripture alone. The mist of private judgement seemed always to cling around the *via media*, even when its promoters try to detach themselves as far as they could from it. The general theory of religious knowledge of the Tractarians provided, however, what they felt to be an escape route from unchecked private judgement: *ethos* – working on probabilities – is the means through which God's guidance is granted to individuals, and what is true of individuals can be said to be true of the Church as well. The process, however, also involved a delicate antecedent judgement on the probability of being, or not being, in possession of the right *ethos*. This was a recurring nightmare. Furthermore, did not many who supported the doctrine of private judgement hold similar ideas about the guidance given by the Holy Spirit to individual

Christians? Wyclif and Luther could probably have signed Wood's answer to the problem, without changing much in it.

It is worth noticing that 'in accordance', the term used by Wood in his sixth proposition, introduces a subtle change in the formulation of Article 6. The term goes beyond the article's formula: 'whatsoever is not read therein [in Scripture], nor may be proved thereby, is not to be required of any man, that it should be believed as an article of the Faith'. The doctrine in question is to be explicitly found in Scripture, or clearly deduced from it. Wood's usage of 'in accordance' is to be related to what he had said in respect of the appeal to the Fathers. Scripture is a positive test for doctrines contained in it, but a negative one for those not found there, in so far as it shows whether they are or are not in opposition to the truths contained in it but in general agreement with them. A doctrine might have developed from Scripture or even from extra-Scriptural Tradition, given that Scripture does not contain the whole Christian revelation. These doctrines have been subsequently taught by the Church, and have been professed by the faithful. In his controversy with the Abbé Jager, Newman admitted this possibility and considered that they should be accepted by the faithful, although this fact did not identify them as necessary for salvation. Jager had argued that the Church considered the Donatists excluded from salvation even though their error was not against Scripture. Newman answered that those obdurate in their rejection of the teaching of the Church nowadays could not do so without sin: 'to maintain an opinion against the voice of the whole Church stubbornly and publicly is of itself without any doubt a mortal sin',[119] and those who so offended were thereby excluded from salvation. Was this primarily because it constituted a sin of pride or because it amounted to a sin against faith, or both? Newman thought that the faithful should have a filial trust that the Church would always teach orthodox doctrine, but this did not mean that they should receive as divine all truths she considered as coming directly from the Apostles.

Manning's and Newman's objections had helped Wood to clarify some obscure points in his theory and to develop further the ideas expressed in the original paper. In the last of his letters on the subject, Wood confessed to Manning that he had not had opportunity to reflect on all the implications and relationships of his theory. His hypothesis was still very schematic, and he admitted as much: 'I find it extremely difficult to develop my meaning, and must go on slowly feeling my way and trusting to your sympathy.'[120] He was, however, fully confident of the soundness of his hypothesis: 'Surely in thoughts like these one may see glimpses of a beautiful and comprehensive system which holding fast primitive antiquity on the one hand, does not reject the later teaching of the Church on the other, but bringing out of its stores things new and old, is eminently calculated to break up existing parties in the Church, and unite the children of light against those of darkness.'[121] He thought, however, that he should keep their disagreements private, so as not to harm the progress of the Movement: 'I am most anxious to avoid the semblance of a difference between those who hold so much in common, and who may so usefully co-operate together.'[122]

Notes

1. Oakeley also dwelt on the subject in his article 'Bishop Jewel', *British Critic* 30/59 (July 1841), pp. 11–45.
2. J. H. Newman, 'Wilfulness, the Sin of Saul' (2 December 1832), *US*, p. 151.
3. J. H. Newman, 'Personal Influence, the Means of Propagating the Truth' (26 January 1832), *US*, p. 66.
4. J. H. Newman, *The Arians of the Fourth Century* (London: Rivington, 1833), pp. 255, 281 etc.
5. J. H. Newman, 'The Theory of Developments in Religious Doctrine' (2 February 1843) *US*, p. 319. Archdeacon Daubeny had pointed out before Newman the progressive nature of error and schism, in particular: the fall into error of those promoting it would run like water till it had reached the lowest ground, destroying in its final stages the very thing they had initially professed to defend (C. Daubeney, *On the Nature, Progress and Consequences of Schism; with Immediate Reference to the Present State of Religious Affairs in this Country* (London: Rivington, 1818), pp. 4, 30, 126 ff.).
6. Newman to H. Froude, 9 August 1835, *LD*, V, pp. 118–19.
7. Newman to H. Wilberforce, 27 April 45, ibid., X, pp. 639–41.
8. Newman to S. Wilberforce, 10 November 1834, ibid., IV, pp. 354–5; similar ideas can be foud in H. Wilberforce, *The Foundations of Faith Assailed in Oxford* (London: Rivington, 1835), p. 38.
9. S. Thomas, *Newman and Heresy. The Anglican Years* (Cambridge: Cambridge University Press, 1991), pp. 65–6, 95, 107, 117, 231–2, etc.
10. Froude to Keble, 9 January 1834, *Remains*, I–I, p. 336.
11. Froude to Newman, 1 November 1835, *LD*, V, p. 156.
12. Froude to Newman, 18 August 1835, ibid., p. 128.
13. [J. Keble], *On the Mysticism Attributed to the Early Fathers of the Church, Tracts for the Times*, 89 (London: Rivington, 1841), p. 124.
14. Thomas, *Newman and Heresy*, pp. 117, 181–4 etc.
15. Newman, *Arians*, p. 37. See also W. A. Beek, in his *John Keble's Literary and Religious Contribution to the Oxford Movement* (Nijmegen: Centrale Drukkerij, 1959), p. 37.
16. By 1836, however, he was asking for the formation of a proper Anglican theology (Newman to Rose, 1 and 11 May 1836, *LD*, V, pp. 291 and 294).
17. J. H. Newman, *Lectures on the Prophetical Office of the Church Viewed Relatively to Romanism and Popular Protestantism* (London: Rivington, 1837), p. 106. The words in brackets are Newman's new wording in the second edition of 1838, p. 109.
18. Ibid., p. 121.
19. Newman, *Arians*, p. 41.
20. Newman, ibid., p. 41–2.
21. Newman, ibid., p. 42.
22. Newman, ibid., p. 147 ff.
23. Newman, ibid., p. 161.
24. Newman, 'Theory of Developments', p. 330 (my italics).
25. Newman, *Arians*, p. 70.
26. 'In ipsa item catholica ecclesia magnopere curandum est, ut id teneamus quod ubique, quod semper, quod ab omnibus creditum est' [In the Catholic Church every care should be taken to hold fast to what has been believed everywhere, always, and by all]. (Vincentius Lerinensis, *Commonitorium or Pro Catholicae Fidei Antiquitate et Universitate adversus Profanas Omnium Haereticorum Novitates*, in

Corpus Christianorum, Series Latina 64 (Turnholti: Brepol, 1985), ch. ii, par. 5, lin. 24–6, p. 149).

27. Newman, *Prophetical Office*, 63.
28. Ibid., p. 384.
29. Newman, 'First Letter to Jager', in L. Allen, *John Henry Newman and the Abbé Jager. A Controversy on Scripture and Tradition (1834–1836)* (London: Oxford University Press, 1975), p. 36. See also Newman, *Prophetical Office*, p. 259. Newman also uses here the expression 'essentials of the faith' to refer to the fundamentals. There is at times a certain ambiguity in Newman's distinctions between fundamental, necessary, and other doctrines (see for example *Prophetical Office*, pp. 246 ff., 286 ff.).
30. Newman, 'Second Letter to Jager', in Allen, *Newman and Jager*, pp. 76–83, 97, 99.
31. Newman, 'Third Letter to Jager', ibid., p. 122.
32. Newman, 'First Letter to Jager', ibid., p. 45; see also pp. 38–9 and 41.
33. Harrison considered Newman's theory Ultra-Protestant, destined to sweep away the teaching of the Church altogether (B. Harrison to Newman, no date, ibid., p. 158).
34. Newman, 'Second Letter to Jager', ibid., pp. 94–5.
35. Newman, *Arians*, p. 55; see also [J. H. Newman], 'Apostolical Tradition', *British Critic* 20/39 (July 1836), pp. 170, 184 ff.
36. Newman, *Arians*, pp. 60–1.
37. Froude to Newman, 2 July 1835, *LD*, V, p. 98.
38. Froude to Newman, 17 July 1835, ibid., p. 101.
39. Newman to Froude, 20 July 1835, ibid., p. 103–4.
40. Froude to Newman, 30 July and 3 September 1835, ibid., pp. 117 and 128. In a letter to Newman (17 November 1833) he had already set the theoretical question being raised now: 'May one not broadly maintain, that no one has any right to call any opinion necessary unless he believes its *necessity* as distinct from its truth to be revealed (I mean in Scripture or tradition)?' (ibid., IV, p. 112). G. Spencer had asked the question earlier in a similar form with respect to the Athanasian Creed: 'no passage in Scripture could be found which declares that whosoever will be saved must hold the orthodox faith on the Trinity' (G. Spencer, *A Short Account of the Conversion of the Hon. and Rev. G. Spencer to the Catholic Faith Written by Himself* (London: Catholic Institute Tracts, n. 11, n.d.), p. 4.
41. Newman to Froude, 20 July 1835, *LD*, V, p. 104.
42. [J. H. Newman], *On the Mode of Conducting the Controversy with Rome, Tracts for the Times*, 71 (London: Rivington, 1836), p. 28.
43. Jager, 'Seventh Letter to Newman', in Allen, *Newman and Jager*, p. 110.
44. J. H. Newman, *An Essay on the Development of Christian Doctrine* (London: Toovey, 1845), p. 58.
45. Ibid., pp. 2, 27–8.
46. Wood to Manning, 29 Jan. 1836, Manning MSS Bod., c. 654, fo. 447. Wood included among them 'the high evangelical doctrines, delivered from the exaggerated and distorted guise in which some have dressed them, and reduced to their true position in the system' (ibid., fo. 446).
47. E. Hawkins, *A Dissertation upon the Use and Importance of Unauthoritative Tradition* (Oxford: Parker, 1819), pp. 1–2.
48. Ibid., p. 18.
49. Ibid., p. 41.
50. Ibid., p. 36. Hawkins, in his 1840 Bampton Lectures, tried to disqualify the conclusions that some Tractarians had drawn from his expressions. Even then, he would not entirely abandon his previous formula (E. Hawkins, *An Inquiry*

into the Connected Uses of the Principal Means of Attaining Christian Truth (Oxford: Parker, 1840), pp. x and 27–8).

51. Wood, as he informed Manning, had read Hawkins's book, and recommended his friend to get hold of a copy (Wood to Manning, 18 December 1835, Manning MSS Bod., c. 654, fo. 445).
52. J. H. Newman, *Apologia pro Vita Sua. Being a History of his Religious Opinions* (London: Longman, Green and Co., 1913, new impression), pp. 9–10.
53. Wood to Manning, 19 November 1835, Manning MSS Bod., c. 654, fo. 440.
54. Wood to Manning, 29 January 1836, ibid., fo. 446. Keble would make a similar point in his sermon on Tradition (27 September 1836): the Fathers of the Church employed Tradition not as derived from Scripture but as parallel to it. The interpretation of the Scriptures is only one of the functions of Tradition; even here Tradition fixed 'the interpretation of disputed texts, not simply by judgement of the Church, but by the authority of that Holy Spirit which inspired the oral teaching, of which such tradition is the record' (J. Keble, *Primitive Tradition Recognised in Holy Scripture* (London: Rivington, 1837, 3rd ed.), pp. 23–4).
55. Keble would develop at length the scriptural theme of a pre-scriptural deposit of faith made up of the substance of Christian doctrine, and of a certain system of practices, government, discipline and worship previous to the writing of the Scriptures. This was a system almost wholly unwritten at the time, complete in itself, and only requiring fidelity in its transmission. He felt that to think lightly of Tradition is as sinful as thinking lightly of God's word in Scripture (Keble, *Primitive Tradition*, pp. 17 ff., 26, 28).
56. Wood to Manning, 19 November1835, Manning MSS Bod., c. 654, fo. 440. Wood, although aware of the Vincentian canon, does not seem to have yet read Vincent's *Commonitorium*. At the end of the accompanying letter he asks Manning where he can obtain a copy (ibid., fo. 439). In his next letter Wood already referred to various passages of the *Communitorium*.
57. Wood to Manning, December 1835, ibid., fo. 442.
58. H. E. Manning, *The Rule of Faith* (London: Rivington, 1839, 2nd ed.), p. 27.
59. Ibid., p. 28.
60. Newman, 'First Letter to Jager', in Allen, *Newman and Jager*, pp. 36–7.
61. [J. H. Newman], *Lectures on the Scripture Proof of the Doctrines of the Church, Tracts for the Times*, 85 (London: Rivington, 1838), pp. 22–3, 31–3, 43.
62. Keble, *Primitive Tradition*, p. 26; see also p. 21.
63. Ibid., p. 28 n. 1.
64. Newman, *Prophetical Office*, p. 297.
65. Ibid., p. 62.
66. Froude, 'Remarks on the Grounds of Orthodox Belief' (November 1835), *Remains*, II–I, pp. 348–50, 352.
67. Froude, 'Essay on Rationalism' (1834), *Remains*, II–I, p. 76.
68. Froude, *Remains*, II–I, Preface, p. xiii.
69. [Newman], *Lectures on the Scripture Proof*, pp. 18, 23, 32.
70. Newman, *Prophetical Office*, p. 288.
71. Wood to Manning, 19 November 1835, Manning MSS Bod., c. 654, fo. 440.
72. Wood to Newman, 1 January1836, Halifax Papers, A2/42, fo. 2R-2V.
73. Wood to Manning, 18 December 1835, Manning MSS Bod., c. 654, fo. 442.
74. Wood to Newman, 1 January 1836, Halifax Papers, A2/42, fo. 1R.
75. Wood to Manning, 18 December 1836, Manning MSS Bod., c. 654, fo. 442. The mind and consciousness of the Church would operate along similar lines.
76. Wood to Manning, 18 December 1835, Manning MSS Bod., c. 654, fo. 442.
77. Wood to Manning, 19 November 1835, ibid., fo. 441. Newman's theory of

development did not dwell on this particular psychological element.
78. Wood to Newman, 1 January 1836, Halifax Papers, A2/42, fo. 2R.
79. Wood to Manning, 29 January 1836, Manning MSS Bod., c. 654, fo. 449.
80. Newman, *Prophetical Office*, p. 65; see also Manning to R. Wilberforce, 30 December 1845, Manning MSS Bod., c. 655, fo. 34.
81. Manning, *Rule of Faith*, p. 49.
82. Ibid., p. 50. When Newman published his *Development*, Manning thought that, among other things, it begged the question: *Quo judice?* (Manning to R. Wilberforce, 30 December 1845, Manning MSS Bod., c. 655, fo. 35).
83. Newman, *Prophetical Office*, p. 79.
84. Denis Pétau (Dyonisius Petavius), Jesuit priest, one of the most learned theologians of the seventeenth century. Newman seems to be referring to his *Dogmata Theologica*, published in three volumes (1644–50), the most widely read of his works.
85. Newman, *Prophetical Office*, p. 77. In later editions he would change this statement, adding a note exonerating Petavius.
86. Wood to Newman, 1 January 1836, Halifax Papers, A2/42, fo. 2V.
87. Wood to Manning, 18 December 1835, Manning MSS Bod., c. 654, fo. 442. These chapters, in the edition of the *Commonitorium* used by Wood, correspond to ch. xxiii in the Corpus Christianorum edition (see Appendix I, nts 4 and 29).
88. Wood to Manning, 18 December 1835, Manning MSS Bod., c. 654, fo. 442.
89. Wood to Newman, 1 January 1836, Halifax Papers, A2/42, fo. 2R.
90. Wood to Manning, 18 December 1835, Manning MSS Bod., c. 654, fo. 442.
91. Wood to Manning, 19 November 1835, ibid., fo. 440.
92. Wood to Manning, 18 December 1835, ibid., fo. 443.
93. Ibid.
94. Ibid.
95. Wood to Manning, 29 January 1836, ibid., fo. 447. In 1838 Newman would affirm that 'justification by faith alone' was a doctrine which emerged at the Reformation, invented by Luther, against previous Christian teaching (J. H. Newman, *Lectures on Justification* (London: Rivington, 1838), p. 389). Froude, on his part, had doubted at an earlier date whether justification by faith was a doctrine necessary for salvation (Froude to Newman, 17 November 1833, *LD*, IV, p. 112).
96. Newman to Froude, 24 December1835, *LD*, V, p. 185. Froude published some of the ideas contained in his exchanges with Newman in his review of Blanco White's autobiography ([R. H. Froude], 'Blanco White's *Heresy and Orthodoxy*', *British Critic* 19/37 (January 1836), pp. 204–25).
97. Newman, *Prophetical Office*, p. 65.
98. Ibid., p. 369.
99. Ibid., p. 64.
100. Wood to Manning, 29 January 1836, Manning MSS Bod., c. 654, fo. 448. Froude had made a similar point in 1834: 'it is to no purpose to say that we can find no proof of it [a practical development] in the writings of the six first centuries; they must find a *dis*proof if they would do any thing' (Froude to Keble, 9 January 1834, *Remains*, I–I, p. 336).
101. Newman, in 1843, would say that Scripture began development; it did not finish it. It would be a mistake to look for every separate proposition of Christian doctrine in Scripture. The question to ask is not whether the doctrine is to be found in the sacred text, in those or similar words, but whether it is contrary to the doctrines found in it (Newman, 'Theory of Developments', pp. 337–8); see also *Development*, p. 110.
102. Wood to Manning, 29 January 1836, Manning MSS Bod., c. 654, fo. 446.

103. In 1834 Newman affirmed that the Reformers did not add to the Creed: 'they *added* protests against the corruption of faith, worship and discipline, which had grown up around them' ([J. H. Newman], *'Via Media' (II), Tracts for the Times*, 41 (London: Rivington, 1840, 4th ed.), p. 3).
104. Newman, *Prophetical Office*, pp. 90–1.
105. The context of Wood's letter and his theory of development, together with Newman contemporary and later writings, make clear that Newman was not speaking of doctrinal developments as such, as some have recently claimed, but was referring to explanations of already professed credal doctrines (see I. Ker, *Newman on Vatican II* (Oxford: Oxford University Press, 2014), p. 48). For a detailed analysis of this point see Chapter IV.
106. Wood to Manning, 29 January 1836, Manning MSS Bod., c. 654, fol. 447.
107. Wood to Manning, 19 November 1835, ibid., fo. 441.
108. Wood to Manning, 18 December 1835, ibid., fo. 442.
109. Manning, *Rule of Faith*, p. 22, n. 1. They seem to have used the Vulgate translation in the controversy. The King James Bible, following Tyndale, translated the Greek original for 'other than', and so did the *RSV*. The Douay Bible (1609) translated it as 'besides that'; the modern Catholic edition of the *RSV* as 'contrary to'; the *Jerusalem Bible* as 'different from'.
110. Wood to Manning, 29 January 1836, Manning MSS Bod., c. 654, fo. 447.
111. Newman, *Prophetical Office*, p. 79.
112. Wood to Manning, December 1835, Manning MSS Bod., c. 654, fo. 444.
113. Wood to Newman, 1 January 1836, Halifax Papers, A2/42, fol. 1R. In the 'Third Letter to Jager', Newman had written: 'Moreover not a word is said to debar Tradition from teaching doctrines additional to those which are emphatically called the Faith, . . . only that it does not come to us as an independent and sufficient informant in necessary truth' (Allen, *Newman and Jager*, p. 123). On 3 January 1836 Newman answered Wood's letter and enclosed a copy of the Recapitulation – a second paper on the subject read at the Theological Society on 11 Dec. (Newman's diary, 11 December 1835 and 3 January 1836, *LD*, V, pp. 176 and 189).
114. Wood to Manning, Dec. 1835, Manning MSS Bod., c. 654, fo. 443.
115. Wood to Manning, 29 January 1836, ibid., fo. 448.
116. [J. H. Newman], *Remarks on Certain Passages in the Thirty-Nine Articles, Tracts for the Times*, 90 (London: Rivington, 1841), pp. 81 and 8. He reinforced this point in later editions, i.e.: 'there is a silence in the Sixth Article about a *judge* of the scripturalness of doctrine, yet a judge there must be' (J. H. Newman, *The Via Media of the Anglican Church*, II (London: Longman, Green and Co., 1889), p. 287.
117. Wood to Manning, 19 November1835, Manning MSS Bod., c. 654, fol.441.
118. Wood to Manning, 19 November 1835, ibid., fo. 441. Newman would affirm in his *Development* that an infallible doctrinal authority is to be expected (antecedent probability), and that this expectation is fulfilled in the Catholic Church (Newman, *Development*, pp. 117 ff.).
119. Newman, 'Second Letter to Jager', in Allen, *Newman and Jager*, p. 103; see also his *Prophetical Office*, pp. 255 ff.
120. Wood to Manning, 29 January 1836, Manning MSS Bod., c. 654, fo. 446.
121. Ibid., fos 448–9.
122. Ibid., fo. 446.

CHAPTER IV

'Out of Shadows'

William George Ward's articles in the *British Critic*

It might be queried whether Wood's description of Newman's reaction to his theory of development, and his summary of their conversations, portrayed Newman's true position on this matter. Wood himself was cautious about this last point, and did not want to commit his friend too narrowly. Having said that, the study of Newman's intellectual development during those years seems to confirm Wood's estimate of his friend's opinions at the time. By 1840, however, Newman could formulate a theory of development, and present it to his brother Francis. What had happened in the intervening years? How had he reached such a conclusion after his emphatic rejection of development some four or five years before?

Different hypotheses have been put forward in an attempt to explain the genesis of Newman's theory of development and to trace its sources. Owen Chadwick's account of the origins of Newman's theory of development, although no longer sustainable in the face of more recent evidence, has a long tradition and does not lack supporters even today. In his view, the doctrine marked a dramatic change of direction in Newman's thought, brought about by the reverses of the year 1841: the attacks against *Tract 90*, the bishops' anti-Tractarian charges, the Jerusalem bishopric and other factors. According to Chadwick, up to that very year of 1841 Newman had been declaring with Bossuet, Keble and Pusey that novelty in doctrine was heresy. William George Ward, according to Chadwick, would have played an important role at this juncture. He introduced Möhler's ideas into his articles in the *British Critic* and, in so doing, brought them to Newman's attention, nudging him towards the theory of doctrinal development. As a result, Newman, while not directly influenced by the reading of Möhler's work, would have been inspired by him through the medium of Ward's articles. Then, as was usually the case, Newman would have imposed his own pattern and originality on the ideas suggested there. As a result, between 1841 and the spring of 1843, when he preached his university sermon on development, Newman's mind – as Chadwick put it – crossed the Rubicon. His passage to the idea of development represented a fracture of continuity, an intellectual leap, without connection with his earlier doctrines. Chadwick considered that there were no mediating steps between Newman's stance in the *Development* and his early ideas on the *via media*.[1]

Newman did obviously know Ward's articles in the *British Critic*. Furthermore, in the first two editions of his *University Sermons*, he did include a reference to some 'admirable articles' about the divinely appointed mode of seeking truth. They sketched an important theory of religious knowledge. Newman went as far as quoting the issues and pages in the *British Critic* where they could be found, and he expressed the hope that those ideas might appear in a more systematic form.[2] He did not mention that some of them had a long tradition in the Oxford Movement, that they had been at the very heart of it from before its inception. Ward, however, had acknowledged that he was not presenting a theory of his own: he was trying to harmonize and develop what the Oxford writers had said on the subject.[3]

Ward pointed out how the Oxford Movement's notions about the acquisition of religious knowledge had originated with Butler, and that Butler's principles had been expanded in a most striking and convincing way by Froude.[4] The latter and the other Tractarians maintained that revelation is a knowledge addressed primarily to man's moral nature, secondarily to the intellect.[5] Experience teaches us that it is difficult to form unbiased judgements on questions in which feelings are really and deeply involved. As a result, high spiritual doctrines can only be spiritually discerned by the spiritual; only the spirit can understand the spirit.[6] Moral truth cannot be really apprehended unless practised. Only in the measure in which man obeys it will he be able to understand the doctrine.[7] Thus, the more conscientious the following of Christ, the deeper and more stable would be the apprehension of truth. By acting on the truth, the person reaches a certainty and infallible conviction of its reality and truthfulness. Although conscience, in the abstract, only discerns moral truth, it also disposes the mind to discriminate doctrinal truth, as it perceives its conformity with the path to holiness. Theory must in general come after rather than precede experience. Ward, following Newman, said that doctrine needs to be *realized* to carry forward reasoning. As a result, individuals would necessarily develop intellectually at different speeds in respect to religious knowledge.[8] He felt that the reliance on conscience made necessary the counterbalance of an external authority in order to avoid the pitfalls of private judgement; an external authority which could only be trusted in so far as it had the mark of holiness.[9] Tractarian theory was still running in circles.

Some of the articles made frequent references to Möhler's *Unity of the Church*, recently published in French translation. In it, Möhler, within the general theoretical framework of the Tübingen Catholic school of theology, described the unfolding of revelation in the life of the Church and compared it to that of a living organism. Revealed truth developed in continuity with the original 'idea' or principle, preserving not changing its substance.[10] As we have seen, however, the Tractarian ideas on religious knowledge and even on development preceded Ward's articles; they did not originate with or were influenced in any significant degree by the Tübingen School, against what Chadwick seems to suggest.[11] It is safe to assume that by the early forties ideas of doctrinal development were being shared by those in the inner circle of the Oxford Movement,[12] and Ward seems to have used Möhler's growing reputation to reinforce the credentials of Tractarian ideas on the subject.

Ward, quoting Möhler, affirmed that the identity of the present day Church with the early one did not imply immobility.[13] Changes, and a progressive deeper apprehension of divine truth, are necessary tokens of the existence of life within the Church and the individual. A life that should always grow and develop, otherwise the Church risked losing even the perception of truths she had already attained.[14] The Apostles had taught principles without their detailed *analysis* or *expression*, not carrying them to their furthest limits; they had also taught the correlative doctrines to those principles without their *development;* real principles contain within them indefinite results. Ward, therefore, considered that there was a need to put development of doctrine at the centre of the history of the Church.[15] She could not be understood without it, and the richness of the Christian message would remain forever hidden from the believer. Development is a law of the Church's history. One cannot swim against the tide of fifteen centuries of history to return to the early Church, as one cannot return the grown man to childhood. The Medieval Church, Ward added provocatively, had the same claim on us as the ancient one. What changes might be found in it, merely represented a further stage of growth, while preserving its identity of doctrine and of ethical character.[16] All present Roman doctrines had quite conceivably arisen from the development of doctrines declared by the Apostles.

Ward established a direct connection between ethos, or moral nature, and development. Man, he affirmed, is indebted to his moral nature for his first principles and for the meaning of the terms he uses. These constitute the starting point of any development and determine also its direction. An increase of spiritual life tends to be accompanied by an increase of spiritual knowledge.[17] If one were to act upon each light granted him, it would be difficult to predict how far they would carry him. The righteous man would be guided by an instinct of truth, while heretical developments would follow from erroneous principles and moral disorder.

Later, in the *Ideal of a Christian Church*, Ward would accept Palmer's distinction between two different types of development: *inferences*, conclusions drawn from known principles; and *expressions*, new and clearer conceptual formulations of known truths. Palmer did not accept that inferences could be demanded as matters of faith, while Newman and Ward affirmed the opposite. The latter, in his *Ideal*, went on to claim that his articles in the *British Critic* had gone beyond what Newman had said in his 1843 sermon on development. In the articles Ward had suggested that the Church might declare as doctrines of necessary faith those not held, even implicitly, by the early Fathers, though they might have held premises which led morally or intellectually to those doctrines.[18]

Dating problems

Newman's letters of 1840 render unsustainable Chadwick's opinion about the genesis of the *Development of Christian Doctrine*. His theory, however, had the merit of directing scholars' attention towards Ward's illuminating articles in the *British Critic*. Stephen Dessain, for his part, proposed that the 'theory was something almost entirely new, although Newman had first adumbrated it in his *Arians of the Fourth Century*'.[19] Ian Ker's biography of Newman follows Dessain's view in seeing in *Arians* a first suggestion of development. The second tract of the *Via Media*, according to Ker, already 'shows how even at this point Newman took the principle of doctrinal development for granted'.[20] Newman himself referred to *Arians* as containing the first expressions of a theory of development, and, in the personal recollections of his *Apologia*, he would write: 'I am brought (now) to the principle of development of doctrine in the Christian Church, to which I gave my mind at the end of 1842. I had spoken of it in a passage which I quoted many pages back, in *Home Thoughts Abroad*, published in 1836; (and even at an earlier date I had introduced it into my *History of the Arians* in 1832) but it had been a favourite subject with me all along.'[21] When republishing in later years his early writings, he would point out in the footnotes that some of his remarks in the early thirties had already presupposed the theory of development. In particular, *Tract 38* and *Tract 40* (1834) on the *Via Media* were identified by Newman as offering some of those instances. There, in words put forward by a layman, there is a reference to doctrinal development: 'as time goes on, fresh and fresh articles of faith are necessary to secure the Church's purity, according to the rise of successive heresies and errors. These articles are all hidden, as it were, from the first, in the Church's bosom, and brought out into form according to the occasion. Such was the Nicene Confession against Arius.'[22] In the 1885 edition he appended a note to this passage: 'Here, as above, the principle of doctrinal development is accepted as true and necessary for the Christian Church.'[23]

Although Newman, in later years, would say that some of his remarks in the early thirties already 'presupposed' a theory of development he was not always consistent in his dating of it. In

1843 he wrote to his sister Jemima, telling her: 'I have now for 12 years been working out a theory', and 'I have kept the same views and arguments for 12 years'.[24] On the other hand, in a letter to Mrs W. Froude two years later, he would say that he had had it in his mind from the time he had written *Arians*, or at least from 1836, although he could not bring it out.[25] As a matter of fact, the evidence against Newman having held a well defined and more or less complete theory of development much before 1839–40 is compelling. With respect to the *Arians*, one could say with Allen that, then, 'Newman's attention was not focused on the increase of doctrine. He merely saw another way of expressing the object of faith. That object itself remained identical and invariable. Far from approving this need to find other ways of expressing the object of faith, he seems to regard the translation of it as inadequate and dangerous. It is nothing more than a necessary evil. His idea of faith is therefore, at this time, a static one.'[26] Newman's articles of faith are not new truths but only more accurate expression of truths already believed: in the case of the Nicene Creed, the divinity of Christ. The same could be said of his words in *Tract 38* and *Tract 40*. These were written before Newman's exchange of letters with Jager and his rejection of Wood's ideas on development. It is therefore unlikely that he would have professed in 1833–4 what he would deny so emphatically some months later. Besides, Laicus's words were also applicable to the *Disciplina Arcani*. Newman himself, in his *Development*, would say that the *Disciplina* could be used, and had been used, to 'account for that apparent variation and growth of doctrine which embarrasses us when we would consult history for the true idea of Christianity'.[27] According to the *Disciplina*, the variations were only 'apparent', and the existence of Christian doctrine hidden from public view 'accounted' for them and for their late appearance. In his *Prophetical Office* (1837), however, he had chased out of the *Disciplina* those who had taken refuge in it to justify what in truth amounted to doctrinal developments, whether Roman or otherwise.[28] He repeated that doctrinal development was a Roman doctrine, in direct contraposition to the rule of faith accepted by the Anglican Church.

Ian Ker has recently asserted that in 1834 Newman, in a letter (not sent) to Thomas Falconer, had already made reference to a theory of development.[29] In Newman's own words: 'it [the *Disciplina Arcani*] existed rather as a feeling and a principle than as a rule in the early Church. This is the case with the greatest part of the theological and ecclesiastical system which is implicitly contained in the writings and acts of the Apostles, but was developed at various times according to circumstances. I should in a certain sense say that this was true of the doctrine of the Trinity – and of the Incarnation as opposed to Nestorianism.'[30] The language Newman uses in this and other places should be analysed carefully. The use of the term 'develop' does not by any means necessarily imply that he had a theory of doctrinal development at this point, and even less that it was the theory of development he later described in his 1845 work. In this case, as in others, references to the doctrines of the Incarnation and of the Blessed Trinity suggest that what Newman had in mind are explanations of the Creed, not additional doctrines.[31]

Ten years later, in a letter to Mrs Froude (June 1844), Newman himself would make this very point. As he wrote, two considerations had hitherto kept him satisfied and secure in the Church of England: namely, that it had Apostolic succession and that some Roman doctrines were not to be found in Antiquity. The second consideration had been undermined by the principle of development. He said that he had always accepted development of doctrine, 'at least in some great points in theology', although he had confined it to the apostolic time or at least to the first ages of the Church. For Newman, apostolic developments were guaranteed by the Apostles' specific and unique charism, but the same could not be said to the same extent of early post-apostolic times. In the same letter to Mrs Froude, he went on to add that his view of development in 1843 differed from that held before 'not in principle, but in two respects':

> 1. In considering that developments may be made at any time, for the Church is always under the guidance of Divine Grace [though he felt he had granted this implicitly in some comments he had quoted from his previous works]
>
> 2. that developments are not only *explanations* of the sense of the Creed, but further doctrines involved in and arising from its articles.

> The direct contrary is maintained in the paragraph following the last extract [taken from his *Prophetical Office*].[32]

Newman, constrained by the *quod semper*, had for many years conceived 'developments' as 'explanations' of the sense of the Creed, not as new doctrinal developments. Samuel Wood, for his part, had propounded a theory of doctrinal development in his 1835 paper including both points. Newman and Manning had rejected them at the time. Ian Ker has recently affirmed that to 'say that Newman did not believe in doctrinal development because he rejected the Roman concept of it would be like saying that as a Tractarian he did not believe in the Real Presence in the Eucharist, when he manifestly did, . . . because he rejected the Tridentine doctrine of Transubstantiation'.[33] It would be more accurate to say that besides not believing the Roman concept of development Newman, in the 1830s, was also far from believing what was to be his own post 1840 concept of it.

How then ought we to interpret Newman's later references to the presence of a theory of development in his 1830s writings? It might be possible to claim that in those instances Newman was applying some of his own principles from the *Essay*. There he had spoken about the legitimacy of interpreting previous steps in development by later ones. The latter might throw light upon, and draw out, what had before been obscure and barely perceived. Newman added that, in the course of a development, there are intimations of tendencies, even flashes of anticipation, of what the final result of development will be, and that these can only be recognized in the light of the fully realized idea.[34] Looking back from the standpoint of a later theory of development, Newman could see clearly those intimations of tendencies and flashes of anticipation, and could perceive development where he had not seen it before. In the *Apologia*, and others of his Catholic writings and commentaries, Newman wrote from positions reached long after the years 1834–7. He was then able to see in retrospect continuity in his thought, leading him to opinions reached later; how some of the principles he had held in those years pointed towards (or implied) development; that some of his expressions might be read in that light, although they had not actually been written under it; that his words, in fact, said more than he actually meant at the time. Ideas found in Newman's early writings might thereby serve as building blocks for a theory of development, and, as a matter of fact, he did eventually use them to this end. It seems clear, however, that in the middle thirties Newman did not recognize all the virtualities contained in those concepts. Only later, and in very different circumstances, would he discover the life hidden in them.

Some scholars have identified particular doctrines as the likely origin of Newman's development. Selby, for example, thought that 'a direct link may be traced between the theory of development and the principle of reserve'.[35] He suggested that Newman 'may have conceived of ideas as informed by the principle of reserve, disclosing their secrets gradually to the earnest seeker of truth'.[36] Selby, however, did not adduce compelling arguments to support his contention, although some evidence favourable to this hypothesis may be gathered from *Tract 85* (1838), where Newman said that the Creeds and the other doctrines professed by the Church are contained in Holy Scripture, yet not on the surface of it but in a latent form.[37] Günter Biemer, for his part, detected in Newman's notion of Prophetical Tradition the seeds of his later theory of the development of doctrine, a suggestion shared by Louis Allen and others.[38] This approach requires qualification: Prophetical Tradition was not conceived by Newman in order to support development of doctrine, but to exclude it. The distinction tried to explain a rather obvious phenomenon: the fact that from the early days of the Church there had been a continuous accumulation of the results of theological enquiry. Theological developments had taken place and were still taking place. The point in question was whether the Church could impose those developments, and the new doctrines resulting from them, as truths to be believed by the faithful. Newman drew the line here. In 1837 he still wielded what he considered his most powerful weapon against the Church of Rome: the 'creed of Romanism is ever subject to increase; ours is fixed once for all'.[39]

In the late 1830s it would perhaps be closer to the truth to say that a series of strands in Newman's thought, some of them part of the common intellectual baggage of the Oxford Movement, pointed Newman's mind in the direction of a theory of development: the Tractarian concept of *ethos*, the doctrine of reserve, the gradual unfolding of God's revelation (as it appears in Holy Scripture), his distinction between Prophetical and Apostolic Tradition, and so on. In the years 1834–7 they did not, however, form part of a coherently structured theory of development. The fact is that, whenever he confronted the question, whether in his 1835 controversy with Jager, in his conversations with Wood or in the *Prophetical Office*, he resisted the principle of development and fought against it. As Allen put it, when development 'is referred to in Newman's early work it is usually an attribute of "Romanism", in other words it is a case *against* which he argues'.[40]

A CENTRAL 'IDEA'

At the heart of Newman's theory of development is to be found the 'idea', that is the object of a process of development. He did not formulate the concept of the *idea* in a clear and systematic way until 1843, in his fourteenth university sermon. This might suggest that Möhler could perhaps have provided him with assistance in conceiving so important an aspect of his theory, but this again is unlikely. There are obvious differences between Newman's concept of the *idea*, and that of the Tübingen School. As a matter of fact, Newman seems to dismiss in the *Essay* the notion of the 'leading idea' of Christianity,[41] given the difficulty in determining it. We need to look elsewhere. Might Coleridge have influenced Newman, and provided him with the illumination under which he discovered the keystone for his theory? This does not seem to be the case either. Newman confessed that had read Coleridge in 1835, and was impressed by how much of himself was in Coleridge; which is far from saying that he had made his own the poet's ideas. The fact that he continued fighting against any theories suggesting doctrinal development, seems to suggest that the reading of Coleridge had not had the dramatic effect of an Augustinian *Tolle, lege*. There was no instantaneous conversion.

There seems to be a Lockeian ambiguity in Newman's 'idea', and in his use of the term. It at times stands for the mind's image of an external object or quality, while, in other instances, it refers to the external object being the subject of apprehension. Besides, as Stanley Jaki has pointed out, the constant use of this term might obscure the fact that Newman is dealing with 'facts'. In the case of the *Essay*, with the reality of the one Church, having kept its identity from apostolic times to the present. Newman saw that entity, even though, as Jaki went on to say, 'for the sake of argument, he writes at times as if it were a mere idea'.[42]

The dramatic quality of Newman's prose is particularly in evidence when writing about the 'idea'; he seems to have been carried away by the rhetorical possibilities of his imagery. Some passages in the *Essay*, and in his 1843 sermon on development, appear to present the idea as a living principle, germinating and growing, almost parasitically, in the individual mind, feeding off its substance, and depending on it for its survival, growth and transmission. Its development is the result of its enlargement and maturing in the minds of men during a sufficient period of time. And Newman would add, somewhat provocatively, that the idea 'employs their minds as instruments, and depends upon them while it uses them'.[43] Earlier on, in his sermon on development, he had applied this same approach to the Christian idea: it seems, he said, 'to employ the minds of Christians, [rather] than occupy them'.[44] And, in a later edition of the sermon, he would make this sentence even more explicit: 'the doctrine may rather be said to use the minds of Christians, than to be used by them'.[45] These expressions, however, do not support a Hegelian interpretation of the *Essay*. Newman's 'idea', in its fundamental doctrinal dimension, is the representation of a transcendent and pre-existent reality, previous and complete before it becomes the object of knowledge and is formulated conceptually. Aidan Nichols is much closer to the mark when he says that the 1878 edition of the *Essay* 'made clear that by 'idea' Newman means the self-expression of some rich and complex reality'.[46]

The most obvious route in search of the sources for the concept of the 'idea' points in the direction of Newman's own Patristic studies. In the early 1830s he had studied in depth the Arian heresy, and was familiar with the controversy surrounding it and with the subsequent conciliar dogmatic formulations. Ten years later, we find him revising his *Arians*, and working on the translation of Athanasius' treatises against them.[47] It is not unreasonable, therefore, to infer that the Christological dimension of these studies might have been the ground from which his concept of the idea was to develop. The Council of Nicaea had defined that the Word (the Logos, the Idea) is consubstantial to the Father, the perfect expression (self-expression becomes truly appropriate in this context) of his substance, the Father's perfect representation or image. The Incarnation (revelation's summit and summing up) was, analogically, the self-expression of the divine Idea through the rather imperfect medium of a human nature, in human words and deeds. At this level, however, the divine so far exceeds human nature's powers of representation that the resulting 'idea' is infinitely poorer than the being it represents. Still, in spite of its imperfection, it conveys a rich and multifaceted knowledge of divine reality; it contains inexhaustible riches. Man's apprehension of the divine manifested in revelation is – because of the very nature of his knowledge – partial and limited, capturing different aspects of revelation in sequence. These different aspects, once they are integrated in the human mind, offer a complex vision of the object. Newman calls this, too, the 'idea', the sum total of the aspects perceived at a given moment in time, the present state of its development in the human mind or in the perception of the Church at a given time. Doctrinal developments of themselves do not involve change in the reality apprehended, but are stages in the process of apprehension. The first is not subject to development, the second is.

Newman's different uses of the term 'idea' seem to support the above interpretation. Sometimes the 'idea' seems to stand for the Idea, manifesting itself in revelation; on other occasions, it refers to the revelation itself; at times it designates the image apprehended by the human intellect. Moreover, Newman's dramatic description of the development of the idea seems to correspond to the doctrinal and institutional development of Christianity. In the case of revelation it may truly be said that the Idea itself is active in the mind. The Idea (a divine Person, although referred to here as *it*) does not only reveal itself in revelation; it also opens the Christian mind to it, and helps the mind 'realize' truth, making possible the mind's progress from notional to real and from implicit to explicit knowledge. It is in the context of Christian revelation that one may properly say that the Idea employs Christian minds as instruments for its full manifestation in the world, and needs a multitude of minds to develop and grow to full stature. It is a process which, while enriching and achieving its purpose in the individual minds, does not end in them; they serve God's providential plan for the perfect development of the 'idea', doctrinally and institutionally, until it will reach its final fulfilment, when the Idea will be all in all. Only divine revelation seems to match adequately all the aspects of Newman's concept of the 'idea' and its development, and it is not difficult to reconstruct the possible intellectual path he was to follow, drawing inspiration from his patristic and historical studies.

Newman's Final Journey towards the Theory of Development

It is beyond dispute that a well defined theory of development had already taken shape in Newman's mind by 1840, as shown by his letters to his brother Francis towards the end of that year, especially the one of 10 November of that month. The letters – almost contemporary with Wood's 'Revival' – clearly show that by then Newman had already formulated a comprehensive theory of doctrinal development, and its degree of elaboration suggests that it was the fruit of a long period of reflection. He ordered his ideas in several numbered propositions: all living beings develop without changing their identity; the living Church develops as well, while the temper and principles that define its identity remain the same; doctrines develop from external and internal causes; and he went on to list most of the notes identifying true developments that he would later describe in his *Essay*.[48] The substance of his theory, and a good number of the concepts he would later employ when describing it, are already present in the letter. Besides, Newman was confident enough to expose his theory to the critical examination of his brother Francis, by no means a sympathetic or gullible judge.

The theory had not been conceived, however, without a struggle. In the mid 1830s a number of dearly held (and strenuously defended) principles and doctrines occupied Newman's intellectual horizon, and prevented him from perceiving the convergence of his ideas towards a theory of development. The process of shedding those principles and doctrines was long and laborious. Peter Nockles argued that Newman's 'Patristic fundamentalism', and his looking at Antiquity using his own eyes, were the cause of his gradual rejection of the Tractarians' original High Church positions. The casualties, he added, soon piled up: the old controversial method against Rome, the existing liturgies, the Thirty-Nine Articles, even the Vincentian Rule had all fallen and were abandoned as a result.[49] This is true in some respects, but not all. Newman's strict adherence to the Vincentian Rule (an essential part of his 'Patristic fundamentalism') long held him back, and prevented him – as his conversations with Wood show – from accepting the possibility of development. The fact is that what really entered into crisis was Newman's 'Patristic fundamentalism' itself. Only when he had abandoned it was he able to free himself from a narrow interpretation of the Vincentian Rule, and to move forward towards a theory of development. This happened before November 1840. By then, he was ready to grant that doctrinal differences could be found before the fourth century; that development was already taking place then.[50] As he wrote to his brother, the question of development affected not only the identity of the nineteenth-century Church with that of the fourth or fifth centuries, but also the identity of the fourth-century Church with that of the first.

The process leading Newman to that new intellectual position seems to have involved several steps. In 1837–8 Newman was still far from discovering two fundamental principles of a proper doctrine of development. The first, that it had always been God's plan for the revelation to disclose its riches in a progressive way, even though it had reached its summit in Christ. Revelation is full and complete in Jesus – *unu afflatu*, as they liked to say – but it requires a process of reception on the part of those to whom it has been made; a reception never fully completed. The second, that it is part of God's providence to provide a continuous divine intercession to preserve the original revelation and guarantee orthodox doctrinal development within the Church. There were also some obstacles to be removed on the road towards the *Essay*. One of them, the strict doctrine of fundamentals exhibited during the controversy with the Abbé Jager, was abandoned by Newman after his discussions with Froude.[51] Next, he slowly made his own Froude's understanding of the role of Antiquity, reinforcing in the process (but not for long) his own 'Patristic fundamentalism'. He had become increasingly aware of the difficulties and internal contradictions arising from some of the principles involved in the recourse to Antiquity, and he described them in his Introduction to the *Essay*.

The Vincentian Rule was seemingly a useful principle to identify those truths to be believed and also a serviceable weapon in the controversy with Rome. The rule cuts off and casts away as corruptions all usages, opinions, and doctrines that had not the sanction of primitive times. The late appearance of a particular doctrine told against it, and Rome, having added to the creed, stood condemned by Vincent. The thesis that '"Christianity is what has been held always, everywhere, and by all," certainly promises a solution of the perplexities, an interpretation of the meaning of history'.[52] The clear spring of early Church doctrine and practice had been later disturbed both in East and West. As a result, doctrine and practice had become confused and corrupt. The only way of recovering primitive purity was by going back to the sources using Vincent of Lerins's rule. The principle was simple but, as Newman himself had pointed out in the *Prophetical Office*, its application was rather more complex, given the difficulty of agreeing on a precise definition of what constitutes or is meant by always, everywhere, and by all. The consent of the Fathers, as we have seen, had similar problems of definition.[53] The strict interpretation of the dictum would require a whole doctrine stated by a whole Church, clear and distinct from the first, with no room for variations and developments between the early and the later Fathers. Newman admitted that 'if it [the Vincentian Rule] be narrowed for the purpose of disproving the Catholicity of the Creed of Pope Pius, it becomes also an objection to the Athanasian'.[54]

Might the *Disciplina Arcani*, come here to the rescue of the Vincentian Rule? It had originally been put forward by Roman divines and enthusiastically endorsed by the Tractarians, although Newman was suspicious of its use by the Church of Rome. That the *Disciplina Arcani* existed was a fact generally granted. In Newman's interpretation, it could be said that 'the subsequent profession of the doctrine in the Universal Church creates a presumption that it was held instinctively even before it was professed; and it is fair to interpret the early Fathers by the later. There had been no variations in the teaching of the Church from first to last: 'doctrines which are associated with the later ages of the Church were really in the Church from the first, but not publicly taught, and that for various reasons: as, for the sake of reverence, that sacred subjects might not be profaned by the heathen; and for the sake of catechumens, that they might not be oppressed or carried away by a sudden communication of the whole circle of revealed truth'. But, Newman countered, 'there is as little room for antecedent probabilities as for the argument from intimations in the *Quod semper, quod ubique, quod ab omnibus*'.[55] Moreover, it did not seem to be the key 'to the whole difficulty, as we find it, for an obvious reason; – the variations continue beyond the time when it is conceivable that the discipline was in force'.[56] In later editions of the *Essay*, he would add that those variations seemed to follow a pattern of progress, to conform to a law of slow and ordered organic development, which continued to the present time, and showed no sign of coming to an end.[57]

But the Vincentian Rule and the *Disciplina Arcani* were not abandoned as explanations of the 'apparent' changes in the Church's doctrine merely because of their internal contradictions. They seem to have been damaged beyond recovery by the traumatic crisis which suddenly overtook Newman in 1839. The occasion was Wiseman's article on the Donatists in the *Dublin Review*,[58] in it Wiseman quoted St Augustine's dictum: *securus iudicat orbis terrarum*,[59] adding as a comment: 'any one Church, in one portion of the world, could not possibly be allowed to be right, while protesting against the union of other Churches over the rest of the world. The very fact of its being in such position, at once condemns it, and proves it to be in schism'.[60] Newman did not feel at first touched by the thrust of Wiseman's argument. When he felt it, it was not merely in the point at which it had been aimed, schism; it also had seismic effects in the area of Antiquity and development. Newman had decided to go by Antiquity, and here one of its main oracles was advancing a simpler rule to settle doctrinal and other ecclesiastical questions. By those words of St Augustine, Newman later confessed, his *via media* was 'pulverized': 'Antiquity was deciding against itself.'[61] Catholicity had now acquired in his eyes a new dimension. Newman had taken it for a one-dimensional and static concept: the universal acceptance of a particular belief in antiquity. In Augustine's hands, as Newman clearly perceived, Catholicity was dynamic: it made allusion to the authority of the living Catholic Church of all times to define doctrine and to impose it as a matter of necessary belief. His study of the Monophysite controversy had made him consider the possibility that Rome might be proved right after all. It was a first crack in his apologia for the Church of England. Wiseman's article continued the work of demolition. Newman strove to recover from the initial shock, and tried to fill the breach opened on the walls of his theory of Anglicanism. The repair work, however, would not hold for long. His main line of defence (and attack) – that Rome had added to the Creed – seemed to have been breached, and was perhaps irretrievably lost. A symptomatic sign of his new intellectual perspective was the fact that, as he later confessed, in his defence of the Church of England he was now reduced to use arguments against Rome's 'political character'.[62]

Nevertheless, Newman did not surrender his positions without a fight. As soon as he felt the force of Wiseman's argument he started preparing his counter-attack, and by the end of the year he had ready for publication a long article, his 'Catholicity of the Anglican Church'. It appeared in the *British Critic* of January 1840. In it, Newman confronted the principle of Antiquity and that of Catholicity, confessing that each disputant sheltering behind one or the other (Anglo-Catholic and Roman Catholic) held a strong position. He tried to parry the thrust of the *securus* by putting forward the argument that this was not intended by St Augustine as a theological verity as sacred as an article of the Creed. Wiseman would have conceded the point: Augustine's *securus* was not a credal truth or as sacred as an article of the Creed, but then – Wiseman would have probably added – neither was

Vincent's *quod semper*. Both were in the order of basic principles. Newman found himself in an unenviable position. Could he deny the force of the one without undermining the authority of the other? He wrote in the article that St Augustine's maxim was a 'presumption rather than a law, not a criterion but a general evidence'.[63] But, once again, what determined one as a presumption and the other as a law? The question was left undecided. Newman moved on to consider Catholicity from what he called its 'political' aspect: whether the Church was designed by God to be under a single government or jurisdiction, as being of the essence of the Church. He passed judgement against this proposition, and went on to secure the position of the Anglican Church by claiming for it the note of sanctity, an essential note of the Church Catholic and, according to the Tractarians, a guarantee of orthodoxy. St Augustine was against the Anglican position, Meletius' sanctity – in spite of his separation from Rome – for it. The balance between Catholicity and Antiquity, Catholicity and Sanctity, seemed to be finely poised.

Newman was relieved by the positive reception of the article on the part of Isaac Williams, Pusey, Keble and others. Was he equally satisfied by it himself? He would later say that the article had kept him quiet till the Autumn of 1841.[64] How quiet? The main question – Catholicity versus Antiquity – continued to haunt him, and his despondency soon returned. In February of 1840 he confessed to Bowden that Wiseman's article was one of its causes,[65] and he wrote in similar terms to other correspondents. His letters do not, however, allow a clear view into his thoughts at the time, beyond showing the unsettled state of his mind. His musings about how much Catholic truth the Church of England could bear were perhaps the first external expression of his new ideas. The letters he wrote to his brother Francis in October-November 1840 clearly showed that a dramatic change had been taking place in Newman's mind during the intervening months, and how far he had travelled since January of that year. We do not know how long the tug of war between Augustine's and Vincent's principles lasted, and we do not know the steps he followed to resolve the apparent opposition between them. The outcome, however, of those months of spiritual and intellectual turmoil seems to have involved the reconciliation between the *securus* and the *quod semper*, probably on the basis of a new understanding of the latter along the lines of *Tract 85*. There he had spoken of how all things necessary for salvation are contained in Scripture, although points of faith may lie *under* the surface of it. This may have offered a stepping stone towards admitting the concept of *implicit* faith, as described in his 1840 article on Catholicity when explaining the Roman doctrine of development. As he would write in 1843, any new doctrine or doctrines adopted by the Church were implicitly included in the primitive creed, and thus held by earlier Christians. If one of these doctrines were 'now to be received, as surely it must be, as part of the Creed, it [means that this doctrine] was really held everywhere from the beginning, and therefore, in a measure, held as a mere religious impression, and perhaps an unconscious one'.[66] Newman had not abandoned the Vincentian Rule; rather it could be claimed, within the Tractarian doctrine of reserve, that the Vincentian Rule had revealed its deeper meaning.

Newman appears to have discovered in the Tractarian concept of *ethos* another key to the theory of development. The ideas in his letter to his brother Francis hinge on it. Some time between January and November 1840, Newman seems to have newly 'realized' the old Tractarian principle: that *ethos* is a better guide than doctrine, and that the main component of the *quod semper* is first and foremost the *ethos* of Antiquity. Continuity of temper is, therefore, a better indication and guarantee of the Church's identity than holding the same doctrinal tenets. Newman saw the continuity of moral temper as the guarantee of continuity in doctrine and of the identity of the Church. A new vision was taking shape before his eyes, integrating many previously held ideas – *ethos*, reserve, the Vincentian Rule – and presenting them under a new light and in a new order. There was only a short lapse of time (just under a year) between the ideas expressed in the *British Critic* article on Catholicity and Newman's letters to his brother. This should not offer cause for surprise. The elements for a theory of development were at hand, and he had already dealt with its principles when refuting Jager and Wood. Still, what Wood had said of his *presumptio*, could also be said of Newman's theory in 1840: it was not yet fully formed. He required some further years of work and reflexion in order to consider from different perspectives the arguments and principles involved; to fill the inevitable gaps; and to be able to offer a well-argued doctrine of development. The sermon on development will be published in 1843 and the *Essay* not until 1845, but the letters of 1840 already contained most of the essential elements of his theory.

Newman's letter to Francis of November 1840 included a determined assertion of continuity in the *ethos* of the Church: 'The *temper and principles* of the Church have been precisely the same from first to last, from the Apostolic age to this'.[67] With these words, Newman declared that the path leading to a theory of development was opened: a legitimate development would be that in harmony with the temper, principles and doctrines of the ancient Church. All the signposts seemed to be pointing Newman in the same direction, but he did not follow them without hesitation. There are indications that the matter was not completely settled in his mind. In his letter (29 March 1841) to the Bishop of Oxford in explanation of *Tract 90*, written barely four months after the letters to Francis, he would repeat those passages of his January 1840 article in the *British Critic* where, while granting for the sake of argument, the possibility of development, he added: does the Church know more than the Apostles knew? Besides, he added, the Roman Church, which claimed development, had developed doctrines clearly erroneous.[68] A letter to Miss Holmes in September 1841 reiterated similar themes. Newman questioned whether the Church of Rome had authority to vary or add to primitive religion. Rome's ground of defence, according to him, was that the Church did not reveal new truths; it only taught 'developments from germs held in primitive times'. He thought that in some cases – Mary's cult for example – this was trifling with words; the only solid ground for Rome was to 'maintain that the Church has the power of adding new truths to the Apostolic revelation'.[69] The cult of Mary in the Catholic Church loomed large before Newman's eyes for some more years, a considerable obstacle on his path to Rome. The Church of Rome claimed Catholicity and infallibility. Apparently she had the first, but Newman could not accept that she possessed infallibility when Rome maintained something which, at the time, appeared to him an obvious error. Had he abandoned his November 1840 profession of development? It does not seem that this is necessarily the case. Newman seems in both instances to be contemplating the possibility either of a false development or that of a new revelation. He could not accept the latter, given that the summit of revelation had been reached with Christ. He would dismiss Mary's cult on both counts. During 1841 he seems to have maintained his new concept of Catholicity, while rejecting the doctrine of infallibility as capable of founding doctrine on its own, 'not on Scripture, not on reason, not on Antiquity, not on Catholicity'.[70] Catholicity in this enumeration was presented, by itself, as a criterion of doctrinal truth. Those were to be trying times. Like Wood before him, Newman had caught a glimpse of the solution to a problem which had exercised him for years; also like Wood, he could still see the dark areas and unexplained facts within the theory.

The course of clarification and integration was to continue in the following years. Newman's concept of 'realizing' helped him find his way towards the solution of the problem of development. His *Parochial and Plain Sermons* had dealt with a particular dimension of 'realizing': the manner of passing from 'notional' to 'real' knowledge. The later *University Sermons* – the 'Theory of Developments' (1843), in particular – concentrate their attention on another, and closely related, aspect of the same process of 'realizing': the progress from 'implicit' to 'explicit' knowledge. Implicit and explicit knowledge are not two categories without intermediate stages. The Church's progressive 'realizing' of revealed truths grows in 'intenseness', and manifests itself in verbal expression, theological treatment, dogmatic definition and the like. As a result of this process, revealed doctrines are more or less present to the consciousness of the Church: dogmatic definitions are more present to the consciousness of the Church than non-defined revealed truths, those expressed in words more than those that are not.[71]

Newman recorded his musings on the subject in the 1843 diaries: what are the doctrines about purgatory, invocation of saints, and so on but 'vivid realizations' or 'vivid representations' of truths professed, of doctrines, feelings, ideas involved in primitive principles?[72] Truths which even a peasant holds implicitly in the creed he confesses, become explicitly known when, out of love and reverence, they are made the object of contemplation and reason: the 'inward idea of divine truth . . . passes into explicit form by the activity of our reflective powers'.[73] Development involves 'the sustained and steady march of the sacred science from implicit belief to formal statement'.[74] It is not a purely intellectual process: developments arise out 'of a keen and vivid realizing of the Divine Depositum of faith'.[75] The result of these developments is a whole world of truth and a body of dogmatic definitions, which 'is the expansion of the few words, uttered, as if casually, by the fishermen of Galilee'[76] – words which only surrender their treasures to those who approached them with due humility and reverence. In this way, what was at first an impression in the imagination becomes a dogmatic statement. 'Realizing is the very life of true developments; it is peculiar to the Church, and the justification of her definitions'.[77] The whole process of development would be authenticated by the act of 'realizing'. Newman refused heretics a share in it: realizing involves a divine action guiding man to truth, and this is obviously missing in the path of heresy, not because of God's denial of light but of man's rejection of it. Heretics, no doubt, played a role in this process but theirs was a negative role, not a constructive one; their errors were merely an occasion for development, not its cause. Newman admitted that in many of the Church's dogmatic decisions, that progress had been fashioned into shape by opposite strokes, defining orthodox doctrine against conflicting errors. He also admitted the pacific development of dogma, where truth grows as a result of study and contemplation, and is subsequently promulgated by the Church.[78]

It took a long time for Newman's ideas to crystallize into a new system. They seem to have lived for years a kind of separate existence, without discovering their natural connections, their affinities among themselves, or their latent oppositions. Possibilities and paradoxes revealed themselves to Newman's mind slowly, and, at times, resolved themselves painfully. Wood had preceded his friend with the 'presumptio' he had formulated in 1835; unfortunately, he did not develop further. Did he have any inklings of what had been going through Newman's mind since 1840? There are no indications that he did. Wood died on 22 April 1843, as the *University Sermons* were being prepared for publication.

Ethos and first principles in the Essay

Newman thought that his new theory reconciled the process of doctrinal development with the immutability demanded by the substantial identity of the Church in time. If the concept of *ethos* had played an important role in the theory's process of gestation, it went on to occupy a central position in the final structure of the *Essay*. Newman, however, did not employ the word *ethos* anywhere in the 1845 edition of the *Essay*. When referring to what he had described elsewhere as *ethos*, he used now expressions like 'temper' or 'moral temper; or, more often, 'first principles' or 'principles'. This latter concept, although intrinsically connected with that of *ethos*, was not its exact equivalent. The terminological change is less surprising than it would appear at first. The Tractarian concept of *ethos* had a restricted circulation, being confined mostly to the inner circle of the Movement, but 'principles', 'first principles', 'fundamental' or 'ultimate' principles were terms which had a recognizable content and were easily understandable by the general reader. They had been in use since at least the seventeenth century to refer to the basic laws of life and organization of churches, and of political and religious parties. There were innumerable publications describing Tory principles, Protestant principles, Church principles, Jacobite and Nonjuring principles, Catholic principles, the principles of revealed religion, and so on. The expression 'first principles' was less frequently used in that type of publication, but it is not exclusive to the Tractarians. Christopher Wordsworth, for example, employed it in his pamphlet *Church Principles and Church Measures* (1845), and Joseph Fletcher had used similar terms –'fundamental principles' or 'ultimate principles' – in 1817.[79]

Newman had made use of the expressions 'principles' or 'first principles' in his *Prophetical Office* (1838), when speaking of the differences between Protestantism and the Roman Church. There he had affirmed that the controversy with Rome turned more upon facts than upon first principles, while that with Protestants was more about principles than about facts; Roman developments were the result of a 'perverted' right principle of true Catholicism.[80] He had also spoken about temper and principles in his letters to Francis Newman, and elsewhere.[81] Other Tractarians had also used these expressions. Keble, in his tract on *Mysticism* (1841), spoke about 'principles' and 'first principles' when comparing the difference in *moral sentiment* between the Primitive Church and the nineteenth-century Anglican Church: the differences between the two ages were occasioned by differences in first principles, rather than being the result of accidental, local or temporary circumstances.

The concept of 'principle' or 'first principle' was nowhere clearly defined. Neither did Newman define it, though his use of the term clarified how he conceived it.[82] First principles, as he understood them, are not self-evident notions, incapable of demonstration. Newman did not view them either from a logical point of view, as premises in a particular reasoning process, from which conclusions might be drawn; nor are they general rules for correct thinking; neither did he consider them merely from a mere moral perspective. Newman's use of the term principle combined both the intellectual and moral dimensions. He conceived principles, within the general literature of the time, as the fundamental inner laws ruling the thought and activity of a particular person or institution, growing from deep moral roots and endowed with moral content. Principles lay deeper than doctrines; they are fundamental assumptions or general approaches to reality. They are abstract, general, permanent, more immediately ethical and practical than doctrines. Doctrines are intellectual and relate to facts; they develop, grow and enlarge.[83] First principles might be formulated – as they were by Newman himself – in ethical concepts, but even then they do not tend to become speculative truths. As to their genesis, principles have a double origin: the individual and the idea itself. They are the result, on the one hand, of the ethical history of the person – of his actions and of the habits that have arisen from them – and of his experience of reality; a particular *ethos* manifests itself in a series of first principles, determining also their relative rank, and shaping the thought of the person possessing it. Newman considered the individual's thought as governed by a number of principles which proceed from our personality as a whole, and that the predominant principle or tendency governs the interplay of their respective influences, defining the character of the individual and of his thought. As a result, an idea or argument might strike two minds very differently, awake dissimilar associations, and lead to even opposite conclusions, depending on their respective intellectual principles, which rest ultimately on the dominant moral ones.[84]

It was not Newman's intention, however, to establish too narrow a correlation between the peculiarities of the individual's mind, antecedent to the reception of a particular doctrine, and its future development. As already mentioned above, an idea has its own proper principles in which it lives and develops. The 'life of doctrines may be said to consist in the law or principle which they embody', and doctrines 'are developed by the operation of principles, and develop differently according to those principles'.[85] In that sense, principle is a better test of heresy and orthodoxy than doctrine: the doctrines of heresy are transient but its principles remain.[86] These act as the moving force pushing forward the development of the idea, and structuring it. Besides, the idea's principles have an influence on the *ethos* of the individual receiving them, i.e.: Church principles have a tendency to produce in individuals a Church *ethos*, and the principles of Dissent a Dissenting one.[87] The greater the openness to the idea, the deeper the forming influence it has on the person. The relationship between first principles and doctrines, therefore, involves a complex interplay of the individual's first principles and those of the doctrine, and the direction of the development of the idea in the individual depends on the dominant principle resulting from that interplay. Newman considered that a doctrine without its corresponding principles would at best remain barren, a 'sham' supported by circumstances external to it; at worst – as in the case of a revealed doctrine developed on the basis of an alien principle – it would generate heresy. A true development, on the other hand, would retain 'both the doctrine and the principle with which it started'.[88]

It may be said that principles generate doctrine but, on another level, they follow doctrines: *ethos* shapes concepts, and facts shape *ethos*. This is particularly the case with revelation. Once it has been received, the supernatural character of revelation as a reality beyond human experience defines and imposes some particular first principles distinct from those naturally acquired. Revealed doctrines generate Catholic principles, at least some of them, in 'absolute terms'. They are doctrines (facts) beyond human reach, and, consequently, their principles cannot be generated by any human agency, although a certain temper of mind may prepare the way for the reception of revealed doctrine. It is in this sense that Newman could say that pagans might have the same principles as Catholics, although, naturally, not *all* Catholic principles. Formal heretics, on the other hand, would not share principles with Catholics, even though Catholics and heretics might share particular doctrines. If some 'heretics' were to have the same principles as Catholics, they would be in ignorance rather than in heresy.[89] The right human *ethos* involves a series of principles which facilitate the acceptance of external reality (whether natural or supernatural) on its proper terms, with its own essential qualities and laws.

The link between moral temper, principles and development, is evident in Newman's letter to his brother Francis of 11 November 1840. There he affirmed that all systems that have life have a development, without thereby losing necessarily their identity. He acknowledged that development might also lead to corruption, but affirmed that continuity of temper and principles guaranteed orthodox development and served to distinguish it from a false one. He went on to claim that 'the temper, cast of principle, doctrine, conduct' of the present day Church was consistent with the temper of the early Church, and that this fact supported the argument of consistency and continuity of doctrine. Newman described them using the terms of abuse employed by her enemies: dogmatic, mystical, credulous, superstitious, bigoted, legal etc. His tenth proposition added that there was no antecedent objection to developments in doctrine, provided that these harmonized with Catholic temper and principles, that the doctrines were consistent with the ideas from which they profess to spring, and that they were professed unanimously by its members.[90]

The ethical dimension thus continued to be present in the different stages of the genesis of the *Essay*. In the 1844 preliminary draft, Newman stated that he wanted to write 'historically, not argumentatively'. He was not intending to produce a complete, step-by-step history of dogma(s); nor did he want to produce a 'theory' as such. He had a different aim in mind: he wanted to find which among the Churches had preserved incorrupt the inheritance of primitive doctrine – that is, where could the true Church be found. At first sight, neither of the two claimants to that title – Protestantism and Roman Catholicism – coincided with Primitive doctrine or theology. Developments had taken place in both (as they had in Apostolic and post-Apostolic times), and it was not always practicable, or even possible, to follow the gradual historical unfolding of a truth or to establish all the logical connections linking primitive doctrine to modern dogma. Agreement could, however, be found between Primitive and Roman theology 'in its *principles* and *ethical* character'.[91]

Newman, in later editions of the *Essay*, listed the notes of a true development in a short sentence: 'There is no corruption [of the original idea]', he would say, 'if it retains one and the same type, the same principles, the same organization; if its beginnings anticipated its subsequent phases, and its later phenomena protect and subserve its earlier; if it has a power of assimilation and revival, and a vigorous action first to last.'[92] Here, like in the table of contents of the first edition, the first two notes are listed at the head of the rest. This order is nor accidental: most of the other tests or notes are in a certain degree dependent on or connected with the first two, and these, at heart, are fundamentally ethical. The continuity of principles depends in good measure on the preservation of the right *ethos* (type); both endow the idea with life, and a living idea enjoys continuous vigour and has a power of assimilation. In a sense, it might be said that the different notes result from the 'development' – conceptual and historical – of the idea of *ethos*.

The influence of *ethos* on development is further illustrated by the fact that although true developments can be shown to result by logical sequence from given premises, in the majority of cases they are not the fruit of a logical process. A development follows as a result of the fuller 'realization' of the idea. As Newman put it: an 'idea grows in the mind by remaining there; it becomes familiar and distinct, and is viewed in its relations; it suggests other ideas, and these again others, subtle, recondite, original, according to the character, intellectual and moral, of the recipient; and thus a body of thought is gradually formed without his recognizing what is going on within him'.[93] The general process is not a wholly unconscious one; rather, the mind is not fully aware of the full range of it, and needs to go through an experience of realizing. At times, external circumstances serve as 'midwives' of this intellectual process, helping or forcing to the surface those thoughts that were coming into being in the depth of the mind. Then, they take formal expression, 'discerned by a moral perception, and adopted on sympathy'. Logic had had little or no part in this discovery (or realizing) but is called in afterwards to present the ideas in intelligible order, arranging scientifically 'what no science was employed in gaining'; showing them as conclusions from previous truths, analogies and the like. Newman and the Tractarians considered this spontaneous process 'higher and choicer than that which is logical'. Logic was common property and, once it had structured the results of the development, made them accessible to those who were strangers to the ideas, their principles, and their development. But for Newman and his friends, a purely logical and scientific knowledge of truths which have an ethical dimension was in clear danger of perverting them.[94]

The fundamental element in the development of Christian doctrine is the fact of it being a divine revelation, and Newman, from among the principles of Christian doctrine, singled out the principle of faith as the one that must rule supreme. This implied the acceptance of authority as a guide when approaching revelation. The dogmatic principle, the corollary of the principle of faith, was the first principle of Tractarian theology. It was directed both against Rationalist as well as Evangelical theology. The first prefers reason to faith, setting reason above revelation, and holding that doctrines are to be considered true in so far as they are proved and logically demonstrated.[95] In so doing it ignores faith's supernatural character transcending human reason. The second subordinates dogma to subjective emotion, making the creed of secondary importance. These hostile principles would generate different and irreconcilable systems.

At the natural level, humility and the love of truth associated with it seem to offer the only soil in which faith is able to grow and prosper. In this respect, Tractarians thought that Catholic truth has in itself the guarantee of right *ethos*, being deficient in all those 'suspicious attractions which other systems hold out to the pride of intellect, to the originality of mind, to powers of eloquence, to susceptibility of emotion, to impatience of restraint'.[96] Catholic views elevated the Church and pushed down the pride of the individual, and the resulting humility was the foundation on which the edifice of supernatural knowledge could be properly built.

It has been pointed out that Newman did not mention the word *ethos* in his 1845 edition of the *Development*. He introduced the term, however, into the later editions, when speaking of the two fundamental characters of a true development of Christian doctrine: its continuity with previous teaching, and its sharing in the *ethos* of the Primitive or Apostolic Church.[97] He would also use this term in other occasions, as when he wrote to Mozley that Christianity arose as a definite ethical system – '*ethos* we used to call it at Oxford' – which is 'the living principle also of present Catholicism'.[98] His intellectual roots, hidden from view, remained solidly planted in the Tractarian theory of religious knowledge.

Notes

1. O. Chadwick, *From Bossuet to Newman* (Cambridge: Cambridge University Press, 1987, 2nd ed.), pp. 102, 111, 119–21. Frank Turner's biography of the Anglican Newman offered a variation on this theme. Development was a theory owing more to external circumstances than to a proper intellectual process. Newman's beliefs changed in response to those of newly found friends: changes in affection, more often than modifications of intellect, drove his theological progress; he embraced development for the purpose of not losing his ascendancy over his friends, or in order to justify particular devotional practices he and they wanted to embrace. Turner, however, does not give any clear indication of when Newman adopted the theory or about who those friends and those devotions were (F. M. Turner, *John Henry Newman. The Challenge to Evangelical Theology* (Newhaven: Yale University Press, 2002), pp. 514, 622–3 etc.).
2. J. H. Newman, 'Love the Safeguard of Faith against Superstition', *US*, p. 242.
3. [W. G. Ward], 'The Divine Rule of Faith and Practice, by W. Goode', *British Critic* 32/63 (July 1842), p. 38.
4. [W. G. Ward] 'Christian Life, its Course, its Hindrances, and its Helps. Dr Arnold's Sermons', *British Critic* 30/60 (October 1841), p. 309.
5. [W. G. Ward], 'Select Treatises of St Athanasius, Archbishop of Alexandria, in his Controversy with the Arians', *British Critic* 32/64 (October 1842), p. 417.
6. [Ward], 'Christian Life', p. 327.
7. Ibid., p. 352; see also [Ward], 'Divine Rule of Faith', pp. 45–6, 47–9, 55.
8. [Ward], 'Christian Life', p. 359; see also 'Divine Rule of Faith', p. 85.
9. [Ward], 'Divine Rule of Faith', p. 90.
10. There is a considerable and growing bibliography on Möhler's views on the development of doctrine. See for example J. A. Möhler, *Unity in the Church or The Principle of Catholicism*, ed. P. C. Erb (Washington, DC: Catholic University of America, 1996), p. 11 n.
11. Chadwick , *From Bossuet to Newman*, p. 102.
12. Some of Ward's expressions resemble those of Newman letter to his brother Francis of 10 November 1840.
13. [Ward], 'Christian Life', pp. 332–3.
14. [Ward], 'Dr Whately's Sermons', *British Critic* 31/62 (April 1842), p. 273.
15. [Ward], 'Divine Rule of Faith', pp. 91–101; 'St Athanasius', p. 403.
16. [Ward], 'St Athanasius', p. 408.
17. [Ward], 'Christian Life', pp. 332–3.
18. W. G. Ward, *The Ideal of a Christian Church Considered in Comparison with Present Practice* (London: Toovey, 1844, 2nd ed.), pp. 547–9.
19. C. S. Dessain, *John Henry Newman* (London: Catholic Book Club, 1966), p. 81.
20. I. Ker, *John Henry Newman. A Biography* (Oxford: Oxford University Press, 1988), p. 105.
21. J. H. Newman, *Apologia pro Vita Sua. Being a Brief History of his Religious Opinions* (London: Longman, Green and Co., 1913, new impression), p. 289.
22. [J. H. Newman], *Via Media' (II), Tracts for the Times*, 41 (London: Rivington, 1840, 4th ed.), p. 5.
23. J. H. Newman, *The Via Media of the Anglican Church*, II (London: Longman, Green and Co, 1885), p. 40 n.
24. Newman to Mrs J. Mozley, 23 January 1843, *LD*, IX, p. 214.
25. Newman to Mrs Froude, 14 July 1844, ibid., X, p. 297; see also *Apologia*, p. 289.

26. L. Allen, *John Henry Newman and the Abbé Jager. A Controversy on Scripture and Tradition (1834–1836)* (London: Oxford University Press, 1975), p. 13.
27. J. H. Newman, *An Essay on the Development of Christian Doctrine* (London: Toovey, 1845), p. 26.
28. J. H. Newman, *Lectures on the Prophetical Office of the Church Viewed Relatively to Romanism and Popular Protestantism* (London: Rivington, 1837), pp. 85–6, 97–8.
29. I. Ker, *Newman on Vatican II* (Oxford: Oxford University Press, 2014), p. 47.
30. J. H. Newman to T. Falconer, about 26 January 1834 (*LD*, iv, p. 180).
31. A too literal interpretation of Newman's words later led some critics of his theory of development to claim that it was impossible to know what he considered to be the faith of the Church in its early days: did the first Christians believe Jesus was God and man, and that the Holy Spirit was God? See Conclusion.
32. Letter 9 June 1844, *LD*, X, p. 266; see also Newman to Mrs Froude, 14 July 1844, ibid., p. 297–8.
33. Ker, *Newman on Vatican II*, p. 48.
34. Newman, *Development*, pp. 77, 132, 153 etc.
35. R. C. Selby, *The Principle of Reserve in the Writings of John Henry Cardinal Newman* (Oxford: Oxford University Press, 1975), pp. 72–3.
36. Ibid., p. 53.
37. [J. H. Newman], *Lectures on the Scripture Proof of the Doctrines of the Church, Tracts for the Times*, 85 (London: Rivington, 1838), pp. 14, 46 etc.
38. G. Biemer, *Newman on Tradition* (London: Burns & Oates, 1967), pp. 48 ff.; see also G. Biemer, 'Newman on Tradition as a Subjective Process', in A. McClelland, ed., *By Whose Authority? Newman, Manning and the Magisterium* (Bath: Downside, 1996), pp. 155 ff.; and Allen, *Newman and Jager*, p. 14.
39. Newman, *Prophetical Office*, 253.
40. Allen, *Newman and Jager*, p. 12.
41. Newman, *Development*, p. 34.
42. J. H. Newman, *An Essay on the Development of Christian Doctrine*, ed. S. Jaki (Pinckney: Real View Books, 2003), p. xviii.
43. Newman, *Development*, p. 37; see also pp. 35 ff. Anglican and Catholic critics of Newman's *Development* found it difficult to grapple with his presentation of the idea as having a life of its own, apart from the mind (see for example W. Irons, *The Theory of Development Examined with Reference Specially to Mr Newman's Essay and the Rule of St Vincent of Lerins* (London: Rivington, 1846), pp. 35 ff. James Mozley would criticize Newman's concept of the 'idea' from a different point of view: an idea cannot develop into an institution (J. Mozley, 'An Essay on the Development on Christian Doctrine', *Christian Remembrancer*, LVI (January 1847), pp. 264–5). He quoted a Catholic commentator, Orestes Brownson: 'If Christianity had come into the world as an idea, it would have left the world as it found it' (O. Brownson, 'Newman's Development of Christian Doctrine', *Brownson's Quarterly Review*, III/III (July 1846), p. 356). To understand the institutional implications of the 'idea', it is necessary to consider the roots of Newman's ecclesiology of communion (see for example J. Pereiro, 'Newman and Manning: the Ecclesiological Issues', *International Journal for the Study of the Christian Church*, 1.1 (2001), pp. 86–102).
44. J. H. Newman, 'The Theory of Developments in Religious Doctrine' (2 February 1843), *US*, p. 316.
45. J. H. Newman, 'The Theory of Developments in Religious Doctrine', in *Fifteen Sermons Preached before the University of Oxford* (London: Longman, Green and Co., 1872, 3rd ed.), p. 317.
46. A. Nichols, *From Newman to Congar. The Idea of Doctrinal Development from the Victorians to the Second Vatican Council* (Edinburgh: T&T Clark, 1990), p. 49.

47. See Newman to Keble, 23 January 1844, *LD*, X, pp. 101–2.
48. J. H. Newman to F. Newman, 10 November 1840, ibid., VII, p. 441.
49. P. B. Nockles, 'Continuity and Change in Anglican High Churchmanship in Britain, 1792–1850' (Oxford, D.Phil. thesis, 1982), I, p. 162.
50. J. H. Newman to F. Newman, 10 November 1840, *LD*, VII, pp. 436–42.
51. V. Blehl, *Pilgrim Journey. John Henry Newman 1801–1845* (London: Burns & Oates, 2001), p. 170.
52. Newman, *Development*, p. 8.
53. Newman, *Prophetical Office*, pp. 68–9.
54. Newman, *Development*, p. 9.
55. Ibid., pp. 12 and 25; see also Newman to Mrs Froude, 19 May 1844, *LD*, X, p. 243.
56. Newman, *Development*, pp. 26–7.
57. J. H. Newman, *An Essay on the Development of Christian Doctrine* (London: Pickering, 1878, new ed.), p. 29.
58. [N. Wiseman], 'Tracts for the Times: Anglican Claim of Apostolical Succession', *Dublin Review*, VII/XIII (August 1839), pp. 139–80.
59. 'securus iudicat orbis terrarum bonos non esse, qui se diuidunt ab orbe terrarum in quacumque parte terrarum' (Aurelius Augustinus, *Contra. Ep. Parmeniani*, lib iii, cap. 4, 24, in *Corpus Scriptorum Ecclesiasticorum*, 51 (Vindibonae-Lipsiae, 1908), p. 131, lins 4–6).
60. [Wiseman], *Anglican Claim*, p. 155.
61. Newman, *Apologia*, p. 117.
62. Newman, ibid., pp.120 ff.
63. [J. H. Newman], 'Catholicity of the Anglican Church', *British Critic* 27/53 (January 1840), p. 79.
64. Newman to Mrs Froude, 9 April 1844, *LD*, X, p. 201.
65. Newman to J. W. Bowden, 21 February 1840, ibid., VII, p. 241.
66. Newman, 'Theory of Developments', p. 324; these words resemble the ones he had used in his 'Catholicity of the Anglican Church' (pp. 12–13), when speaking of the Roman theory of development.
67. Newman to F. Newman, 10 November 1840, *LD*, VII, p. 440. He did not mention to which Church he was referring, whether the Anglican Church, the Church Catholic (made up of three branches), or the Roman Catholic Church.
68. J. H. Newman, *A Letter to the Right Reverend Father in God, Richard, Lord Bishop of Oxford, on Occasion of No. 90 in the Series Called The Tracts for the Times* (Oxford: Parker; London: Rivington, 1841), pp. 23 ff.
69. Newman to Miss Holmes, 6 September 1841, *LD*, VIII, p. 262.
70. Newman, 'Letter to Jelf' (13 March 1841), *Via Media of the Anglican Church*, II, p. 377.
71. At times, Newman gives the impression of considering non-dogmatically-defined doctrines as implicit truths, even though they may be acknowledged by the faithful, e.g.: the infallibility of the Church or the inspiration of Scripture ('Notebook on Development' (1844), p. 31, and 'Diary', 22 February 1844, BOA).
72. Newman, *Diary*, 18 March and 7 April 1843, BOA.
73. Newman, 'Theory of Developments', p. 321.
74. Newman, *Development*, p. 448.
75. Newman to Keble, 4 May 1843, *LD*, IX, p. 328.
76. Newman, 'Theory of Developments', p. 317.
77. Ibid., p. 339.
78. Newman would later use the example of a disciple of Aristotle to illustrate the relationship/distinction between implicit and explicit knowledge. The learned Aristotelian does not have all the doctrine of Aristotle present in his mind, buried in memory. He could nonetheless answer any whatever philosophical questions

in the way that Aristotle would have answered them, even if they were questions which could not occur in Aristotle's age. He does so by two means: a) by the instinct that a thoroughly Aristotelian intellect possesses, i.e.: the habit formed in his mind by long years of study; b) by a process of ratiocination. Thus the Apostles had the fullness of revealed knowledge, a fullness which they could as little realize themselves, as the human mind as such, can have all its thought present before it at once. In the Apostle's mind great part of his knowledge was, from the nature of the case, latent or implicit. As a result, the Church nowadays does in fact answer questions which the Apostles did not answer, and in one sense did not know, though they would have known them –i.e. made them present to their consciousness – had the questions been asked (manuscript Paper on Development, 15 February 1868, BOA, pp. 5–10).

79. C. Wordsworth, *Church Principles and Church Measures. A Letter to Lord John Manners* (London: Rivington, 1845), p. 26; J. Fletcher, *Lectures on the Principles and Institutions of the Roman Church* (London: Conder, 1817), pp. xxi, xxiii.
80. Newman, *Prophetical Office*, pp. 50 ff.
81. See for example references to 'first principles' in *Tract 90*, p. 8; and in his *Letter to the Bishop of Oxford*, pp. 6, 12, 17, etc.
82. See in this respect N. Lash, *Newman on Development. The Search for an Explanation in History* (London: Sheed and Ward, 1979), pp. 107–8, and J. H. Waldgrave, *Newman the Theologian. The Nature of Belief and Doctrine as Exemplified in his Life and Works* (London: Geoffrey Chapman, 1960), pp. 114 ff.
83. Newman, *Development*, p. 70.
84. Newman, *Grammar of Assent*, pp. 245 ff.
85. Newman, *Development*, pp. 67 and 71.
86. Ibid., p. 72.
87. J. H. Newman, 'Prospects of the Anglican Church', in *Essays Critical and Historical*, I (London: Longman, Green and Co., 1897, new ed.), p. 278; see also J. H. Newman to F. Newman, 10 November 1840, *LD*, VII, p. 438.
88. Newman, *Development*, p. 72.
89. Ibid., p. 72.
90. J. H. Newman to F. Newman, 10 November 1840, *LD*, VII, pp. 436–43.
91. J. H. Newman, 'Preliminary Draft of the Development of Christian Doctrine', Manuscript in BOA, pp. 1–2.
92. Newman, *Development* (1878), p. 171. Oakley claimed as a reason for his conversion that the Roman Church 'plainly corresponds with that Type of the Catholic Church, which is deeply and habitually impressed upon my whole moral and spiritual nature' (F. Oakeley, *A Letter on Submitting to the Catholic Church. Addressed to a Friend* (London: Toovey, 1845), p. 18).
93. Newman, *Development*, p. 81.
94. Ibid., pp. 81 and 83.
95. Ibid., p. 328.
96. Newman, 'Prospects', p. 282.
97. Newman, *Development* (1878), p. 100 .
98. Newman to Mozley, letter, *Contemporary Review* (September 1899), quoted in Walgrave, *Newman*, p. 266.

CONCLUSION

NEWMAN, in his *University Sermons*, had mentioned how he looked forward to a systematic exposition of the ideas contained in Ward's articles in the *British Critic*. When the *Ideal of a Christian Church* came out, he was disappointed by the book; 'It won't do', he told John Dobree Dalgairns.[1] Its polemical character, Ward's attacks on the Reformation, and his unbounded praise for the Church of Rome as a model for the renewal of the Anglican Church, obscured the Tractarian theory of knowledge and made the book inadequate to convey it. Newman's *Essay*, on the other hand, being focused on the question of development, left the Tractarian general doctrine of religious knowledge dispersed in sermons and articles. The closest he got to a systematic exposition of it is to be found in his *University Sermons*, and so it was to remain until he would give it new form and scope in the *Grammar of Assent*.

That *ethos* was important for the Tractarians has been universally recognized. Familiarity with the term, however, has hardly ever been accompanied by clear analysis of its content. Contemporaries ignored the radical nature of the new principle, and modern historians have generally overlooked it. This neglect has distorted the perception of important aspects of the Oxford Movement and of Newman's intellectual history. J. T. Coleridge's description of *ethos* became generally accepted, leading Owen Chadwick, among others, to consider the distinction between the old-fashioned High Churchmen and the Tractarians to have been primarily one of feeling and atmosphere. Tractarianism, in Chadwick's estimation, was fundamentally an ethical phenomenon: the Oxford men were more interested in holiness than in doctrine; it was a movement of the heart rather than of the head.[2] The Tractarians would have agreed with him, up to a point. In their opinion, divine revelation had been granted man first and foremost for the sake of his eternal salvation, rather than to offer him raw materials for the development of the theological sciences. It would be a serious error, however, to conclude from this that the Tractarians lacked deep concern for doctrinal matters. As far as they were concerned, only truth is capable of shaping man into the likeness of Christ, which is the object of man's sanctification. Any kind of 'divorce' between doctrine and ethics was alien to the minds of Keble, Froude, Newman and their friends. They thought that orthodoxy could not be separated from orthopraxis; both are intimately and inseparably united, and cannot survive or prosper in isolation from each other. Holiness is the aim of God's revelation; it is to be achieved in truth; and truth opens up its treasures to those who search after holiness.

As Christopher Dawson remarked, the Oxford Movement stood, among other things, for scientific theology against the emotional religiosity of popular Protestantism.[3] Tractarianism was an intellectual movement that proposed new answers to a considerable number of theological questions, being in many areas well in advance of contemporary Anglican thinking. As they saw it, the Church of England had lost the Catholic *ethos*; she needed to regain it, if she were to recover from her parlous condition. Without a Catholic *ethos*, doctrine, principles and life would always be in danger of decay, unable to lodge in fertile ground, find sustenance and develop. As Newman came to see it, *ethos* also contained a progressive element, and pointed to doctrinal development. When confronted by the challenge of Augustine's *securus*, Newman had discovered in the concept of *ethos* a way forward to escape from the intellectual cul-de-sac in which he found himself. The identity and continuity of the Primitive *ethos* was more important as a hallmark of the true Church than exact numerical doctrinal identity; it was a sign of the Catholic Church's identity and also the guarantee of proper doctrinal development.

Initially, after the publication of Newman's *University Sermons*, there had been a certain pregnant pause, while people pondered the implications of the sermon on development. Palmer, in 1843, would not express outright disagreement with Newman's theory of development, 'rightly understood'; while condemning the dangerous and reckless call for 'changes' and 'development' of the *British Critic*. He considered that Newman's sermon of 1843 did not go the whole length of the theory necessary to justify the Roman system, but he would however criticize 'the eminent writer' for inaccuracy and lack of clarity in a number of substantial points.[4] The panorama was to change with the publication of the *Essay* and the news of Newman's conversion. Here was a book that had led the author into the Roman Catholic Church. Henry Wilberforce, afraid of the influence that Newman had exerted on him over the years, refused at first to read it. William Palmer of Worcester was one of the first to come out against it. Although Palmer's High Churchmanship had some points of contact with that of Newman and his friends, he had never been fully privy to Tractarian ideas about the connexion between right *ethos* and right doctrine. As a result, he was led to the conclusion that, according to Newman, conscience shaped by the exercise of moral rectitude is the '*sole* arbiter of religious truth, and that all *external evidence* is either worthless or absolutely subordinate to this inward voice'.[5] Palmer thought that this, ironically, was equivalent to accepting the *right of private judgement*, against which Tractarians had constantly declaimed.[6] He went on to connect Newman's idea of development with Schleiermacher's theories, where mysticism becomes the sole test of religious truth, and revelation a continuous and erratic process. As was to be expected, Palmer dismissed the doctrine of the infallibility of the Church, and, therefore, Newman's definitive external hall-mark guaranteeing the orthodoxy of doctrinal developments.

James Mozley, who had started to distance himself from Newman's influence towards the end of 1843, published in 1847 a lengthy critical review of the *Essay* in the *Christian Remembrancer*. He considered that Newman had not taken sufficiently into consideration the possibility of a corrupt development, which, while preserving the original type, was the result of an exaggeration of Christian principles and *ethos*. He recognized that the doctrine of infallibility was the keystone of Newman's theory, and that this would stand or fall depending on whether he proved it or not. Newman, according to Mozley, had not done so satisfactorily.[7] He also rejected the argument that Newman had used to reconcile development and the *quod semper*: implicit knowledge. Mozley would say in response: implicit knowledge is not knowledge.[8] He could only admit development as explanation of what was already held. In this respect, a main focus of his critique was centred on whether the definition of the council of Nicaea about the divinity of Christ was a development or an explanation. If the first, it would be difficult, if not impossible, to maintain that the divinity of Christ had been part of the Church's faith from the beginning. In Newman's theory, Mozley added, it was difficult to determine what the faith of the Church was in apostolic times.[9] He had a point. Newman, however, did not intend in his *Essay* to define what early Christian belief had been. His was a theory of development, not a history of dogmas, although he illustrated his ideas with some historical examples.

The Tractarian theory of knowledge is a vital element for a proper and comprehensive understanding of Newman's *Essay* and also of the other approaches to development within the Oxford Movement. It underlies some of the central concepts used by Newman – particularly those like type, temper or principles – and helps to understand the ethical engine propelling and guiding the development, whether orthodox or heretical. Many Tractarian concepts found in it their proper setting and unveiled their role within the theory of development; *ethos*, realizing and reserve among them. They pointed towards development, but not all those involved in the Oxford Movement would go so far as to accept development of doctrine when clearly presented to them.

Owen Chadwick, following R. W. Church and others, thought that Newman's final step (doctrinal development and infallibility) marked a clear discontinuity with his previous positions as a Tractarian. The opposite seems to be the case, though Newman is partly at fault in this respect. In the *Apologia* he tried to provide a guide to the history of his religious opinions but, although he wrote a useful biographical document of great literary merit, it would be misleading to see it as a full record of his progress from early Evangelical conversion to joining the Catholic Church. The *Apologia* veils as much as it reveals. Some of the steps are missing; events and ideas are sometimes mentioned without giving a clear indication of their full import or of the effect they had on him, even though they are said to have had momentous consequences;

personal influences, while given considerable space in Newman's early recollections, fade from view in the later stages of his development. The results of the present study tend to reinforce the impression that Newman owed more to the intellectual bases of the Oxford Movement and to the interaction with his friends – Keble, Wood and in particular Froude – than the *Apologia* gives the reader to understand. Some studies tend to ignore the richness of the intellectual milieu in which the Movement was born and developed, its intellectual dynamism, as well as Newman's roots and originality.

James Stephen thought that the theology of Newman differed from that of Keble 'as a substance in a solidified form differs from itself when in a gaseous form'.[10] There is some truth in this judgement. Keble's ideas never crystallized into a clear system of thought, and his influence over contemporary intellectual life and events would have been almost negligible, had he not inspired Froude and Newman. Principles took shape under the hammer of Froude's logical powers and intellectual intuition; ideas acquired a clarity and consistency they had not previously had; connexions were established and conclusions drawn. Froude's life was too short and his intellect too restless. Newman would offer some mature fruits of the Movement in his *University Sermons*, the *Essay on the Development of Christian Doctrine*, and in the *Grammar of Assent*. As Richard Holt Hutton pointed out, Newman showed as nobody had previously the influence exerted by unconscious assumptions – intellectual, moral and spiritual – over man's thought and action:[11] he had unmasked the pretence of rationalism, and revealed under it that core of unconscious prejudices – the result of moral habit and inclination – that guide thought or influence judgement.

The theory of development of doctrine had its roots firmly set in Tractarian soil. Wood, after encountering Manning's and Newman's opposition to his ideas, decided to keep the theory to himself. He seems to have been guided in this decision by the principle of reserve. Wood did not want to press his ideas on his friends at a time when they were not ready for them. Minds, even when moving in the same direction, develop at a different pace according to their circumstances and intellectual history. If his 'presumptio' was right, and it was the natural development of their principles, others would in time reach similar conclusions. Events seem to have justified his decision. Ward's articles were an indication that development was in the air within the Oxford Movement. It is not easy to determine whether and to what an extent other minds influenced Newman's theory of doctrinal development. He included among the notes of a true development a power of assimilation. This was a power that Newman himself possessed in considerable measure. Ideas put forward by others or current in the intellectual atmosphere of the environment in which he moved were absorbed, integrated with others, transformed, and enriched by his fertile mind, giving mature fruit in intellectual contributions of the first order to the history of thought.

The theological studies and historiography of the Oxford Movement seem to navigate uneasily between a near denial of its originality and long-term influence, on the one hand, and the presentation of Tractarianism as the single-handed work of John Henry Newman, on the other. Some see it as a High Church epiphenomenon gone rogue. Others as the work of an intellectual giant: ideas growing from Newman's mind as Athena grew fully formed from Zeus's head. Both approaches have tended to distort the perception of the genesis and nature of the Oxford Movement, and also of Newman's own intellectual development. The present study tries to contribute a more balanced view of the intellectual character of the period and to help identify the personal contributions of those who took part in the Oxford Movement. Further studies are needed in order to bring into light some of those, who like Wood, played an important part in the Movement – both in the realm of ideas and action – but have remained for far too long in the shadow of its main protagonists.

Notes

1. W. Ward, *William George Ward and the Oxford Movement* (London: Macmillan and Co., 1889), p. 295.
2. O. Chadwick, *The Spirit of the Oxford Movement* (Cambridge, Cambridge University Press, 1990, 2nd ed.), pp. 1–2.
3. C. Dawson, *The Spirit of the Oxford Movement* (London: Sheed & Ward, 1833), p. xi.
4. W. Palmer, A *Narrative of Events Connected with the Publication of the Tracts for the Times* (London: Rivington, 1843): pp. ix and 57–64.
5. W. Palmer *The Doctrine of Development and Conscience Considered in Relation to the Evidences of Christianity and of the Catholic System* (London: Rivington, 1846), p. 72.
6. Ibid., pp. 154–5.
7. J. Mozley, 'An Essay on the Development on Christian Doctrine', *Christian Remembrancer*, LVI (January 1847), pp. 171 ff.
8. Ibid., p. 251.
9. Ibid., pp. 211 ff.
10. J. Stephen, *Essays in Ecclesiastical Biography*, II (London: Longman, Brown, Green and Longman, 1850, 2nd ed.), p. 173.
11. R. H. Hutton, *Essays on Some Modern Guides of English Thought in Matters of Faith* (London: Macmillan, 1887), p. 92.

APPENDICES

Appendix I contains four letters: three to Manning and one to Newman, and Wood's paper on the development of Christian doctrine sent as an attachment to Letter I. Appendix II is the transcription of the paper Wood wrote for Tholuck on the revival of Primitive Doctrine.

The archival foliation numbers of the manuscripts have been preserved in the letters and the paper in Appendix I. In Appendix II the numbering of the folios is that used by Wood. The paper is made up of twenty-eight folios, and the last three folios (containing his notes to the main text) are not numbered in the manuscript; they are here numbered in italics for easier reference. The paper is written only on one side of the folios.

Wood's spelling, punctuation marks, and use of capitals has been preserved. Square brackets denote editorial additions, whether punctuation marks or expansion of Wood's abbreviations. The most frequent abbreviations have been silently expanded in order to facilitate the reading of the text: thus 'would' (wod.), 'should' (shod.), 'though' (tho'), 'could' (cod.), 'and' (&), 'etc' (&c). Wood's erasures and additions are noted in the footnotes.

The bibliographical references are given in full in the appendices; in some cases, the edition of books quoted in the appendices differs from that of the same book referred to in the preceding chapters.

APPENDIX I

LETTER I

Bodleian Library. Oxford, 'Correspondence and papers of Cardinal Henry Edward Manning and members of his family, 1751–1901'.
MS. Eng. lett. c.654, letter 212, fos 438–41.

[*fo.* 438r] Temple. Thursday night. [Novembe]r. 19 [1835]

My Dear Manning,

Being returned to town, and removed from the constant round of society, and present tangible objects, which extrude more distant ones from the thoughts, the desire of learning from you, and thanking you for your last affectionate letter more frequently recurs. Who has not experienced the feelings you describe, when forced to enter upon the realities of the world and their consequent responsibilities and anxieties? Wordsworth[']s beautiful lines always instruct and console my heart under these thoughts

> So changes mortal life with fleeting years,
> A mournful change, should Reason fail to bring
> The timely insight that can temper fears,
> And from vicissitude remove the sting;
> While Faith aspires to seats in that domain
> Where joys are perfect, neither wax nor wane[1]

[*fo.* 438v] I have spent a holiday strenua inertia,[2] busily engaged in all the out of doors pursuits and social duties of a rural neighbourhood, and have returned in vigorous health. Rob[er]t. Wilberforce spent a few days with me, and though suffering from a bad cold, seemed in very comfortable spirits. I have lately been distressed by an old friend of mine – L[or]d. Milton[3] – having been cut off by a fortnight of typhus fever, leaving his poor wife near confinement and his family in very deep affliction. I never was intimate with him, but it so happens that I was staying some days last month at Wentworth, and [a] saw him a good deal in other ways, and our acquaintance was fast ripening into regard. He was of a guileless affectionate temper, and had, I think, enjoyed this world's gifts, which were all at his feet, without abusing them.[b] To have his horses to ride, and his brothers and sisters to converse with, seemed to him an [*fo.* 439r] ever springing source of gratification. Nor were his intellectual powers inadequate to the station he would have filled. When there are such strong ties to life, and strong reasons why one should live, it is hard to believe that the "last Enemy" can do his work so swiftly.

I am looking forward to the fulfilment of your promise respecting Apostolical Tradition with much interest I assure you – pray indicate to me the sources which you have discovered, and tell me where the Tractate of Vincentius[4] is to be found. Meanwhile I offer you a few dogmas of my own on the same subject. They profess to state the offices fulfilled by the Apostolical Tradition and the Scriptures, relatively to each other, in the Church. I am aware that the view generally taken of Apost[olic]: Trad[ition]: specifically regards its [*words missing*] the interpretation of Scripture [*lines missing*] once see [*fo.* 439v] that it supersedes the necessity of this consideration. But at any rate it is (to my mind) a trivial one, for, 1st. how few really are the points on which candid minds differ in Scripture interpretation, and 2dly. they are for the most part of a kind not within the scope of Apostol[ic]: Trad[ition]: The numbered propositions contain the outlines of my idea – the notes are merely illustrative, and put in this way not to interrupt the series of the other. I hope you will not think me very Popish.

Your friends[c] Pearson[5] and Twisleton[6] are quite well – Acland is at All Souls, Wilson[7] is going to be Keble's curate, what a privilege. I rather look for Newman in town, as I am told a 3d. volume is forth-coming. Pray read Pusey on Baptism in the Oxford Tracts.[8] I shall be delighted to hear good [*lines missing*]

a had] crossed out.
b It seem] crossed out.
c Illegible word crossed out.

[*fo.* 440ʳ] Tradition and Scripture

1. Under the direction of the Spirit, and pursuant to Christ's commands, the Apostles committed to the charge of the Church[a] a formal system of doctrines[,] ordinances[,] discipline etc. And this orally, their writings imply or presuppose, but do not contain, it.+

Note. e.g. There is no systematic or complete exposition in Scripture of the doctrine of the Trinity or of the Sacraments – i.e. – the knowledge of the object of worship and of the means of grace is traditional.

And if the ultra Protestant insists on taking the Scriptures for his sole rule of faith from a mistrust of the primitive Church; I ask, to whom, from the nature of the case, was necessarily committed the office of settling that Canon or rule of faith? Well may the Church say (to him)

> 'Quam temere in nosmet legem sancimus iniquam'[9]
> +Comp: 2 Thess 2, 14.[10] 2 Tim: 1, 13.[11]

[*fo.* 440ᵛ] 2. It is therefore only incidentally that the obligation to receive doctrines arises from their being found in Scripture; primarily, it results from their being of ascertained + Apostolical Tradition.

+. The canon of Vincentius,[12] or of Augustine, (lib. 4 contra Donatistas)[13] "Quod universa tenet Ecclesia, nec in conciliis nec alibi institutum esse referitur, sed semper retentum est, non nisi auctoritate Apostolica traditum esse certissime creditur", is here to be applied.

3. In common with other societies the Church has the inherent power of expanding or modifying her organisation, of bringing her ideas of the Truth into more distinct consciousness, or of developing the Truth itself more fully.

4. It follows then that doctrines may be true, though not traceable* to the Apostles:

*i.e. we may not have need to trace them etc[14]

[*fo.* 441ʳ] [b] Note. e.g. Admitting that "Predestination["] did not assume a definite shape till St Augustine's time – this is not con-

[a] to the charge of the Church] inserted.

[b] And further, that the Church retain the] crossed out.

clusive against it. (Newman vol 2 ad loc:)[15] And the prima facie presumption ag[ain]st. it, from its late rise, may be rebutted by the consideration of the natural course of the mind, first, to regard the external Objects of faith, next, to turn the eye inwards upon their operations in the soul, and its condition as affected by them.

NB. I only bring this forward, illustratively, not asserting either that the Church has adopted the doctrine (§ 5) or that it is capable of Scripture proof (§5 and 6).

5. And further, that the Church retains the right of authoritatively exhibiting them, subject only to the condition – arising from the withdrawal of her inspired guides and from her fallibility – of their being true.

6. But the only mode of proving this is by showing their accordance with Scripture. [*fo.* 441^{v}][a] So that while the Church has ever been our sole expositrix, we have now two co-ordinate tests of doctrine – Apostolical Tradition and Scripture.

Note to §5 and 6: It is not[b] intended to [c] deny that Scriptural proof may be found for all doctrines, or that this was not designed: Nor again, that practically, and regard being had to past events, Scripture may not be our chief standard. But it is submitted that the theory that is duly stated in §6, which nearly agrees with that[d] of the Roman Catholic[e] Church,[f] however grievously in practice they make "Scripture of none effect by their tradition." But have not some[g] Protestants fallen into the opposite error by needlessly throwing off[h] tradition, and refusing obedience to all ordinances not expressly recognised in Scripture? And do they not boast of this (so-called) liberty? Rather than exult, we should feel pained at being obliged, – a caution imposed by the sad experience of past errors – to test what the Church may propound to us by Scripture, instead of yielding an implicit confidence to our holy Mother.

a In the manuscript the number 6 is inserted again at the beginning of fo. 441v.
b not] inserted.
c assert] crossed out.
d that] inserted.
e theory] crossed out.
f Church] inserted.
g some] inserted.
h primitive] crossed out.

LETTER II

Bodleian Library. Oxford, 'Correspondence and papers of Cardinal Henry Edward Manning and members of his family, 1751–1901'.
MS. Eng. lett. c. 654, letter 213, fos 442–4.

[*fo.* 442^{r}] Temple. Friday Night. Dec[embe]r 18/[18]35

My dear Manning

Your paper on Tradition, and your general concurrence in my view gave me very sincere delight; but I will not spend time in compliments, but at once address myself to the subject.

Our sole difference appears to me to consist in our notions of the development of truth in the Church, as stated in my 3d. proposition, and in your 4th. § – "Therefore the Ch[urch]: has no warrant to promulgate new truths." And I am not at all sure that we differ in fact, for I believe my idea coincides with that of Vincentius in his 28th, 29th and 30th[16] sections. But I will state it more fully that you may judge for yourself (insert +. at the end of 2d sheet) What[a] would be the state of the Church on the removal of her Inspired Guides? To the divinely instructed minds of the Apostles, glancing to and fro' over the whole range of Christian[b] doctrine, the whole body and perfection of truth was indeed ever present. But was this the case with the early Church also? Would [*fo.* 442^{v}] She not dwell on those parts of the scheme to which the mind is naturally first directed, however completely she might be informed in all truth? And as a consequence of this, such parts would be more fully developed in her teaching, and form the basis of the ecclesiastical Traditive structure. The question then occurs: – Is the structure to be arrested at this stage? are we to be deprived of the benefit of a great truth clearly deducible from Scripture, merely because the constitution of the human mind was not intirely changed in the case of the early Church, and made capable of at once conceiving and expressing a stupendous system? Surely it is more analogous to God[']s general dealings

a then] crossed out.
b Xtan in the text.

with us to suppose that the Church should gradually and carefully, taking the divine word for her guide, and proceeding in the course which is natural to the mind and which successive heresies required, (that course being identical, for the intellect, heretical or catholic[,] is governed by the same laws) evolve[,] comment on and exhibit the whole counsel of God.

[*fo.* 443[r]] But it will be said this is a mere "presumptio" as to what the case was; it is so, and therefore casts not a shadow of disparagement on the primitive Church, because it shows the moral necessity of the progress I contend for. I now proceed to the practical proof of this. I might bring several instances, but I will confine myself to one which you at least will not dispute. The great doctrine of Justification by faith lay hid (latitaverit Vinc[entius]: §29)[17] in the bosom of the Church[18] for a considerable time, and perhaps was not evolved in her teaching before Luther.

I think I might rest my case with you here, and that you will let my 4th proposition stand: (only it must be[a] modified thus "doctrines may be true, though not apparent in the teaching of the primitive Church." Of course if doctrines are provable from Scripture they must be "traceable to the Apostles") But I will say a word or two to reconcile my 5th prop[osition]: with the doctrine of the Anglican Church with which it may seem at variance.

The Canons of 1571 contain this directive – [*fo.* 443[v]] "Preachers shall be careful not to preach aught to be religiously held and believed by the people, except what is agreable to the teaching of the O[ld]. and N[ew]. Testament, and collected, as such, from that very teaching by the Catholic Fathers and ancient Bishops."[19]

By the 1st. of Elizabeth c 155 it is determined that such matter and cause only shall be adjudged to be heresy, as heretofore has been adjudged to be so "by authority of the Canonical Scr[iptures]: or by some of the 1st. 4 Councils, or by any other general council wherein the same was declared heresy by the express and plain words of the S[acre]d. Canonical Scr[criptures]:"[20] Now the Canon at least would appear adverse to my view. But in comparing it with the 6th Article[21] it is evident that they both have reference to the "condition of communion"[,] "the things

a Illegible word crossed out.

necessary to salvation", which a Church has a right to impose on her members, and in default of them to excommunicate[,] anathematize and the like. In this painful duty of fixing the minimum of faith our Reformers did not enter into abstract reasoning as to what the terms of communion ought to be, but took those of the Primitive Church as an historical fact.

[*fo.* 444[r]] Wisely they did do so, and least of all would one like to meddle on such a point. My intention merely is to consider the "authentic Records from whence the whole body of divine Truth is derived."[22] And this when ascertained may well be called the "rule of faith", in as much as it is the duty of every Christian[a] man to receive truths so warranted. But I raise no question as to whether all or what part of these truths are "necessary to salvation" etc.

But again, allowing for a moment this distinction not to be[b] well founded, there is perhaps sufficient resiliency to be discovered in these documents from the Popish errors, to warrant me not following them out too rigorously.[c] This is very observable in the Act, which would save harmless all subsequent heresies, however flagrant, thus[d] disarming the Church and leaving her powerless. I think I have now at least unfolded [e] my meaning, and will proceed to an incidental point in your paper.

Your distinction between the μαρτυριον[23] and μυστηριον[24] [*fo.* 444[v]] is a very valuable one, and I quite admit that on the whole the Gospels record the facts, and the Epistles build up the doctrinal structure thereupon. Still as a matter (a)[f] of fact, consider[g] how many of the doctrines of our faith are really promulgated by Christ,[h] though His Apostles declare them more fully. e.g. The Trinity "in the name of the Father, the Son, and ye Holy Ghost." His Divinity – "the only begotten Son etc." His Eternity – "having glory with the Father before the world was." His Atonement – ["]

a Xtan in the manuscript.
b to be] inserted.
c Originally spelt rigourously.
d thus] inserted.
e your] crossed out.
f (a)] inserted.
g what] crossed out.
h Xt. in the manuscript.

giving his flesh for ye life of ye world", "giving His life a ransom for many." The doctrine of the Sacraments as distinguished from their institution, viz of the Eucharist John 6, of Holy Baptism John 3. Again, (b)[a] antecedently; Christ[b] was the Prophet of His Church, and as such would himself declare his doctrines, and the sententious depth of his discourses agrees hereto, in that they would seem to require the Epistles etc. as commentaries, and to bring out and fix their meaning.

[*fo.* 445^r] And now I will relieve you from my diatribe. Hawkins on Tradition[25] I have had for some years. It is a Tract of 100 pages, well written, and though not much to the matter in hand I think you would like to posses it. By Tradition he means that "oral teaching which introduces to us Christian[c] doctrine,"[26] and his object is to show its use in arranging[,] systematizing etc Scripture. He touches incidentally on interpretative Tradition, to which he only gives the weight of a "faint presumption",[27] and Scr[ipture]: is to prove all. You may extort it from Henry William Wilberforce,[d] who has or had 2 copies, for I recollect his offering one to me. If you are writing to Sam,[28] please say I shall be very glad to have my 10s applied as he prefers, I don't want to trouble him with a substantive letter on the subject.

This one to you has run out to such a [*fo.* 445^v] length that I must defer one or two other subjects I wish to write on, and confine myself to one thing more on the old one! What shape did I see Vincentius in at Lavington? I have got it in a little old duodecimo the text of which is very corrupt.[29]

How are you and yours in health? I long to see you again – I am thankful to say I am quite well, and shall be pretty stationary here till Easter. I am going down to Farleigh, and will remember your suggestion de vita etc.

Ever dear Manning
Very affectionately yours
S. F. WOOD

a (b)] inserted.
b Xt. in the manuscript.
c Xtan in the manuscript.
d H.W.W. in the manuscript.

+. It is not contended for a moment that the Rule of faith, the summa Fidei was not concluded by the Apostles, or that any addition was to be made to Scripture. But was their Faith fully exhibited in the teaching of the infant Church? This depends upon the question What would be etc

LETTER III

The Borthwick Institute of Historical Research. York. Halifax Papers. Ref. A2/42: letter 1, fos 1–2

[*fo.1r*] Temple. Jan[uar]y. 1st 1836

My Dear Newman,

As time passes on without your appearance in town I begin to think you may be wanting your paper on Tradition for some purpose, and therefore return it with very many thanks. I need hardly add that I have received much light and instruction from it, and I am rejoiced to find nothing in it which seems contrariant to my own notion. For the fact that we use the term 'Rule of Faith' in different senses is sufficient to reconcile an apparent discrepancy. You intend by it the measure of 'things necessary to salvation' of 'the terms of communion', while I employed it so as to comprehend what you call 'doctrines additional to those which are emphatically called the Faith', p.7[30]: – 'In short as 'that which so warrants any doctrine to a Catholic Churchman as to make it his duty to receive it'.[31]

[*fo. 1v*] As I am writing, I will just add a word or two on this subject, but without at all looking for an answer or wishing to draw you into any discussion. I do not see how my notion can disparage the early Church, even as an historical fact. I propound it merely as a 'presumptio' of what were Divinely intended to be the means of dispensing truth in the Church, this 'presumptio' being founded on the nature of the case, and the general analogy of God's dealings with us, and wholly irrespective of what the early Church was in fact. I assume indeed that it was intended there should be a 'profectus religionis'[32] in the Church, but I believe my view falls under what Vincentius says in his 28th, 29th, 30th and 32d chapters.[33] But that you may judge whether I am justified in thinking so, I will make a remark which may perhaps explain my meaning.

[*fo.* 2r] To satisfy the requirements of the intellect and to discover heresy, the early Church collected and arranged the Scripture notices of the Trinity, and built thereupon the doctrines of the Hypostatic Union e[t]c, exposing them in her symbols. People complain even of this. Now I consider that it ought to have been but the foundation (and a most precious one) of the doctrinal Ecclesiastical Structure, and that if the Church in after times had fulfilled her office as well as the early Church did, She would have proceeded to arrange and expand (excurare[34] et dilatare,[35] Vinc[entius]:) other doctrines, in the same manner. It surely will not be said that Her authority was exhausted by its first exercise. The course of events, corruptions, and schisms, might interrupt its subsequent application, and this is our grievous loss, but no invalidation of the authority itself, or disproof that a 'profectus' was designed. Now the view assumes indeed that the full body and perfection of Divine truth could not be ecclesiastically exhibited at once, in [*fo.* 2v] a moment, without a violation of the ordinary course of the Divine dealings with us and also, of the constitution of the human mind, but it ascribes to the early Church the praise of having alone borne Her share of that 'profectus' which has been more or less neglected ever since. In other words, it does not depreciate what she did, but attempts to show that it was humanly impossible she could do more.

I have just returned from Farleigh, where I found Wilberforce[36] in fair spirit, with 2 very fine children, who are a great blessing and consolation to him, poor fellow. Now, I am stationary till Easter, and trust I shall see you ere then – meanwhile

Believe me dear Newman
affectionately yours
S. F. WOOD

LETTER IV

Bodleian Library. Oxford, 'Correspondence and papers of Cardinal Henry Edward Manning and members of his family, 1751–1901'.
MS. Eng. lett. c. 654, letter 214, fos 446–9. This letter was published by Purcell, *Cardinal Manning*, i, 221–2; the paragraphs he omitted in the transcription of the letter are enclosed here between two lines.

[*fo.* 446[r]] private

Temple. Wed[nesday]: Jan[uar]y. 29. 1836

My dear Manning,

During part of last and of the present week I have enjoyed the great privilege of having Newman living in my chambers, and I believe you will receive a paper from him in this cover about the Oxford tracts, and also about a plan of Dodsworth's[37] for getting up a spring lecture on Church matters in London.

Of course Newman and I have had a great deal of interesting talk together, one result of which has been to confirm certain parts of the view about Church teaching etc I lately sent you, and to convince and satisfy me that it is not mere matter of idle speculation, but involves practical consequences of very great weight in our present condition, and about which I earnestly desire to confer with you above all other persons. And in the outset I must beseech you not to communicate the sentiments herein contained to anyone in their present shape. (1st) because, though I am confident I state the substance[a] of N[ewman]'s opinion accurately I would not pledge him to any thing thrown out to a friend; and (2d) because I am most anxious to avoid the semblance of a difference between those who hold so much in common, and who may so usefully co-operate together.

[*fo.* 446[v]] I will begin by[b] professing my intire and cordial and active assent to all the great features of their system – to the Apostolical succession, to the virtue and efficacy derived therefrom on

a tendency] written above substance.
b by] inserted.

the Sacraments, to their view of the Sacraments themselves, to the reverence due to antiquity and Catholicism; and by owning that the times require the most prominent assertion of them. But I had hoped that the high evangelical doctrines, delivered from the exaggerated and distorted guise in which some had dressed them, and reduced to their true position in the system, would have been[a] allowed a place therein. I grieve to think that I have discovered in one person at least a violent repugnance to them, and to justify this an adoption of principles which go so far (as to be available they must) that they have at least this advantage viz – they open one's eyes to their unsoundness. I will first state what they are, and then try to show how some part of the view before alluded to is the only bulwark ag[ain]st. them. But you must not look for any plan, for I find it extremely difficult[b] to develop my meaning, and must go on slowly, feeling my way and trusting to your sympathy.

[*fo.* 447^{r}] 1.Well then! Newman holds that from the time the Church ceased to be One, the right of any part of it to propound Articles of faith, as such, is suspended, all that remains to them is to impose terms of communion, articles of peace etc. Further, he[c] says that before the Reformation the Church never deduced any doctrine from Scripture, and by inference blames our Reformers for doing so. Moreover he objects to their doctrine in itself as to Justification by faith, and complains of their attempt to prove it from the Fathers, as a perversion of their meaning. Generally, his result is, not merely to refer us to antiquity but to shut us up in it, and to deprive, not only individuals but the church, of all those[d] doctrines of Scripture not fully[e] commented on by the Fathers: and he seems to consider that our Reformed Church has erred as much in one direction as the Council of Trent in another, and that the fact of other churches holding different views e[.]g[.] on justification, requires the suspension of our judgment, or at least[f] prevents full acceptance of our own doctrine concerning it.

a been] inserted.
b y] crossed out at the end of difficult.
c denies] crossed out.
d Illegible word crossed out; doctrines] inserted.
e fully] inserted.
f Illegible word crossed out.

[*fo.* 447v] 2. Now all this occurs to me to do despite to a large portion of the experience and Tradition of the Church under pretence of [a] respect for primitive antiquity, and to slight doctrines which to many holy men have appeared most surely founded on God's word, and the preaching of which have to say the least been outwardly eminently blest. How then am I to prevent them from being wrested from me? Of course I should be ashamed of myself if I wanted any practical reassurance of truths to which my heart and conscience bear testimony. But on what theory are they to be defended? I reply there is a poor hint of it in my paper on Tradition which I am confident will bear development. I there assume that there is a natural course of the mind (whether of the individual Christian or of the Christian Church), and this course is first to regard the external Objects of faith, next, to regard their inward operations on the soul, and its condition as affected by them. Accordingly, the doctrine of the Trinity, of Church order, ordinances, etc, would first engage the attention of the Church and be exhibited fully in Her teaching. In due course the 2d. class of[b] subjects e.g. the Atonement, [*fo.* 448r] the nature of faith, etc would likewise have been brought before Her, and authoritatively expounded. Unhappily corruptions and schisms interrupted this, and severing the unity of the Church left Her divided members to complete the Ecclesiastical structure each for itself. Accordingly we have some doctrines e.g. Justification by faith,[38] exhibited indeed in our[c] own and the[d] Reformed Confessions but without the full authority of Oecumenical consent. Again, we have other doctrines not so exhibited at all, but delivered by one party in the Church in a distorted form, and by another slighted and denied. But does this compel us to abandon the doctrines themselves, or diminish their intrinsic importance? Surely not, surely each Church must not shrink[e] from Her part in building the temple of the Lord, though deprived of Catholic authority, and at the risk of mixing hay[,] wood and stubble with her gold and silver. And

a Illegible word crossed out.
b doc] crossed out.
c our] inserted.
d other] crossed out.
e ing] crossed out at the end of shrink.

though the fabric be purged by fire the foundation standeth sure (I Cor:3).

[*fo.* 448*v*] My answer then to the attack on our Reformers for adducing the Fathers as witnesses of their doctrine is, – not that they did systematically hold it, for I admit they did not, but – that we have no business to look to the Fathers about it further than to be satisfied their general teaching was not contrariant to it.[39] For the nature of things, and the matter of fact, in that there were no disputes on the subject then, prove that the attention of the Church was not[a] and could not then be directed on it, and it is no disparagement to the early Church not to look for things at her hands which it is impossible[b] she could perform.

Surely in thoughts like these one may see glimpses of a beautiful and comprehensive system which holding fast primitive antiquity on the one hand, does not reject the later teaching of the Church on the other, but bringing out of its stores things new and old, is eminently calculated to break up existing [*fo.* 449*r*] parties in the Church, and unite the children of light against those of darkness. I have endeavoured in vain to gain an entrance into N[ewman]'s. mind on this subject, and have tried each joint of his intellectual panoply, but its hard and polished temper glances off all my arrows. Still I feel so fully the truth and importance of all the positive parts of his system, that it does not at all damp my devotion to[c] it. And I try not to be restless or anxious[d] about such difficulties, but wait calmly in the sure trust that if any of us be otherwise minded God will reveal this also unto us. You cannot conceive what satisfaction it will give me to know your sentiments and hear your counsel on this matter. I trust and believe that what I[e] object to[f] in N[ewman]. is merely owing to[g] his resiliency from opposite error, and that Pusey and others[h] do not share it. And I

a then] crossed out.
b Illegible word crossed out.
c to] inserted.
d for] crossed out.
e Two illegible words crossed out.
f object to] inserted.
g the res] crossed out.
h did] crossed out.

am sure he will not seek to put forward such views, and this is another reason why I earnestly entreat this subject may be confined to our[a] two selves.

[*fo.* 449^v] I had other things to say, but this has absorbed my letter. We hear nothing of who is to be poor Burton's[40] successor yet. I am quite well and trust to hear good acc[oun]ts. of you and yours.

Ever y[ou]r aff[ectiona]te friend
S. F. WOOD

[a] Two illegible words crossed out.

Notes

1. William Wordsworth, 'Once I could hail', *The Poems*, ii (New Haven: Yale University Press, 1981), p. 623. Probably composed in 1826. Wood's line 4 has 'its' in lieu of 'the' in the 1981 edition.
2. Q. Horatius Flaccus (Horace), *Epistulae* 1, 11, 28: 'Strenua nos exercet inertia' ('A busy idleness is tiring us').
3. William-Charles Fitzwilliam (1812–35), Viscount Milton, first son of the 5th Earl Fitzwilliam, died on 8 Nov. 1835, leaving a posthumous daughter by Lady Selina Jenkinson, daughter of the 3rd Earl Liverpool.
4. Vincentius Lerinensis, *Commonitorium or Pro Catholicae Fidei Antiquitate et Universitate adversus Profanas Omnium Haereticorum Novitiates*, in Corpus Christianorum, Series Latina 64 (Turnholti: Brepol, 1985). The quotations from the *Commonitorium* in the notes are taken from this edition. See n. 29 ref. the edition used by Wood.
5. John Pearson, Manning's contemporary at Balliol, a few years his senior; barrister, Lincoln's Inn. There are some letters of Pearson to Manning in Manning MS.Bod., Eng. lett. c. 663.
6. Probably Edward T. B. Twisleton (1809–74), Wykhamist, contemporary of Manning at Oxford, fellow of Balliol College (1830–8); barrister, Inner Temple; member of several parliamentary commissions.
7. Robert Francis Wilson (1809–88); entered Oriel College in 1827; first curate of Keble at Hursley; when Hursley parish was divided he became the first Perpetual Curate of Ampfield, the newly created parish (1841); contributed some articles to the *British Critic*.
8. E. B. Pusey, *Scriptural Views of Holy Baptism, Tracts for the Times*, 67–9 (London: Rivington,1835), they were dated on the feasts of St Bartholomew (24 August), St Michael (29 September), and St Luke (18 October).
9. Q. Horatius Flaccus (Horace), *Satirae* 1, 3, 67: 'How ready we are to sanction a law that presses hard on ourselves'.
10. Does he mean 2 Th 2: 15? This verse reads: 'So then, brethren, stand firm and hold to the traditions which you were taught by us, either by word of mouth or by letter.' This would fit better with the passage from the letter to Timothy, and with the point Wood is trying to make. 2 Th 2: 14 reads: 'To this [belief in truth] he called you through our gospel, so that you may obtain the glory of our Lord Jesus Christ'.
11. 'Follow the pattern of the sound words which you have heard from me, in the faith and love which are in Christ Jesus.'
12. 'In ipsa item catholica ecclesia magnopere curandum est, ut id teneamus quod ubique, quod semper, quod ab omnibus creditum est' (*Commonitorium*, ch. ii, par. 5, lin. 24–6, p. 149) ('In the Catholic Church every care should be taken to hold fast to what has been believed everywhere, always, and by all').
13. Aurelius Augustinus, *De Baptismo Libri Septem* ('On Baptism', against the Donatists), lib. 4, ch. 24, par. 31, linea 2, in Corpus Scriptorum Ecclesiasticorum, 51 (Vindibonae-Lipsiae: Tempski-Freytag, 1908), p. 259: 'quod uniuersa tenet ecclesia nec conciliis institutum, sed semper retentum est, non nisi auctoritate apostolica traditum rectissime creditur' ('what is held by the universal Church, not having been established by the councils but has always been held, is rightly believed to have been handed down by apostolic authority').
14. The note is difficult to read. The present reading is an interpretation matching the tone of Wood's thought.

15. J. H. Newman, 'Human Responsibility', *Parochial Sermons*, II (London: Rivington, 1835), pp. 360 ff.
16. These three 'sections' of Vincent of Lerins's *Commonitorium* are all included within ch. xxiii of the Corpus Christianorum edition.
17. 'Quot paruulorum artus, tot uirorum, et si qua illa sunt, quae aeui maturioris aetate pariuntur, iam in seminis ratione proserta sunt, ut nihil nouum postea proferatur in senibus, quod non in pueris iam ante latitauerit' (*Commonitorium*, ch. xxiii, par. 6, lin. 20–4, p. 178) ('The limbs of the young child are as many as those of the adult man, even though some only become apparent in maturity they already existed virtually in the embryo, in such a way that nothing is later produced in old men that had not been previously latent in the child').
18. The expression 'hid (...) in the bosom of the Church' is almost a literal quotation from Newman (J. H. Newman, *The Arians of the Fourth Century* (London: Rivington, 1833), p. 41); Newman would also use similar expressions in his *'Via Media' II*, *Tracts for the Times*, 41 (London: Rivington, 1834), p. [5]; and in his 'Second Letter to Jager', in L. Allen, *John Henry Newman and the Abbé Jager. A Controversy on Scripture and Tradition (1834–1836)* (London: Oxford University Press, 1975), p. 95.
19. Canons of 1571, 6.2 'Imprimis vero videbunt, ne quid unquam doceant pro contione quod a populo religiose teneri et credi velint nisi quod consentaneum sit doctrinae Veteris et Novi Testamenti, quodque ex illa ipsa doctrina catholici patres, et veteres epicopi collegerint', in G. Bray, ed., *The Anglican Canons 1529–1947*, Church of England Record Society, VI (Woodbridge: Boydell Press, 1998), pp. 196 and 198. Canon 6 in *A booke of certaine canons, concernyng some parte of the discipline of the Churche of England: in the yeare of the Lord 1571* (London, [1571]), p. 23: 'But chiefly they shall take heede, that they teach nothing in their preaching, which they would have the people religiously to observe, and beleve, but that which is agreeable to the doctrine of the olde Testament, or the newe, and that which the catholike fathers, and auncient Bishops have gathered out of that doctrine.'
20. 'by virtue of this Acte, shall not in anny wise have Auctoritie or Power to order determine or adjudged to anny Matter or Cause to bee Heresie but onelye suche as heretofore have been determined ordred or adjudged to be Heresie by thautoritatie of the Canonicall Scriptures, or by the first fowre general Councelles, or anny of them, or by anny other Generall Councell wherein the same was declared Heresie by thexpresse and playne woordes of the say Canonicall Scriptures', An Acte Restoring to the Crowne thauncyent Jurisdiction over the State Ecclesiasticall and Spuall, and abolishing all Forrreine Power repugnaunt to the same [Act of Supremacy], XX, c. 1, in *The Statutes of the Realm. Printed by Command of His Majesty King George the Third*, IV (London: Eyre and Strachan, 1819), p. 354.
21. Thirty-Nine Articles, Art VI: 'Holy Scripture containeth all things necessary to salvation: so that whatsoever is not read therein, nor may be proved thereby, is not to be required of any man, that it should be believed as an article of the Faith, or be thought requisite or necessary to salvation.'
22. This seems to be a quotation from Manning's paper on Tradition. Manning would express similar ideas in his *Rule of Faith* (H. E. Manning, *Rule of Faith* (London: Rivington, 1838), p. 13).
23. Witness, testimony.
24. Revealed truth.
25. E. Hawkins, *A Dissertation upon the Use and Importance of Unauthoritative Tradition, as an Introduction to Christian Doctrines* (Oxford: Parker, 1819), viii+88.
26. Not a literal quotation; see ibid., pp. v, 18, 64, 69 etc.

27. Not a literal quotation; see ibid., pp. 42–5.
28. Samuel Wilberforce; see Chapter III, n. 161.
29. There are a number of Latin duodecimo editions of the *Commonitorium* in the sixteenth and seventeenth centuries; there seems to be no record of later latin duodecimo editions until 1836. The most widely distributed editions appear to have been the Cambridge edition: Vincentii Lerinensis, *Adversus Profanas Omnium Novitates Haereticorum Commonitorium. Cum notis V. C. Stephani Baluzii* (Cantabrigiae, 1687); and Campion's editions. There are several duodecimo Campion's editions of the *Commonitorium*, giving different places of publication on the Continent (although some of the editions may have been printed in England). Both, the Cambridge edition and Campion's, have similar distribution of chapters. Wood probably used one of Campion's editions. He quoted *latitauerit* (ch. 29) in fo. 443, the reading in Campion's editions (and in the Corpus Christianorum), while the Cambridge edition has it as *latitaverat*. See for example Campion's: Vincentii Lerinensis Galli, *Aduersus prophanas haereseon nouationes, libellus vere aureus. Distinctus in capita, et notis breuibus ex Ioannis Costerii commentariis illustratus* (Cracoviae, 1605), p. 80.
30. Newman, 'Third Letter to Jager', in Allen, *Newman and Jager*, p. 123.
31. Wood had made the same point to Manning in his letter of December 1835 (see above fo. 444).
32. On the *profectus* according to Vincent of Lerins, see above all *Commonitorium*, ch. xxiii, par. 1–2, lin.1–7, p. 177: 'Sed ita tamen, ut uere profectus sit ille fidei, non permutatio': see also n. 35 below.
33. Chapter 32 is also included in ch. xxiii of the Corpus Christianorum edition (starts in par. 16, lin. 75).
34. 'Fas es etenim, ut prisca illa caelestis philosophiae dogmata processu temporis *excurentur*, limentur, poliantur, sed nefas est ut commutentur, nefas ut detruncentur, ut mutilentur' (*Commonitorium*, ch xxiii, par. 13, lin. 55–8, p. 179) ('It is right that those ancient dogmas of heavenly philosophy should in the course of time be taken care of, sharpened and polished, but it is sinful to change, decapitate or mutilate them').
35. 'Ita etiam christianae religionis dogma sequatur has decet profectuum leges, ut annis scilicet consolidetur, *dilatetur* tempore, sublimetur aetate, incorruptum tamen inlibatumque permaneat et uniuersis partium suarum mensuris cunctisque quasi membris ac sensibus propriis plenum atque perfectum sit, quod nihil praeterea permutationis admittat, nulla proprietatis dispendia, nullam definitionis sustineat uarietatem' (*Commonitorium*, ch. xxiii, par. 9, lin. 31–8, p.178) ('In a similar way, the dogma of the Christian religion ought to follow these laws of progress, so that it may be consolidated in the course of years, developed in time, and sublimated by age, while remaining incorrupt and unimpaired, complete and perfect in all the proportion of its parts (as it were its limbs and senses); without admitting any change, any loss of its properties or any change of its true substance').
36. Robert Wilberforce: his first wife, Agnes Wrangham, had died at the end of 1834, a few days after the birth of their second child.
37. There seems to be no record of any spring lectures being organized in London at the time. Newman had also referred to this plan, and mentioned among other possible speakers Rose, Copeland, Palmer, S. Wilberforce, Manning, Keble, etc. (Newman to Pusey, 21 January 1836, *LD*, V, p. 208).
38. Manning seems to have made some remarks on Wood's references to Justification. Wood sent Manning a paper on the subject on Passion Sunday 1837: 'It was your hint that set me off', he said in the accompanying letter; it had taken him long

to put it together because of the pressure of business (Manning MSS Bod., c. 654, fo. 452).

39. Compare Wood's words with Froude's in his letter to Keble of 9 January 1834: 'We cannot know about any seemingly indifferent practice of the Church of Rome that is not a development of the apostolic ethos and it is to no purpose to say that we can have no proof of it in the writings of the six first centuries; there must found a *dis*proof if they would do anything' (H. R. Froude, *Remains of the Late Rev. Richard Hurrel Froude*, ed. J. H. Newman and J. Keble, I–I (London: Rivington, 1838), p. 336.

40. Edward Burton (1794–1836), Regius Professor of Divinity at Oxford (1829–36). The election of Renn Dickson Hampden as his successor was to prove highly controversial.

APPENDIX II

REVIVAL OF PRIMITIVE DOCTRINE

UNDATED NOTE ATTACHED TO THE MANUSCRIPT

[*r*] J W Colvile, Esq.[1]
9 New Square
Linc. Inn

[*v*] My dear C.

I send you my Paper which went to Tholuck.[2] How are you? I am busy with some law I want to finish, before (?) I could come and see you.

Yours aff[ectissime].
SFW

Friday

[REVIVAL OF PRIMITIVE DOCTRINE]

[*fo.* 1] The following paper is intended to furnish[a] some particulars on the subject in which persons[b] are taking interest – the revival of primitive doctrine and practice in the English Church. What these doctrines and practices specifically are, and in what form and to what extent they have lately been reproduced[c] will be gathered far more satisfactorily from the publications of those who have mainly contributed to this revival. Indeed one of these publications – Dr. Pusey's Letter to the Bishop of Oxford[3] contains a recapitulation of these very points, and relieves me from the

[a] The following paper is intended to furnish] inserted; replacing: My dear Sir, I sit down to furnish [?] you with some particulars] crossed out.
[b] persons] inserted; you] crossed out.
[c] you] crossed out.

task of attempting to state them with precision. What I propose to do is to offer [a] some collateral information, which may facilitate a[b] study of the writers themselves, and give [c] some clue to their general scope and meaning.

I will begin by speaking shortly of *[fo. 2]* [d] the state of feeling which immediately preceded their promulgation. On this head my knowledge is almost wholly confined within the circle of members of the University of Oxford, but as it was in that quarter that the movement first took a definite and palpable form perhaps this is of less consequence.

Most persons are aware[e] to how low an ebb Theological learning had fallen among the English Clergy at the beginning of the present Century. By one party in the Church, and that the most prominent and active one,[4] it was systematically disparaged, and although this party never gained a footing as Teachers in Oxford, at least in the[f] University, they probably tended to draw into another channel those minds which would naturally have applied themselves to the study of Divinity. In this state the University continued up to the very period of which I am to speak, and as it was popularly considered to be the *[fo. 3]* chief spot where this study still lingered, it may fairly be inferred that the subject was even more neglected elsewhere.

In other respects however considerable intellectual activity manifested itself during the years 1820–30; the Students were excited to a more intelligent study of the Principles of Logic and Rhetoric by the Elementary works of Archbishop Whately[5] on these subjects; and generally, this Author's writings, whose characteristic it is to sharpen and discipline the intellect without giving it matter to feed and rest upon, were a remarkable preparation for what was to follow. The Ethics of Aristotle also, long a text book in the University, became in the hands of more than one College

a you] crossed out.

b facilitate a] inserted; replacing: assist you] crossed out.

c you] crossed out.

d of] crossed out.

e Most persons are aware] inserted; replacing: You are doubtless aware] crossed out.

f at least in the] inserted.

Lecturer the ground work of a very instructive course of Ethical study. Not that this course was either very extensive or scientific, but it led to much useful reflexion on the formation of moral habits, on their influence on opinions[a] and such like practical points. Bishop Butler's great work "The Analogy of Religion, Natural and Revealed, to the [*fo.* 4] Constitution and Course of Nature"[6] was also studied; much more for the sake of the poignant suggestions it incidentally contains on the points just named, than as an argumentative defence of Religion, and in connexion with it was read his Treatise on Morals entitled "Sermons at the Rolls Chapel."[7]

To minds thus engaged the Religious Teaching of the day naturally became unsatisfactory; they found it wanting in practical reality, in any discrimination of character or insight into motives and principles of action. Indeed it was probably this which led them to make so religious a use of a Heathen treatise on morals, to dwell so largely on its details, and to make it as it were the ground work of an education bearing to a great degree a Theological aspect. They employed this indirect means for the inculcation of that which found no place in the explicit system.

While persons within the University were thus supplying for themselves the deficiency of the day, and thereby training [*fo.* 5] their minds in a manner which has remarkably influenced the tone of their subsequent writings, the world without was craving for some religious nutriment more real and satisfactory than what they as yet possessed. Accordingly new religious publications were eagerly sought after and perused; year by year volumes of sermons issued from the press+ [See Note A], and yet the wants of serious minds remained unsatisfied, they had not yet found that system in the authority and fullness of which they could repose. It is curious to remark that together with this unsatisfied feeling there co-existed, as must naturally be the case where there is no recognised standard, no definite landmarks of belief, and great sensitiveness and jealousy of any apparent innovation. "Religious restlessness, and feverishness of speculation in divine things"+ [See Note B] were lamented, at the same time that it was admitted

a on their influence on opinions] inserted. This insertion seems to be in Newman's hand.

that the actual state and temper of the Church stood[a] greatly in need of reformation.+[b]

[fo. 6] It is only just to mention that during these[c] years+ [See Note C] appeared a volume of Sermons by Bishop Jebb,[8] the Appendix to which contained an Essay on the "Peculiar character of the Church of England." This Essay has the praise of having revived after a considerable interval, and reproduced in a modern shape, the Anglican Rule of Faith. On this Rule our learned Divines of the 16th and 17th centuries+ [See Note D] founded[d] their Theology, and it is the intellectual basis on which the whole system, as lately reconstructed, rests. How far the turn men's minds were naturally taking would of itself have gained for it that wide acceptance it has now received, had not external circumstances [e] powerfully contributed to the same result, it is useless perhaps[f] to inquire. Those circumstances did occur just at this period, and to them I will now refer.

In the Autumn of 1830 the Liberal Government came into office, and the passion for reforming the civil institutions *[fo. 7]* of the country which had placed them in power, soon extended itself to Ecclesiastical matters. The payment of tithes and Church-rates was resisted, the Bishops were exposed to popular contumely, and their seats in the Legislature were proposed to be taken away, alterations of the Liturgy and of the internal discipline of the Church were vehemently advocated at public meetings.[9] This hostile clamour roused the Church from the state of security in which she had long reposed, and threw her back on the contemplation of what was her inherent and spiritual strength, now that the support of the Civil arm seemed to be withdrawn from her. In the first instance however, all that was said or written assumed the form of defences against external attacks and objections to proposed Reforms. In 1832 the late lamented Mr. Rose[10]

a was] crossed out.

b +Preface to Miller's Sermons] crossed out.

c app] crossed out.

d 16th and 17th centuries founded] inserted; replacing: Laudian era constructed] crossed out. It seems that 16th and 17th centuries are in Newman's hand

e forf] crossed out.

f perhaps] inserted; replacing: now]crossed out.

established the "British Magazine"[11] expressly for the purpose of disseminating more correct statements of the real amount of the property of the Church, of vindicating its ordinances from misrepresentation, and of enabling [*fo.* 8] the clergy to communicate and co-operate with each other. In 1833 an Association to resist alterations [a] in the Prayer book[12] was projected, and though this project was abandoned, it indicates the defensive posture in which men's minds were then placed. It was in the same year that the Legislature passed an Act suppressing ten Irish Bishoprics,[13] and otherwise naturally affecting the independence of that Church. This offensive measure seems to have satisfied the minds of those, who were the most alive to the course of events in the Church+ [Note E], that a crisis had arrived which called for their protest and exertions. Accordingly in September[b] of the same year the first Number[14] of the "Tracts for the Times" appeared, and was rapidly succeeded by others. They were[c] written in an abrupt and energetic style, confining themselves to the enunciation of a few leading principles, and a protest against specific proposals or prevalent [*fo.* 9] sentiments of the day. It is well to prepare those beforehand for this, who, opening the volume with the expectation of finding an elementary and systematic exposition of doctrine, will find only practical suggestions on single and apparently unconnected points.

Throughout the first Volume,[15] the 'Tracts for the Times' preserved the same character, and thus, not touching directly on controverted points, they[d] were widely [e] circulated without exciting formal opposition.

In 1834 appeared the first volume of Mr. Newman's Sermons.[16] And here the[f] fruits of that course of study in Oxford to which I have adverted became remarkably evident. This volume hardly contains a directly theological Sermon. The scope of the whole

a Illegible words crossed out.

b September] inserted; replacing: December] crossed out. The correction seems to be in Newman's hand.

c were] inserted; replacing: are] crossed out.

d they] inserted.

e Unreadable word crossed out.

f fruits] crossed out.

of it appears to be the production of a certain moral temper – a temper, for the most part, in strong contrast with the prevalent one of the day. It is a very small thing to say of these Sermons [*fo.* 10] that their style and matter, compared with other Sermons, could not fail to produce a great impression on serious minds. They were the first publication which produced a strictly religious effect in this direction, the operation of the Tracts being hitherto more or less ecclesiastical.

In the two years immediately following, 1835 and 1836, events occurred at the University of Oxford which indirectly yet powerfully tended both to bring into prominence those persons who were engaged in the revival of Church principles, and to develop and establish those principles themselves.

The first was an attempt on the part of the Government to induce the University to abandon her practice of requiring subscription of the Thirtynine Articles on the Matriculation (or admission) of Students, and thereby to open the University as a place of Education to Dissenters.[17]

The second was the nomination, by the Government, of a Professor of Divinity, whose published Theological opinions were at least of doubtful [*fo.* 11] accordance with the formularies of the Church.[18]

In the course of the discussion which these events excited the authority of the Creeds of the primitive Church, and the importance of doctrinal truth as such, was brought out and insisted on. The fact that one of their number was charged with holding loosely or imperfectly certain fundamental articles of faith naturally led the Clergy to consider on what grounds their own belief of them rested. And the discussion turning on doctrines in the belief of which the Clergy were unanimous,+ [Note F] such for instance as the doctrine of the Holy Trinity or of the Atonement, a more favourable opportunity could not well have [a] arisen for impressing upon them the weight and value of Apostolical Tradition.

Hitherto then the "Tracts for the Times" and other writings had excited but little formal controversy, for they had treated of points which were either accordant – or not incompatible – with the prevailing sentiments of the day. But they [*fo.* 12] were now

a existed] crossed out.

(1836) brought into direct collision with these sentiments; and this, chiefly, by the publication of Dr Pusey's "Scriptural Views of Holy Baptism,"[19] and of Mr. Keble's Sermon on "Primitive Tradition."[20] The former of these – at its first appearance an elaborate treatise, and still under process of expansion by the author – is in fact a detailed exposition of the antient doctrine of the Sacraments being the instruments of Divine grace, as opposed to the modern notion of grace being obtained by faith – by the active energising of the mind for itself.

The latter, although not differing [a] in its statement of the Rule of Faith from the Essay of Bishop Jebb before noticed, yet now that it was brought forward in connexion with such doctrines as the one just referred to on Baptismal Grace, and that it was felt to be the argumentative[b] basis on which that and other primitive doctrines rest, likewise excited much discussion and remark.+ [Note G]

[fo. 13] It will be observed even from the brief account here given that there is no systematic character about the 'Tracts for the Times'. At first they are chiefly protests against external innovations. Afterwards, on becoming more doctrinal, they develop this or that point incidentally, and according as circumstances elicit it. This is the natural consequence of their being no new theory, but a revival of doctrines already contained in older Anglican Theology, and implied (more or less) in the teaching of our Church. Nevertheless, the foundation of an attempt to harmonise and classify the stores contained in this elder Divinity has been laid by Mr. Newman. It is to his writings that we must chiefly look for traces of this organizing process; he commenced it by a Volume of "Lectures on the Prophetical Office of the Church"[21] (that is, on the Church as a Teacher) in the course of which he expounds the Rule by which she teaches, a true understanding *[fo. 14]* of that Rule, lying, as I have said, at the bottom of the whole matter. Circumstances have since called him off to the subject of "Justification,"[22] but it is his intention (as I understand) to revert to the other branches of the Church's office,[23] + [Note H] in order, while treating of them, to systematize other points of Anglican Theology.

a from] crossed out.

b argumentative] inserted; replacing: intellectual] crossed out.

With reference to this his general object Mr. N[ewman]. states, in the Introduction to his Lectures, that he proposes "to offer helps towards the formation of a recognized Anglican Theology in one of its departments,"[24] – that "we have a vast inheritance, but no inventory of our treasures. All is given us in profusion; it remains for us to catalogue, sort, distribute, harmonize, select,[25] and complete. We have more than we know how to use; stores of learning, but little that is precise and serviceable . . . . We require a recognized Theology, and if the present work, instead of being what it is meant to be, a first approximation to the required solution [*fo.* 15] in one department of a complicated problem, contains after all but a series of illustrations demonstrating our need, and supplying hints for its removal, such a result," etc. etc.[26]

In the meantime, the Tracts have on several points furnished materials for ascertaining the doctrine of Anglican Divines by the publication of 'Catenae' of copious extracts from their writings.[27]

I have as yet made no mention of Mr. Froude's writings. It is difficult to estimate too highly the personal influence which he exercised over those contemporaries who thought and acted with him. It was he who first directed their minds to the study of Catholic antiquity, with a view of bringing its principles to bear on the actual state of the Church around him. These principles, which others had to acquire by means of books and study he seems to have grasped intuitively as it were[a] by instinct [b]. And he not only seems to have done this as regards[c] their general [*fo.* 16] scope and meaning, but also to have rehearsed in his own mind their application to matters of detail and conduct, in such a manner as to be able to give directions on these points which afterwards proved to be in accordance with Catholic usage. To him more specially thanks are due for an exposure of the Rationalistic tendencies of several of the English Reformers, and for having rescued us from that blind veneration for celebrated names which would have placed an obstacle in the way of consistent reception of primitive Truth. Still it is true hitherto that Mr. Froude has operated indi-

a as it were] inserted; replacing: by an] crossed out.
b of his own mind] crossed out.
c as regards] inserted; replacing: as regarded] crossed out.

rectly rather than directly on the minds of Churchmen in general. He has rather given a tone and direction[28] to those writings [a] the influence of which has been widely felt by the public, than himself influenced it.[b] The first Part of his Remains[29] furnish not so much direct contributions to the revival of primitive doctrine as a [*fo.* 17] history of the process by which these doctrines were revived in his own and in other minds. And so far as this process bears the semblance of being personal and accidental merely; – so far its being laid bare has tended to repel rather than to win over.

The second Part of his Remains (lately published)[30] contains Essays of the greatest value. Yet even these, owing to their publication having been delayed, do not meet the wants of the present moment. They are occupied in establishing the grounds of orthodox belief, of Church authority and the like; whereas men's minds, having more or less accepted these principles, are pressing on to a knowledge of the things themselves, and are engaged in explaining the records of Christian antiquity. But this love of Theological study among the Anglican Clergy, whose character and avocations are on the whole so eminently practical, may again languish as it has before languished. In such a case the value of Mr. Froude's [*fo.* 18] Remains will be felt. External tastes and opinions are fluctuating things, but the laws of belief, the deep wants and universal tendencies of the human mind cannot but continue [being] matters of enduring interest, and it is these with which Mr. Froude deals, and that with all the freshness and vigour of reality.

From what I have said it will be apparent that of the task undertaken by these writers that portion which chiefly regards permanence, and which least regards the wants of the passing day, is still in its rudiments. I mean the work of systematizing and completing the Anglican Theology. The Anglican Theology it may with property be called, notwithstanding that in several points it has never been recognized but by a school within the Church. Still it is the only one which at all meets the requisite conditions of the case. To be a <u>Theology</u> at all, it must rest on a scientific [*fo.* 19] basis, and be capable of being maintained at least by probable arguments.

a who] crossed out.

b it] inserted; replacing: them] crossed out.

And to be Anglican it must steer clear, as our Church professes to do, between Romanism and Ultra-Protestantism. Moreover, it must provide a consistent interpretation of our authorised formularies. All this the system to which I refer, and it alone, professes to accomplish. Other schools of doctrine within our Church are manifestly heterogeneous and arbitrary; they adopt this or that dogma, and reject its necessary consequent; they can give no account of their rule of faith, of their standard of interpretation. They do not even attempt to reconcile our formularies with each other, and to give them a Catholic sense, but are content to take them with all the various and conflicting meanings History would impress upon them. The question therefore, viewed theoretically, is between this theology or none. It is another and a different question how far [*fo.* 20] the English Clergy, absorbed as they are by pressing practical duties, will be inclined as a body to embrace this view of the matter. It must in fairness be admitted that the experience of the period since the Reformation is counter to their doing so. The great Divines of the 17th Century, and the school of the Nonjurors could only transmit, they could not propagate these doctrines. On the other hand outward circumstances are certainly more favourable to it now than formerly. There is what has been called 'a fresh start' both in religion and politics; our divines are not fettered by political subservience, by the party obloquy which oppressed the Nonjurors; they have the benefit of the experience and the labours of their predecessors.

But whatever may be the result of this there is at any rate another process already actively at work, in the origination of which these writings have been chiefly instrumental, although [*fo.* 21] seconded by a sympathetic tendency and spirit springing up in other quarters, and without any previous concert and communication. I mean the revival of many ordinances and practices expressly enjoined by the Rubrics of the Prayer book, but which during the last Century had fallen almost universally into neglect. They are such as the following: – the observance of Saints days and festivals of the Church; of Friday in each week as a fast day, and fasting generally; daily public worship and more frequent celebration of the Eucharist; a more reverent attention to the external and symbolical parts of Divine Service, and generally a bringing out into prominence the peculiar functions and powers of the Christian priesthood.

Whatever may be thought of these things viewed separately, when it is remembered that they all bear the same character and tend in the same direction, that they are indications of one line of doctrine and one temper of mind, [*fo.* 22] and that the practice of them has an immediate tendency to reproduce and disseminate this temper, no one who wishes rightly to understand the meaning and extent of the present movement can safely overlook them. They have been revived with a success and rapidity which is a remarkable testimony to the importance of maintaining forms even when their spirit seems to have expired. In all cases when the practice to be restored was enjoined by the Prayer book the Clergy have recognised the obligation when laid before them, little as they had previously acted upon it. On the contrary it is with great difficulty that any doctrine or practice not thus embodied in our formularies, however accordant with them, (however imperatively called for by primitive usage[a]), has been revived.[31] Great delicacy moreover has been felt by the Authors of this revival about pressing any thing upon the Clergy at large before they are prepared and willing to receive it. They [*fo.* 23] have always shown a desire that others should follow out for themselves the principles of our Church, rather than profess themselves the adherents of a party.

Thus, with regard to individual devotion, they are inviting persons to expand and elevate and complete it for themselves by reprinting the manuals and ascetic works of our elder divines.[32] So too with regard to Theology; what is the Translation into English of Select Works of the Fathers[33] in which they are now engaged but an invitation to others to accompany them, in their study of antiquity, in a reverent examination of the doctrine and temper of primitive times? In this study the persons so often alluded to are themselves engaged, preparing themselves thereby for proceeding in their work of systematizing our theology, of separating that which is Catholic in it from that which is accidental, of giving it consistency and completeness.

a usage] inserted; replacing: authority] crossed out.

And on the whole, this is the attitude in which they seem to wish the minds of [*fo.* 24] others at present to rest, to reflect on what they have learnt, to endeavour to realize and deepen their knowledge of it, and to express it in their daily life, before they press on to new acquisitions.[34]

I have now sketched – I am conscious how imperfectly – what are the preparations, external and internal, of this Revival; what the objects are which I conceive the authors of it to have proposed to themselves; what have been[a] the instruments and the mode of their operation; what has been the success which has attended them; what is the present aspect of affairs. I shall not venture on any anticipations of the future.

[*fo.* 25][35] Notes

A. It is curious to compare the Booksellers Advertisements of this period with those of the present. The former announce little else in the way of religious publications but Sermons, the latter are full of Reprints of old Books of Doctrine. That is to say, people were then asking after knowledge, they were enquirers after Truth. A satisfying form of truth is now brought home to them, and they are disposed towards ασκησις, and exercise in it.

B. Quoted from Miller's Sermons, Preface, p. 15.[36] I would draw attention to the whole Preface as throwing light on the character of the period, and also as disclosing the perplexity into which earnest and thoughtful minds were there thrown for lack of some master-principle to guide them.

One symptom of this 'religious restlessness' was the numerous pleas by [b] attached members of the Church to remodel the Prayer book. Perhaps one motive which led to the publication[c] of the 'Christian year'[37] during this period was a wish to counteract this feeling, and to unfold the ηθος of our services. It had [*fo.* 26] the effect of doing so to a remarkable degree.

Subsequently, the apprehension of innovations in an opposite direction has [d] recalled persons who then wished to popularize the

[a] been] inserted.
[b] persons] crossed out.
[c] to the publication] inserted; replacing: the author] crossed out.
[d] been] crossed out.

Prayerbook, and rendered it their standard almost unchangeably.

C. These Sermons originally appeared some years earlier. Bishop Jebb was much indebted to Alexander Knox, a deep and original thinker, whose own writings have greatly contributed to [a] overthrow the narrow dogmatism of the Calvinistic[b] school, and to inculcate more inward and [c] living principles of piety. His Treatise on the Sacraments,[38] only of late years made publici juris,[39] is also peculiarly adapted to lead minds onward to Catholic views. Dr. Hook too was a professed follower of Bishop Jebb, and his writings are an independent [d] testimony to primitive doctrine, earlier than the general movement at Oxford.[40]

[*fo.* 27] D. For a very instructive account of the manner in which Anglican Theology, in the hands of Hooker, emancipated itself from the Puritanical influences of the period immediately succeeding the Reformation, and returned to a more Catholic standard both as to doctrine and as to Church polity, I would refer to Mr. Keble's Preface to his Edition of Hooker's works.[41] In the next century Laud,[42] Hammond,[43] Cosin,[44] Jer[emy]: Taylor[45] and others carried on the work which Hooker had begun.

E. A proof of this is to be found in Mr. Keble's Sermon on 'National Apostasy[']'[46] published during this year.

F. (One of the gentlemen who actively cooperated) *Those who*[e] *cooperated on this occasion were of different shades of opinion, one who took a prominent share* with Dr. Pusey, Mr. Newman etc (in this matter) (was a clergyman of) *would be classed with* the Calvinistic School.[47]

G. A formal attack on Dr. Pusey's Tract was carried on by the 'Christian Observer',[48] and by the 'Record'[49] newspaper, the organ of the Calvinistic party. Dr. P.s.[usey] happening to be the author of the first publication thus [*fo.* 28] controverted led to the vulgar name often applied to those who hold these opinions. This controversy came to no definitive issue, and is only noticeable as having led to a subsequent work of Mr. Newman on "Justification."[50]

a that] crossed out.
b Calvinistic] inserted; replacing: Evangelical] crossed out
c living] crossed out.
d and earlier] crossed out.
e cop] crossed out.

H. That is, to her Sacerdotal[51] and Regal Offices. Under[a] the first I conceive he will touch on Sacraments and sacramental ordinances, and under the last, of Church Government, discipline, etc. This reminds me that the Church's substantive existence, anterior to her connexion with the State, and the spiritual powers of her ministers as Apostolically commissioned has been strongly brought out by the present movement. The hostile spirit manifested towards her in 1830–1835 first led to this; and the measures of the Church Commissioners have subsequently led to much attention being paid to her Diocesan organisation, the functions of Chapters and so forth.

That a young Statesman should in common with others have taken up more primitive views on this subject is not remarkable, but that he should feel called upon to publish an elaborate Essay on the subject is a remarkable indication of the state of men's minds. Mr. Gladstone's "Essay on the State[b] in relation to the Church"[52] has, I am informed, been translated in German.[53]

a Under] inserted; replacing: In] crossed out.
b State] inserted; replacing: Church] crossed out.

Notes

1. James William Colvile (1810–80). Educated at Eton and Trinity College, Cambridge; barrister at Law, Inner Temple (1835); practised at Lincoln's Inn; Chief Justice of Supreme Court of Bengal (1855); early supporter of High Church concerns.
2. The editor of Newman's *Letters and Diaries* seemed to think that Wood was preparing a paper on Tholuck for the *British Critic* that was never published (*LD*, VII, p. 3 n.).
3. E. B. Pusey, *A Letter to the Right Rev. Father in God, Richard Lord Bishop of Oxford, on the Tendency to Romanism Imputed to Doctrines Held of Old, as Now, in the English Church* (Oxford: Parker, 1839).
4. Wood seems to be referring to the Evangelicals.
5. Richard Whately (1787–1863) Fellow of Oriel College, Oxford, and one of the Oriel Noetics. He was appointed Archbishop of Dublin in 1831. The works mentioned by Wood, although hardly original, were very popular and went through many editions: R. Whately, *Elements of Logic* (Oxford: Talboys and Vincent, 1826) and *Elements of Rhetoric* (Oxford: Parker, 1828). Both were initially contributed to the *Encyclopaedia Metropolitana*, and were later published separately, with additions. Copeland remarked how the teaching of the school of the Noetics 'underlay the Movement, which in one sense may be regarded as a reaction from it' (manuscript 'Narrative of the Oxford Movement', notebook I, p. 44, Copeland Papers, Pusey House, Oxford). The Noetics provided the Tractarians with some of the intellectual weapons – logical rigour and devastating irony – which they used to great effect. See also J. H. Newman 'Autobiographical Memoir III, Appendix' in *Autobiographical Writings*, ed. H. Tristam (London: Sheed and Ward, 1956), p. 85, and *Apologia pro Vita Sua. Being a History of his Religious Opinions* (London: Longman, Green and Co., 1913, new impression), Note A, pp. 286 ff.
6. J. Butler, *The Analogy of Religion, Natural and Revealed, to the Constitution and Correct Course of Nature* (London: Knapton, 1736).
7. J. Butler, *Fifteen Sermons Preached at the Rolls Chapel* (London: Knapton, 1726).
8. J. Jebb, *Sermons, on Subjects Chiefly Practical, with Illustrative Note and Appendix, Relating to the Character of the Church of England, as Distinguished both from Other Branches of the Reformation, and from the Modern Church of Rome* (London: Cadell and Davies, 1815; 4th ed. 1824).
9. The first attempts at Constitutional reform failed in 1831. The Reform Bill was rejected in the House of Lords. Twenty-one bishops voted against it and secured its defeat. The rhetoric unleashed against the bishops provoked in places public demonstrations and, at times, violence. As a result, the cries for Church reform both inside and outside Parliament became more persistent (O. Chadwick, *The Victorian Church*, I (London: Black, 1971, 3rd ed.), pp. 24 ff.).
10. Hugh James Rose died in Florence on 22 December 1838.
11. *The British Magazine and Monthly Register of Religious and Ecclesiastical Information, Parochial History and Documents Respecting the State of the Poor, Progress of Education, etc.* (1832–49). The Address presenting the policies of the magazine spoke, among other things, of its intention to refute misrepresentations, falsehoods and misconceptions used to attack the doctrines, discipline and property of the Church, and to bring about its destruction (*British Magazine*, 1 March 1832, vol. I, pp. 4–5). This issue included a lengthy article refuting those who attacked the riches of the Anglican Church: 'Facts Respecting the Church of England and her

Revenues' (ibid., pp. 60–4).

12. He appears to be referring to the 'Society for the Defence of the Church' or 'Association of Friends of the Church' which was one of the results of the Hadleigh meeting in July 1833. One of its main objects was to maintain pure and inviolable the services of the Church, as contained in the Prayer Book (cf. 'Suggestions for an Association for the Defence of the Church', the text of which can be found in A. P. Perceval, *A Collection of Papers Connected with the Theological Movement of 1833* (London: Rivington, 1842), pp. 17–18; also in *LD*, IV, pp. 66–7 and 129–30). Among the Tracts dealing with liturgical matters: [J. H. Newman], *Thoughts Respectfully Addressed to the Clergy on Alterations to the Liturgy, Tracts for the Times*, 3 (London: Rivington, 1833); [J. Keble], *Adherence to Apostolical Succession the Safest Course, Tracts for the Times*, 4 (London: Rivington, 1833) included a final note denying the competence of Parliament to introduce changes in the liturgy. See also Newman to H. Wilberforce, 16 July 1833, *LD*, IV, p. 9.
13. The Irish Church Temporalities Act (1833) abolished two archbishoprics, out of four, and eight bishoprics. Among other measures, it reduced the revenues of the richest sees, abolished church rates, provided for the suspension of redundant benefices, and set up a board of Ecclesiastical Commissioners to administer the money resulting from those proceedings ('A Bill to alter and amend the Laws relating to the Temporalities of the Church of Ireland', *Parliamentary Papers*, 59 (210) (431) (594) (057) I 339, 417, 499, 587, 599).
14. [J. H. Newman], *Thoughts on the Ministerial Commission, Respectfully Addressed to the Clergy, Tracts for the Times*, 1 (London: Rivington, 1833).
15. *Tracts for the Times, by Members of the University of Oxford*, I, for 1833–4 (London: Rivington, 1834).
16. J. H. Newman, *Parochial Sermons*, I (London: Rivington, 1834).
17. The Bill to abrogate subscription to religious test was introduced in the Commons by G. W. Wood. It passed its third reading in the Commons in July 1834, but was subsequently defeated in the Lords. The committee of Oxford campaigners against the measure included Burton (Regius Professor of Divinity), Faussett (Lady Margaret Professor of Divinity), Sewell, Pusey and Newman. The Hebdomadal Board's proposal to substitute a test of conformity for the subscription to the Articles was rejected by Convocation in May 1835. A new attempt at legislation in July 1835 was also defeated (P. Nockles, '"Lost Causes and . . . Impossible Loyalties", The Oxford Movement and the University', in *The History of the University of Oxford*, VI, ed. M. Brock and M. Curthoys (Oxford: Oxford University Press, 1997), pp. 212 ff.).
18. Renn Dickson Hampden (1793–1868) was offered the post of Regius Professor of Divinity by Lord Melbourne in 1836, against the wishes of the University.
19. E. B. Pusey, *Scriptural Views of Holy Baptism, Tracts for the Times*, 67–9 (London: Rivington, 1835). The Tracts were dated on the feasts of St Bartholomew (24 August), St Michael (29 September), and St Luke (18 October).
20. J. Keble, *Primitive Tradition Recognised in Holy Scripture, a Sermon* (London: Rivington, 1836).
21. J. H. Newman, *Lectures on the Prophetical Office of the Church, Viewed Relatively to Romanism and Popular Protestantism* (London: Rivington, 1837).
22. Samuel Charles Wilks, editor of the *Christian Observer*, published an editorial in the December 1836 issue of the magazine (pp. 788–91) attacking Pusey's Tract on Baptism: he suggested that Pusey ought to have lectured at Maynooth or the Vatican. Wilks invited supporters of the Tracts to show how Pusey could remain in the Church of England while upholding those views. Newman took up the challenge. His first letter (dated 11 January 1837) was published in the February

and March issues of the *Christian Observer*; the second letter (dated 11 March) appeared in the April and May issues. The letters were subsequently published as Tract 82. Newman did not send a third letter but rather began a series of lectures on the topic at the University Church; they were later published (J. H. Newman, *Lectures on Justification* (London: Rivington, 1838)). Wood had suggested that Newman should publish a book on the subject, rather than a pamphlet, as the Evangelicals would find it difficult to answer a book (Wood to Newman, 13 April 1837, Halifax Papers, Borthwick Institute, A2/42, fo. 36). Newman wrote on this letter: 'This was an anticipation of Wood to my lectures on Justification published the next year. JHN'. See also Newman to Bowden, 12 April 1837, *LD*, VI, p. 53.

23. Newman when sending the manuscript to Pusey wrote: 'The only thing I object to is the bold way in which he lays down what I am to do next' (Newman to Pusey, 20 August 1840, *LD*, VII, p. 379).
24. Newman, *Prophetical Office*, pp. 30–1.
25. Newman's text: *select, harmonize.*
26. Newman, *Prophetical Office*, p. 29.
27. Catenae I: *Testimony of Writers in the Later English Church, to the Doctrine of the Apostolic Succession, Tracts for the Times*, 74; Catenae II: *Testimony of . . ., to the Doctrine of Baptismal Regeneration, Tracts for the Times*, 76; Catenae III: *Testimony of . . ., to the Duty of maintaining Quod Semper, Quod Ubique, Quod ab Omnibus Traditum est, Tracts for the Times*, 78; Catenae IV: *Testimony of . . ., to the Doctrine of the Eucharistic Sacrifice, Tracts for the Times*, 81.
28. At this point there is a marginal note in Pusey's hand: 'How far did he influence the writers of the Tracts? This is a point upon w[hic]h people would be very jealous and suspicious; if they thought the tone and direction of yours and Keble's writings had been given by Fr[oude]'. Newman added below Pusey's marginal note: 'But it has been JHN'. Below this marginal note there is a pencilled draft of a letter to Wood. Only the words 'My dear Wood' are legible, the rest having been erased.
29. R. H. Froude, *Remains of the Late Rev. Richard Hurrel Froude*, ed. J. H. Newman and J. Keble, Part I, 2 vols (London: Rivington, 1838).
30. R. H. Froude, *Remains of the Late Rev. Richard Hurrel Froude*, ed. J. H. Newman and J. Keble, Part II, 2 vols. (Derby: Mozley, 1839).
31. This section – from 'On the contrary' to 'revived' – has a line in pencil running along it and an interrogation mark in the margin, probably by Pusey. This is one of the points to which he objected, feeling that this was not sanguine enough. Newman referred to it in his letter to Wood of 6 September 1840 (*LD*, VIII, p. 389).
32. The *Library of Anglo-Catholic Theology* was started after the *Library of the Fathers*. The first work published was Bishop Andrewes's first volume of Sermons (1841). William Copeland, Fellow of Trinity College, Oxford, was the editor. Newman showed little interest in the undertaking: 'I do not feel that I could join with any interest into a plan for printing many of the authors whose names you enumerate. Indeed there are some whose works I had rather not see printed' (Newman to H. N. Evans, 10 December 1839, *LD*, VII, p. 191). Some of the offending authors were later dropped from the list of those to be published in the series.
33. The series was called *A Library of the Fathers of the Holy Catholic Church Anterior to the Division of the East and West*. The plan had been conceived by Pusey and Newman in the summer of 1836 (cf. Newman to Bowden, 28 August 1836, *LD*, VI, p. 345; also Pusey to Newman, September 1836, in H. P. Liddon, *Life of Edward Bouverie Pusey*, I (London: Longman, Green and Co., 1893, 3rd ed.), pp. 420–2); and Newman to Pusey, 13 October 1836, *LD*, VI, p. 368). The editors were Pusey, Keble and Newman. The first volume, the *Confessions* of St Augustine, appeared in

1838. At the end of the volume can be found a copy of the Prospectus, containing the aims, plan of publications, contributors and subscribers.

34. This theme was also the subject of letter to Manning around this time. The letter bears no date but is arranged among those of January 1841 (Manning MSS Bod., c. 652, fo. 506 ff.).
35. The pages containing the *Notes* are not numbered in the manuscript; they are numbered in italics here for easy reference.
36. J. Miller, *Sermons Intended to Show a Sober Application of Scriptural Principles to the Realities of Life: with a Preface Adressed to the Clergy* (Oxford: Parker, 1830).
37. J. Keble, *The Christian Year: Thoughts in Verse*, 2 vols (London: Parker, 1827).
38. A. Knox, *Remains of Alexander Knox*, ed. J. J. Hornsby, 4 vols (London: Duncan and Cochran, 1834–7). Volume I contained his treatise on Baptism, and vol. II three treatises on the Eucharist. They were published separately: A. Knox, *The Doctrine of the Sacraments, as Exhibited in Several Treatises First Published in the Remains of A. K., Esq.* (London: Duncan, 1838).
39. Common right or publicly available.
40. The writings referred to by Wood are probably: W. F. Hook, *The Peculiar Character of the Church of England Independently of its Connection with the State* (London: Rivington, 1822) and *An Attempt to Demonstrate the Catholicism of the Church of England* (London: Rivington, 1825).
41. *The Works of that Learned and Judicious Divine Mr. Richard Hooker: with an Account of his Life and Death by Isaac Walton*, ed. J. Keble, 3 vols (Oxford: Oxford University Press, 1836). Keble maintained that Hooker had had his full share in training in succeeding generations Laud, Hammond, Sanderson and many others. They had made possible for the Church of England to remain distant from Geneva and near to primitive truth and apostolic order. Keble felt Hooker's works were an antidote to the rationalism which threatened the Church of England in the nineteenth century (ibid., I, Preface, pp. civ–cv).
42. William Laud (1573–1645), president of St John's College (1611); bishop of St David (1621); bishop of Bath and Wells (1626); bishop of London and Chancellor of Oxford University (1628); Archbishop of Canterbury (1633); laid stress on sacramental grace, the episcopal government of the Church, and ecclesiastical discipline, antagonizing English Calvinists and Scot Presbyterians; his differences with Rome were clearly expressed in his dispute with the Jesuit Percy (alias Fisher); attainted by Parliament (1645).
43. Henry Hammond (1605–60), Anglican divine; fellow of Magdalen College, Oxford (1625); vicar of Penshurst (1633); published *Practical Catechism* (1644); his other best known work was the *Paraphrase and Annotations on the New Testament* (1653); suffered much because of his attachment to the Royalist cause.
44. John Cosin (1594–1672), friend of Laud, accused of Romanist tendencies after the publication of his *Collection of Private Devotions* (1627) compiled at the request of Charles I; deprived of his benefices by Parliament; exiled in Paris (1642–60); defended the real presence in the Eucharist while attacking the Catholic doctrine of transubstantiation; appointed bishop of Durham by Charles II (1660).
45. Jeremy Taylor (1613–67), fellow of All Souls (1635); chaplain to Laud and Charles I; vice-Chancellor Dublin University and bishop of Down and Connor (1661); he was renowned as a moralist; his books *Holy Living* (1650), *Holy Dying* (1651), and *Worthy Communicant* (1660) enjoyed enduring and wide popularity as spiritual classics.
46. J. Keble, *National Apostasy Considered in a Sermon Preached in St. Mary's, Oxford, before Her Majesty's Judges of Assize, on July 14, 1833* (Oxford: Parker, 1833).
47. Newman corrected this note. He put some of Wood's words in brackets, and

added some words of his own (in italics in the main text). The clergyman of the Calvinistic School to whom Newman refers to is John Hill (1786–1855), Vice-Principal of St Edmund Hall.

48. See note 23 above.
49. The *Record* dedicated eight long articles to criticize High Church principles, between 15 August and 22 September 1836. Apostolic Succession and the Sacraments were the main targets, particularly Pusey's tract on Baptism.
50. See note 23 above.
51. The idea of a book on the Sacerdotal Office had appeared in the correspondence between Newman and Wood in 1837. Newman seemed to be wondering at the time whether the book on Justification should be separate or part of the one on the Sacerdotal Office; Wood felt that Newman was the best person to judge this (Wood to Newman, 13 April 1837, Halifax Papers, Borthwick, A2/42, fo. 37R). On 23 July of the same year Wood would wonder whether future Tracts on the Sacrifice of the Eucharist and the Real Presence could prepare people for Newman's Sacerdotal Office (*LD*, VI, p. 113).
52. W. E. Gladstone, *The State in its Relations with the Church* (London: Murray, 1838).
53. In a letter to Manning, dated 8 February 1839, Wood said that Bunsen had asked for the book to be translated into German for the Crown Prince of Prussia (E. S. Purcell, *Life of Cardinal Manning, Archbishop of Westminster*, I (London: Macmillan, 1896), p. 150). The Crown Prince read it, and in April 1839 sent Gladstone a congratulatory letter by the intermediary of Baron Bunsen (cf. Gladstone to Manning, 23 February 1839, British Library Add. MS 44247, fos 61–2; see also *The Gladstone Diaries, 1833–1839*, ed. M. R. D. Foot, II (Oxford: Oxford University Press, 1968), p. 594, entry of 18 April 1839). The fourth edition of Gladstone's book (1841) was published in German in 1843, with a preface by F. G. A. Tholuck (*The Gladstone Diaries, 1840–1847*, ed. M. R. D. Foot and H. C. G. Matthew, III (Oxford: Oxford University Press, 1974), p. 305; entry of 5 August 1843). Tholuck's Preface was later published in English (A. Tholuck, *Dr. Tholuck's Preface to Julius Treuherz's Translation of Gladstone's 'State in its Relations with the Church'* (London: Murray, 1845).

INDEX

www.ingramcontent.com/pod-product-compliance
Ingram Content Group UK Ltd.
Pitfield, Milton Keynes, MK11 3LW, UK
UKHW040025200726
13854UKWH00001B/358